Wealth

—————Doesn't Last—————

3 Generations

How Family Businesses can
Maintain Prosperity

Wealth

Doesn't Last

3 Generations

How Family Businesses can
Maintain Prosperity

Jean Lee
China Europe International Business School, China

Hong Li
Chinese Academy of Social Sciences, China

 **World Scientific**

NEW JERSEY · LONDON · SINGAPORE · BEIJING · SHANGHAI · HONG KONG · TAIPEI · CHENNAI

Published by

World Scientific Publishing Co. Pte. Ltd.

5 Toh Tuck Link, Singapore 596224

USA office: 27 Warren Street, Suite 401-402, Hackensack, NJ 07601

UK office: 57 Shelton Street, Covent Garden, London WC2H 9HE

British Library Cataloguing-in-Publication Data
A catalogue record for this book is available from the British Library.

ISBN-13 978-981-279-751-3
ISBN-10 981-279-751-3

Typeset by Stallion Press
Email: enquiries@stallionpress.com

Printed in Singapore.

Preface

Worldwide, family enterprises play a prevalent role in the business world. Therefore, research on family enterprises is highly significant to the economic development of all countries. Compared to other developed countries and regions, China's family enterprises indicate a divide in terms of their history, scale and strength. The impeding challenge for Chinese family enterprises and its economy is to narrow down this gap in the near future. Chinese family enterprises are witnessing an unprecedented financial boom achieved in the last two decades since the opening up of its market. The pressing question is, when founders of the family enterprises are gradually transferring power to the next generation, what should be done to grow and strengthen the enterprises in the hands of the future generations?

Through the immaculate observation by the authors, this book, *Wealth Doesn't Last 3 Generations*, accurately reflects the development of Chinese family enterprises. This book points out problems and difficulties that might be encountered during the growth of Chinese family enterprises in a systemic and prophetic way. It thereafter proposes some suggestions. By introducing the business models of established family enterprises from developed countries, the book brings a relevant touch. It guides Chinese family enterprise on how to face challenges and handle the problem of power transfer. This book also includes considerations for the Chinese government in its guiding and supporting of family enterprises within its national context.

A departure from other books on family enterprises, this book consciously avoids difficult concepts, theories and discussions. Readers will certainly gain important insights while enjoying its fluent style and interesting cases.

Professor Zhang Weiying
Dean
Guanghua School of Management
Peking University

About the Authors

Jean Lee

Dr. Jean Lee is the Michelin Chair Professor in Leadership and Human Resources Management, Chair of the Management Department and Director of Leadership Behavior Laboratory at China Europe International Business School (CEIBS). Prior to joining CEIBS, she was Professor of Management and Associate Dean at Cheung Kong Graduate School of Business (CKGSB), and former Associate Dean and Associate Professor at the National University of Singapore.

Dr. Lee's research interests include leadership, corporate culture, women in management, family business and cross-cultural management. She has published extensively in local and international journals, such as *Human Relations, Family Business Review, Journal of Managerial Psychology, Asia Pacific Business Review, Journal of Leadership and Organizational Development, Journal of Management Development, Asian Academy of Management Journal, International Journal of Entrepreneurial Behavior Research, Journal of Small Business Management, Women in Management Review, Applied Psychology, Management Education and Development, International Journal of Management*, and *Asia-Pacific Journal of Management*, etc. She has also served as Associate Editor of the *Asia-Pacific Journal of Management*.

Dr. Lee has consulted and conducted training programs for many multinational, local and international organizations. She has received several Teaching Awards and Service Awards based on her excellent teaching and outstanding leadership and contributions to the profession. She also received the 2005 Outstanding HR Educator Award and 2007 Businesswomen Award (Professional Excellence) in China.

Hong Li

Dr. Hong Li obtained her PhD degree in industrial and organizational psychology at the Institute of Psychology, Chinese Academy of Sciences. She currently works as Associate Professor in Management at Graduate School of Management, Graduate University of Chinese Academy of Sciences. She has studied and worked at Cheung Kong Graduate School of Business and Anderson School at UCLA. Her current research interests are on family business, leadership and emotions.

Contents

<u>_____Introduction___</u>

A Curse Upon Family Enterprises?

IBM, Wal-Mart, Ford, LG Electronics, Carrefour and Mercedes-Benz are some examples of evergreen enterprises well-known around the world and undoubtedly apotheosis of fortune-makers and examples of remarkable management. In addition, all these enterprises share another common feature: they are all family enterprises. Other than eminent family wealth and social status, ordinary Chinese family enterprises are also often associated with problems of nepotism, poor management, and even sinister internal power struggles. This fate is epitomized in an old Chinese proverb: "Wealth does not sustain beyond three generations" (which is also known as "from rags to riches and back again in three generations"). In fact, numerous examples in history have testified to the truth of this proverb. As China embraces an unprecedented period of great development in its economy, family enterprises in China have increased by leaps and bounds. While people are delighted by the achievements, they also have their worries. During this peak period of growth, can family enterprises in China make themselves bigger, stronger and sustainable? Can they break away from the tragic cycle of wealth disappearing in three generations? These are the central issues to be discussed in this book.

Family enterprise is the most common form of enterprise around the world. According to the World Competitiveness Report provided by the Lausanne Management Center, 80% of the enterprises around the world are more or less considered family enterprises. In the US, family enterprises contribute half of the gross domestic product and provide half of the job opportunities. In Germany, family enterprises create 66% of GDP and account for 75% of the total national employment. In Great Britain, the number of employees in family enterprises is 50% of the country's workforce. 40% of the World's Top 500 Enterprises are owned or run by families. In developing countries, almost all of the private enterprises are family-owned. In India, the total sale and net profit of family enterprises account for 70% of the country's 250 largest private companies. Family enterprises contribute a lot to GDP of Southeast Asian nations and the region, with Korea reaching 48.2%, Taiwan 61.6% and Malaysia 67.2%. Market capitalization owned by the top ten family enterprises in the Philippines and Indonesia accounts for more than 50% of the total GDP. Market capitalization by the top five family enterprises in Thailand and Hong Kong makes up 26% of the total.

Table I.1

The US	90% of the enterprises are controlled by families
Britain	76% of 8,000 major enterprises are owned by families, with output accounting for 70% of GNP
Germany	80% of the enterprises are family-owned
Italy	46% of industrial companies with more than 50 employees are family enterprises
Holland	80% of the enterprises are owned by families, and 50% of the enterprises with more than 100 employees are family enterprises
Spain	71% of the enterprises with more than $2 million sale are owned by families
Australia	80% of unlisted companies and 25% of listed companies are controlled by families
South Korea	Families control 48.2% of all companies
India	75% of top 500 major enterprises are controlled by families, and 99% of registered companies are family enterprises
Latin American nations	80%–98% of non-state-owned companies are family enterprises

Source: IMD, the World Competitiveness Report, 2000, the Family Business Network, Switzerland.

The proportion of family enterprises in China's economy is becoming increasingly significant. Compared to ordinary enterprises, family enterprises have their unique set of problems in dealing with power transfer, management, employment, internal relationships, strategic planning and governance structure. Proper handling of these problems is of great importance and is most challenging for the survival and development of family enterprises. Moreover, these problems will exert a significant influence over the overall economy and society. The authors' intention is to focus on the problems, so that entrepreneurs in China will reexamine their business practices and decide on the appropriate path to take for long-term success and survival.

There are four sections in this book. In Section I, Interpreting Family Enterprises, the authors use interesting examples to present and analyze the unique and primary problems in family enterprises, and also discuss the challenges posed by these problems toward the development of family enterprises in China. Section II relates stories of family enterprises in other parts of the world, across different cultures. The history of family enterprises in European and American societies, East Asian societies and cases of miracle-creating family enterprises — their operation, management, ups and downs, characteristics and social influence — will be discussed respectively in Section II. It is believed that enterprises face the most serious of challenges when changes in the social environment occur. These changes in China and the alternation of dynasties are directly correlated with the rise and fall of Chinese enterprises: from the Ming to Qing dynasties when family enterprises just took shape; to the period of the Republic of China when family enterprises developed in a capitalist economy and to the present social environment in China. In Section III, these problems will be analyzed from the perspectives of formation, property, family, enterprise and individual entrepreneurship. As the saying goes, "nothing is more practical than a good theory", which would surely benefit businessmen of family enterprises in many ways. In this section, therefore, the authors systematically present the latest research findings and theories, making it possible for readers to analyze the problems of family enterprises from a profound aspect.

Family enterprises in China have only survived a generation of growth and development. There is still a long way to go. In this section, in light of the current environment in China, the authors unravel the traps that Chinese family enterprises may face, and put forward suggestions to sustain long-term development by avoiding the ambushes. In the last section, the authors discuss several break-through approaches for family enterprises. The approaches are specially designed in accordance with the unique nature of family enterprises, and are examined from the organizational system, ownership and unique driving force inside family enterprises.

Presently, there is no universally acknowledged definition for family enterprises. Chandler, a famous American business historian, defines family business as an enterprise where the majority of company shares are held by its founder and his intimate partners (and family). They maintain close personal relations with managers and keep decision-making centralized in top management, especially in financial matters, resource distribution and appointment of key personnel.

Pan Bisheng, a well-known Chinese scholar, considers a family enterprise to consist of a family or several families in intimate alliance, which enjoy full or partial ownership, and are directly or indirectly in control of the enterprise. In addition, Pan divides family enterprises into three types in accordance with the degree of family involvement:

(1) Control of ownership and power of management by the same family;
(2) Control of partial ownership and power of management;
(3) Control of partial ownership but not power of management.

As a widely extended definition, it regards family business as a flexible pattern and leaves vagine boundaries for the definition of family enterprises.

Ye Yinghua, a scholar from Taiwan, puts forward a quantitative definition — bringing the difference of ownership structure of individual company and the degree of family control into the definition by way of critical control shareholding ratio. According to this criterion, enterprises with the following three conditions can be defined as family enterprises:

(1) The proportion of family shareholders is bigger than the critical control shareholding ratio;
(2) Family member or a second-degree kin relative assumes the office of chairman or general manager;
(3) Family members or third-degree kin relatives occupy more than half of all the directorships of the company.

This definition regards family enterprises in a situation of serial distribution from the perspective of shareholding and control right of management. It clearly defines these enterprises that own shareholding and control the right of management, own the majority of control right, or own the critical control right as family business. Once the critical control right is lost, a family enterprise is transformed into a public company.

At present, no definition for family business is globally recognized. Enterprises which have a majority of the following characteristics may be defined as family enterprises.

Organizational basis: Members of a family enterprise are related by blood. As the business expands, the organization is formed by a concentric-circle network of relationship by blood (relatives), quasi-relationship (quasi-relationship by blood, for example, nominal kinship or sworn brothers), geographical relationship (fellow villagers), and fellow student relationship (fellow students).

Organizational structure: Family business is an economic organization in pursuit of profits. As an enterprise, family business generally presents the following development track: when the business is just off or is still small, most enterprises choose to establish individual companies with internal cooperation, partnership or unlimited liability companies; when business expands, they gradually transform to be limited liability companies or limited joint stock companies. Most family enterprises choose direct-line functional structure to be their internal organizational structure as it facilitates power centralization.

Structure of ownership: A family enterprise tends to exercise power by way of ownership control. The smaller the size of an enterprise, the more centralized and singular the ownership structure. As the size expands, some enterprises are capable of adopting proper share-holding structure, but in reality, the actual ownership (or property controller) is still in the hands of one or several core members.

Power arrangement: A family enterprise is generally controlled by core members of the family organization, so as to retain actual control within the family and consequently keep the organization united and the members loyal.

Leadership: In light of experience, achievements, talent and authority of founders, patriarchal and centralized systems of management are generally put into practice in family enterprises. Business founders consolidate the right of decision-making in their hands or in the family, to establish a centralized, stable and authoritative leadership.

Governance: Corresponding to the patriarchal system, enterprises are managed by a ruling leader. They employ kindness and severity; set examples by being strict with themselves and being kind toward others; and take care of matters personally.

Exterior form: From an outsider's perspective, family enterprises possess the features of modern enterprises and may sometimes not reveal any trace of family control. However, certain special informal organization may exist inside the enterprise, posing significant influence over the decision-making and management process (it may be rigorous or relaxed). Members of the informal organization generally come from the same family or share similar relationship networks, deriving special momentum from common experience, identity and language. The most important characteristic is that they may undertake commitment or even self-sacrifice in the name of common interest of the family. Only when enterprises encounter serious problems, setbacks or emergencies will the organization arrange internal negotiation or actions exclusively. The actual control of family enterprises will then surface.

Family Culture: Family enterprises unceasingly instill family identity, patriotism and sense of social responsibility in their development. Invariably, family enterprises are aimed at maximizing family wealth in the beginning. They then gradually integrate business with employees' needs and social responsibility.

There are numerous family enterprises around the globe, many of which are internationally-renowned evergreen enterprises. These family enterprises have not only established strong and powerful business, but have also enjoyed a long history. In the world's top 500 companies, Ford Company is renowned in the motor industry; DuPont Company in the chemical industry; Wal-Mart in the retail industry and Mellon Bank Corporation in the financial industry. Nevertheless, family enterprises in China have not achieved such remarkable successes. People often sum up the fate of Chinese family enterprises as "wealth does not sustain beyond three generations". However, China possess a centuries-old and far-reaching family-oriented culture, which forms the core of Chinese politics, society, economic and cultural life.

Family enterprises boast of a deep cultural root in the history of China, so it is possible for family enterprises to survive on this land. Especially after the 1980s, with deepening of the reform in economic system and transformation of social structure, non-public-owned businesses are developed to be an important part of the market economy in China. At present, most private enterprises in China take the form of family ownership and adopt family-oriented management. In enterprises of other types such as township enterprises, partnership enterprises, joint stock enterprises and private contracted enterprises, family or quasi-family-oriented management exist. It is predicted that family enterprises will play an increasingly important role in the Chinese economy. The problem of family enterprises, therefore, deserves much more concern and research.

Obviously, the difference between family enterprises and other enterprises is the former's connection to a certain family. It is this relationship that makes them special. Will this unique feature bring peculiar problems to the development of family enterprises? What influences will these peculiar problems have over the development of family enterprises?

Section I

INTERPRETING FAMILY ENTERPRISES

Yeo Hiap Seng: A Typical Case Study of a Family Enterprise

Interpreting the Fate of Chinese Family Enterprises Through YHS

In Southeast Asia, Yeo Hiap Seng (YHS) is a well-known brand. Its products can be found everywhere in Hong Kong, Taiwan, Southeast Asia, and even the rest of the world. As a century-old family enterprise in food manufacturing, YHS (Singapore) Ltd focuses its production and sales on beverages and canned food. It also provides bottling service for Pepsi and Cadbury Schweppes. Among the company's most popular products are Asian sauces, canned food, instant noodles and soup stock. After 1995, the company diversified its business and entered the real estate industry. In 1998, the company's revenue from real estate stood at S$74 million, accounting for 25.87% of the company's total revenues of S$286 million.

Established in 1901 in Zhangzhou, Fujian Province by Yeo Keng Lian (Renliu), YHS traded mainly in the sauce industry. Mr. Yeo had eight children, five boys and three girls. Back in 1935, Yeo Keng Lian, because of poor health, handed over his factory to his eldest son, Yeo Thian In, who was only 22 years of age at that time. Young as he was, Thian In, under the guidance of his father, managed the business with painstaking efforts. Thian In first worked as a salesman, traversing around to sell products manufactured in his sauce factory. His hard work eventually paid off. The sauce factory enjoyed a booming business. Soon, YHS products flooded the market in Zhangzhou. Thian In sent his younger brothers and sisters to colleges in inland China and even to Japan. Having suffered tremendously from the political turbulence of China at that time, the Yeo brothers decided to leave their hometown and settle down in Singapore. After their college education, Thian In's brothers and sisters joined the family enterprise. YHS, started from scratch, and over the period of time, witnessed rapid growth in the business. The brothers modernized their food factory through automation, gaining wide recognition from the public. At the same time, the brothers diversified their business by employing the bottled soymilk patent invented by their nephew Chen Chee De. With their success in Singapore, they set out to conquer the market in Malaysia, thus starting the YHS business venture abroad. As the business grew, the family also expanded. In 1956, the five brothers signed an agreement dividing the estate of YHS into seven parts, shared amongst the five brothers, the eldest grandson Chee Ming, and Chee Kiat (see Case 1 for the Yeo family tree). As stated in the agreement, Thian In was recommended to be the permanent chairman and general manager; Thian Soo the vice chairman; and Chee Kiat the permanent finance director. It was also agreed that the number of directors shall be five, but with the provision to add two more in the future. In addition, it was also agreed that three of Thian In's offspring and one each of Thian Soo's, Thian Kiew's and Thian Hwa's offspring shall be directors (by succession). The offspring of Thian In and Thian Soo, if they are interested in the work of the factory, shall be given priority in management positions. Offspring of the Yeo families who have no interest in the work of the factory may find other jobs, but they should never borrow the name of YHS or do anything detrimental to the company. In the agreement, it was also prescribed that the board of directors shall draw a certain portion of the company's earnings to set up a scholarship, providing the Yeo offspring with financial assistance for their college education. Upon their graduation, those offspring funded by the company's scholarship shall be encouraged to work in the company. If they should choose not to work in the company, they would be required to contribute 20% of their income to the company for the first four years of employment.

It was a well-crafted agreement, setting up guidelines for the division of family property, assignment of position to family members, cultivation and education of offspring, which indeed greatly promoted the future development of YHS.

The 1960s witnessed a golden period for YHS. As a pioneer of local companies in Singapore that ventured abroad, YHS established a business network covering Malaysia, Hong Kong and even Europe. Plans for public listing were made in 1968. In order to prevent the company from falling into the hands of others, the family members decided to establish a holding company jointly controlled by the family. In 1969, YHS was listed and YHS Holding Company held 49% of shares of the listed YHS, reinforcing YHS's strength in the industry. The company took the lead in the beverages and canned food market when it was given exclusive dealership in the region by a Pepsi. In 1971, YHS built a factory in Malaysia. Three years later, YHS (Malaysia) Ltd was established and in 1975 listed on the Malaysia Stock Exchange. The 1980s was a pivotal period for YHS, during which the company carried a series of reforms and innovations in strategy, product renovation, operation management and organizational structure. By so doing, the listed company performed well and enjoyed a leading role in the beverage market.

In the 1990s, with the third generation of the Yeo family at its helm, problems emerged in YHS. Family members were divided on investment and management decisions. Although decisions in the company had always been made by a majority vote, it became increasingly difficult for family members to come to a consensus. The relationships among family members became increasingly complicated, which adversely affected the management of the company. When the third generation of the Yeo family was at the helm of YHS, Alan Yeo, a son of the eldest brother Thian In, took the position of chairman and president of YHS Ltd. The listed limited company was controlled by YHS Holding Pte Ltd, with the seven families jointly owning the shares. As the seven families grew and multiplied, they were more concerned about the interests of their own families and were often in conflict with one other. In order to maintain consistency in the running of the company, some family members were asked to relinquish and resign from their senior and managerial positions in the company, resulting in the breakdown of the relationships among family members, and a loss of trust and affection which they had cherished since the founding of the company. In 1992, Thian Seng and three other family members were asked to resign. Devastated, Thian Seng's family decided to sell their shares and rights issue of the holding company. At the same time, Yeo Chee Wei, having been removed from his position as executive director, also planned to sell his shares of the company. It was prescribed in the founding charter of the holding company that any withdrawal of shares of the holding company by any family member must be under the consent of other shareholders. Therefore, the holding company made plans to sell the shares at a higher price to the Keppel Group, a company was interested in acquiring shares of YHS. Part of the fund was to be reserved for the company's use. YHS Holding Company, however, could not reach an agreement on the price with the two families. Furthermore, when the two families discovered that the prospective buyer was a third party rather than a family member, they changed their mind. In the hope of upholding the position of the family as a whole in the holding company, they decided to sell only their shares but not the rights issue, thus bankrupting the share-selling program. The conflict intensified when Alan Yeo, having negotiated with the Keppel Group, communicated with the other families, except two, on the sale price. The management style of Alan Yeo was considered autocratic by other family members, as he made decisions without consulting other directors. On one occasion, he tried to purchase 140,000 shares (4.32%) for his son Timothy Yeo in the hope of obtaining more than 50% share ownership for absolute control. Alan Yeo's move greatly disappointed other family members who felt betrayed by his actions, and the rift between them deepened. In the end, Wing Tai's purchase of YHS resulted in the dissolution of the family enterprise. At that time, Wing Tai Holdings had planned to purchase 25.5% to 40% of the total shares of YHS. The action would net them $25 million profit from the development of a $100 million commercial housing project on a plot of land owned by YHS at Bukit Timah Road. The opinions of family members, however, were completely contradictory. Alan Yeo, acting unilaterally, delivered an announcement in support of the purchase; but other members, jointly holding 53% of YHS shares, disagreed. Instead, they demanded to purchase the other 47% of YHS shares owned by Alan Yeo and two other family members that supported the purchase. In addition, they asked Alan Yeo to resign as chairman. Alan Yeo retaliated, saying that his family and the other two families who were in support of the purchase will not sell their shares to other shareholders, and that his resignation should be decided by the shareholders' vote. To complicate matters, the other six families had mixed feelings and did not share a common standing and view. Under such circumstances, YHS Holding Company had to be dissolved. Only by doing so could each family hold direct shares of YHS and avoid unnecessary disputes in future. The disputes among family members were finally settled in court. On July 1, 1994, the high court adjudicated YHS Holding Company Private Limited to be dissolved. Based on the understanding that the relationship of trust and dependence among the family members no longer existed, the verdict recognized that decision-making by consensus among shareholders in the holding company were impossible. If business decisions were made by vote, it meant that the pattern of a holding company similar to partnership ended and a new structure was born. Under such circumstances, the dissolution of the holding company was an inevitable choice. Sadness and disappointment were felt by the family as the properties inherited from their ancestors were soon to fall into the hands of others. The dramatic family fending over shares and ownership rights, as depicted in many movies or TV series, took place in the story of YHS.

YHS, a well-established and profitable century-old family business empire, was dissolved at the hands of its third generation, as if being cursed by an inextricable fate. Is the saying that "wealth does not last for three generations" an incantation affixed on family enterprises?

Are family enterprises ultimately unable to avoid their short-lived fate? From the case of YHS, we may discover many common and typical problems in family enterprises: complicated family politics, mixed family-style management, and vital changes of power. What impact do those problems have on the development of family enterprises?

Family-Oriented Management: Reasons for Both Success and Failure

From the YHS case, we can see the necessity for an enterprise, at its initial stage, to choose the mode of family management. The first reason is that other modes of management are uneconomical. At the starting stage, family enterprises often lack human and financial resources. Most of the pioneers were driven by the motive of shaking off family poverty. Based on the close kinship among the family members and their social relationship, family enterprises could rapidly assemble committed employees who are devoted to the enterprise, even when facing difficult conditions. Furthermore, they are sometimes willing to compromise their salaries. It is due to these factors that family enterprises survive. Family management also leads to a low communication cost, because under most circumstances, the coherence of interests provides family members with a natural sensitivity to the external environment. Thus, information on the external changes, especially market changes, could be passed to every employee as soon as possible. In addition, the patriarchal leadership enhances efficiency in business decisions. With a culture of close communications and conformity to authority, family members can easily come to a consensus or reach an agreement. This helps to enforce and implement decisions. Due to kinship, there is much cohesion within the enterprise and this helps to indirectly reduce the transaction cost of management. Furthermore, family members usually tend to have a much higher level of commitment to work. As a result, the early stage of a family enterprise involves a much lower management cost than other types of enterprises.

Moreover, family culture is a tradition of Chinese culture. Many Chinese businesses prefer the mode of family enterprise when they embark on business ventures. China is a country with far-reaching family culture spanning centuries. Family forms the core of Chinese ethics, the traditions and social organizations. In the language aspect Chinese is one of the few languages in the world that integrates the state with family so closely. In the Chinese language, state is just an extended family. Individuals are members of the family. According to the traditional Chinese education, promoting family ethos is seen as the most outstanding glory for an individual, and conversely, undermining family property is the most irremissible guilt. This value, which takes family interests to be the most important end, is known as familism. Ever since the Shang and Zhou dynasties, familism has had a long history, during which the most effective rules, dealing with the relationships among family members, between family and society, and between family and state, have been stipulated. Familism was not only promoted by the rulers of every dynasty, financed by the esquires and steered by the academia, it was also propagandized by a variety of sacrifices, etiquettes and even depicted in many plays and literary works. As a result, familism was inherited by every generation of Chinese, and became the ethical standard for judging right and wrong, good and evil. Until the Ming and Qing dynasties, familism was regarded as a key element of the ancient Chinese culture, evolving into a cultural modality reflecting Chinese national values. Being edified by the special familism culture, the Chinese seem to be born with the tendency toward the value of familism. Meanwhile, the family experiences, the mindsets and the patterns of behaviors that the Chinese have accumulated in their family lives have been brought to other social organizations, resulting in family enterprises.

Undoubtedly, in the initial stage, family management is feasible and effective. Due to the high pressure brought on by competition among enterprises, family members realized that with limited capital, only by working hard together could they fight a way out to survival. Secondly, at the initial stage, family members have a deep understanding and trust among themselves; seldom are there interest conflicts. Even if there are, they often avoid shaking the foundation of trust among family members. Furthermore, potential conflicts are often mediated and resolved by the patriarchs. Thirdly, the management radius and relations are comparatively small and simple. Decision-makers can easily get relevant information, and the experiences and capabilities of the managers can generally meet the demands of the enterprise's development. Fourthly, although the property distribution is based on family at the early stage, in every family there is a core person who might be chosen by the patriarchal clan system or who wins the position by his own capability exhibited during the development of enterprise. Generally speaking, the highest prestige of the core person helps him to establish the basis of people and relationship management. The desire of other members for capital and interests of the enterprise is not enough to negate this kind of reverence of patriarch. At least, the interest conflicts among family members could not challenge the authority of the patriarchal prestige. Fifthly, managers and their subordinates can get symmetrical information. And usually those in higher positions can seize much more information than the subordinates. This applies not only to information within the enterprise, but also external information about market changes, product development, and the relationship with government and other social entities. Holding more information channels than the others, the managers can thus protect themselves from being cheated and can exert better and economical supervision. As for the forgoing business proprietors, only the proprietors of the family-managed enterprises could be called the real owners. As property rights are mainly controlled by a few people, the owners are undoubtedly deeply involved in the production and management activities. Owners have enough initiatives and conditions to ensure that the enterprise is operating for its real interests. Therefore, as a form of management system, family-oriented management could meet the demands of the early phase of family enterprises, and also would contribute greatly to the rapid development of private businesses.

For the above reasons, Mr. Yeo Keng Lian had created the embryo YHS with his two eldest sons. Subsequently, he asked his children to manage the company. With the endeavor of the whole family, the company operated and expanded at the bequeathal of their father. Consequently, YHS developed remarkably, due hard work of the whole family.

However, when enterprises reach a certain phase, the mode of family-oriented management would restrict their progress. The reason lies in that with the expansion of the enterprise, requirements for specialty, advanced technology and management techniques become much higher. And with the expansion of the enterprise and the increase in management complexity, weaknesses of family-oriented management are gradually revealed. The management radius becomes much wider and it becomes more and more difficult to supervise the enterprise only by individuals or family members. Moreover, the environment is undergoing tremendous changes. The experiences and knowledge of managers or family members on technology products, markets and finance are insufficient. The management know-how of individual managers starts to fall behind the growing pace of the enterprise. The growth and expansion of family enterprise would inevitably lead to the infusion of many outsiders, especially professionals. The efficiency of the management could be raised, but at the same time, the original patriarchal clan system among the family members would be challenged. Relations among the management become more complicated. Hence, information asymmetry begins to emerge, which makes it difficult for managers to rapidly grasp necessary information to make right decisions.

With the development of family enterprises, the respect for the key players would gradually reduce, especially in fast-developing enterprises. The courage, insight, and the spirit of adventure of the key players would fade. Particularly, after obtaining some social credit and achieving a series of successes, they would become overconfident and arbitrary, which would destroy the cohesion of the enterprise. But what is the most important is that when the enterprise had accumulated much wealth and dividends, the conflicts of interest within the family would be intensified. In the face of temptation, family members would tend to take more care of their own property, other than the property of the enterprises, which would lead to conflict of interests, and this often results in disorganized management. This phenomenon constitutes one of the most important factors that led to the dissolution of YHS.

Both the pros and cons of family-oriented management in family enterprises are so peculiar. It is like a double-edged sword, requiring its master to have a brilliant mind and techniques. Thus, when wielding it in a fight, he must also avoid hurting himself. But whenever unbalanced, that famous saying would come to mind: the key to their success is also their undoing.

Power Transfer: To Be or Not to Be

The transfer of power from generation to generation within the family is inevitable for family businesses. It is of great importance to the development of family enterprises, for it can be a crucial dividing point between prosperity and decline. Power handover is not a simple process of the new replacing the old. It has significant impact and implication on the ownership and strategic development of the enterprise and could even be a life-and-death decision for a family business. Succession planning in family business is uniquely complicated and impactful. There is no exception for any family enterprises in the world. Currently, a majority of family businesses in China are still in the hands of the first generation. Some of them have entered the transitional period from the first generation to the next. As time passes, succession and power transfer of family enterprises will become a major challenge for many family enterprises in China.

In the case of YHS, the power handover from Yeo Keng Lian (first generation) to Yeo Thian In (second generation) was quite successful. With his own efforts, Yeo Thian In established his authority and prestige within the family and among the employees, and thus laid a foundation for YHS to take great strides during his period. When it came to the third generation, the family fell apart into three factions, due to differing management viewpoints and mindsets. Unlike the two predecessors, Alan Yeo, the board chairman at that time was unable to gain absolute authority and consensus within the family. Internal conflicts deteriorated and a total dissolution was inevitable. In the process of power transfer, both generations were faced with big challenges. The older generation had to face problems such as: How to hand over power? How to keep the family together? How to position family members in the enterprise? How to differentiate and balance family role and business role? How to ensure the competitiveness of future leadership? How to instill a sense of family obligation and responsibility among family members? How to keep non-family members in the core positions of the enterprise?

The younger generation has to mull over questions such as: How to exert control over the enterprise? How to grow business? How to acquire support from family members? How to balance conflicting interests if the older generation chooses to divide evenly the inheritance among offspring (a customary practice in China)? Will the successor of the father — the eldest son, for example — enjoy greater privilege and authority? If so, how can we protect our own interests? For the older generation, business handover could mean a loss of power and control. If they cannot adjust themselves to changes and are unwilling to step down from leading positions, obstacles are posed to a smooth power transition. Senior leaders, who have been used to giving orders, may not feel contented being an observer. They may inevitably interfere with the management, thus repressing the performance of the successor. The possible consequences will be: difficulty for successor in establishing authority; political dynamics among employees; difficulty in policy implementation; and decreasing efficiency in organizational operation. Another potential problem in the power transfer process comes from senior employees. They can be the siblings of the former power controller (that is, the elders of the new successor), or the pioneer employees who have made remarkable contributions to the enterprise. A smooth transfer of power cannot be achieved without support from these people. Furthermore, they will exert strong influence on the future development of the business management. This was certainly the case in YHS. Nevertheless, reforms are often necessary for new leaders to advance business development. Successors need to form their new management team and develop new style and culture, which will consequently alter the former organization and power structure. And such alterations may cause certain instability to the enterprise. Under such circumstance, some senior employees may step out to oppose or even destroy the reform especially when their interests are being threatened. Failure to handle such power struggles poses threats to the implementation of new strategies and sustainability of the reform, which may also create disturbances in management, or even more severe consequences in business performance.

Now, let us look at another key issue in family business — the distribution of ownership (or property) during the process of power transfer. In Chinese family businesses, power derives from ownership. Being out of ownership implies being deprived of authority. In the case of YHS, ownership was evenly divided into seven portions. In the Chinese family, it is customary to divide property in similar fashion. While it appears to be reasonable and impartial, it poses a potential threat to the future development of the enterprise. For the new successor, an even distribution of ownership fails to ensure actual control over the enterprise during the initial period. Succession provides nothing more than an opportunity. Actual control is to be gained gradually through managing the business, or even from power struggles. Consequently, redistribution of interests and power causes conflicts and frictions or even dissolution of the enterprise. Nevertheless, equal distribution of property does not necessarily lead to a split in family business, which mainly depends on the dynamic relations among different branches within the extended family. Apart from inheritance of ownership and management, there is another factor playing a role in the process of power transfer — social relations, a non-capital inheritance. If the successor can make full use of the network of social relationship established by the predecessor, the enterprise will suffer a lesser degree of disorder generated by management handover. Therefore, the legal identity of the enterprise can be kept intact in spite of a split in property and stock shares, for which many existent family businesses serve as good examples. What should be done to maintain the integrity of the family enterprise under constant impairment of property and stock shares is an interesting question worth addressing.

In fact, a power transfer process is another pioneering period — a process full of risk and challenge. For any family enterprise, this is a difficult period of adjustment and adaptation with the clash of old and new conceptions and underlying values. It is no exaggeration to refer to power transfer process as a "to be or not to be" issue, which often becomes a crucial dividing line between prosperity and decline.

Internal Conflicts in Family Enterprises: Emotional or Rational

Although we cannot pin the deterioration and dissolution of YHS totally down to family politics, the conflicts within the family can be regarded as an important igniting point. Since the 1990s, opinions of Yeo's family members on matters of investment and management had begun to diverge. YHS had been adopting the decision-making mode of minority subordinating to the majority, but with the number of the family members increasing, the relationship among the same generation, and the relationship between the younger generation and the older generation became more complicated. This had prohibited them from reaching consensus, which undoubtedly had a negative impact on the operation of the enterprise.

The origins of conflicts within family enterprises vary. Some are due to the change in management, which we have briefly discussed in the previous session. In some family enterprises, the old family patriarch has come to the age of retirement, and the younger generation are ready to take over. But being infatuated with power and position, the old patriarch refused to retire, holding the power tightly in his own hands. Therefore, the younger generation would either rely too much on him or feel oppressed. When they find that they cannot take over the management, the younger generation would be extremely discontented and indignant and if not properly addressed, this may affect the stability and development of the enterprise. Of course, the source of conflicts can be the other way round, from the younger generation. If the younger generation lacks the capability and experience of leadership, the older generation would not have trust and confidence in them, and would be unwilling to delegate more power and responsibility. As a result, it would reduce the learning opportunities for the younger generation. The younger generation may become more self-contemptuous, or they would probably go to the other extreme of rushing and making quick fixes; leading the enterprise to vulnerability and possible loss. The conflicts between the two generations would be intensified if this happens.

Conflicts within the same generation would also affect family enterprises. In traditional Chinese families, the elder brothers are usually superior to the younger ones. The distribution of wealth would impact on the relationships among siblings and cousins. Over time, the brothers would become presumed enemies, and the discontent and indignation among the members of the same generation would emerge. As the children grow up, get married and settle down, more parties are involved, and thus the conflicts would become much more complicated across families and generations, which could directly threaten the management, operation and survival of family enterprises. Furthermore, this conflict would become apparent with the passing away of the patriarch. With the number of the family branches increasing and the educational levels widening, the divergences and conflicts within the family would also be intensified. If the conflicts cannot be resolved at an early stage with or without intervention from some objective outsiders, the severity and complexity of internal conflicts would be aggravated. Sometimes, there is even the possibility of ending up in court (which was the case with YHS). The final and worst ending would be the dissolution of both the family and the enterprise.

The main reason why minor and benign divergences can lead to severe conflicts lies in the fact that the intimacy and interdependence among the family members no longer exist. Instead, they become suspicious and jealous. As a result, even some minor differences would turn into ugly conflicts, which would ultimately hurt the solidarity of the family and the operation of the enterprise.

The emergence of these conflicts can be traced back to the family members themselves, to the interior regime of family enterprises and to enterprise culture. If the older generation could accept, with an enlightened and open attitude, the different ideas and reform measures by the younger generation, and at the same time entrust them with important tasks, then many potential divergences would disappear. If family members have the courage to face the divergences, and could carry out discussions with an open attitude and objective views, then many conflicts and disputes could be resolved in constructive ways. With respect to the regime, if work division within family enterprises is not clear, and if there exists overlapping conflicts between rights and obligations, this can easily lead to dissension, estrangement and tension. In addition, the unprofessional, unfair, and non-transparent management system and measures would give way to a sense of distrust among family members and non-family employees. As a result, different power factions would come into being, hence ruining the relationship and morale within the enterprise. If there is no effective channel or regime to alleviate or resolve existing divergence, these minor differences would probably degenerate into ugly conflicts. Therefore, an effective communication channel is crucial.

Distrust and conflict within family enterprises are sometimes caused by informational asymmetry and a lack of communication among family members. To push forward the development of interdependent relations, it is necessary to build up an effective communication system to eliminate misunderstandings and informational obstacles. This communication, formal or informal, face-to-face or conducted by a third party, may help improve the quality of the communication in family enterprise.

In fact, not all divergences and conflicts within family enterprises are negative. Some conflicts can even propel the enterprise to move forward. Conflict can lead to an in-depth understanding and spur profound thinking. Therefore, some win-win solutions can be found to promote better interaction and competition. And the development of the enterprise will also become more healthy and mature. Sometimes, disputes can boost communications among family members, and subsequently eliminate accumulated misunderstanding and prevent the destruction brought on by conflicts. Moreover, some insignificant conflicts can be easily resolved within the family, which would definitely eliminate or suppress potentially overwhelming conflicts. Sometimes, conflicts are just like viruses. Although harmful in nature, they could also stimulate our bodies' immune system at times. But if not effectively controlled, they could turn into cancer cells, and ultimately spread to every inch of our bodies. By that time, it would be too late to seek help.

With as long as 95 years of operation, YHS also could not escape the curse of the old Chinese saying that "wealth does not sustain beyond three generations". It was dissolved in the hands of the third generation. The key to their success was also their undoing. The family solidarity once helped it to thrive and boom, but the family conflicts also plunged it into a dilemma. The complicated relationships between families, and between younger generation and older generation have not only influenced the objectivity of the enterprise management, but also influenced rationality of the enterprise decision making. What is most important and tragic is that the long-term and sustainable development of the enterprise was prohibited.

Can Chinese family enterprises be evergreen, transcending one generation to another? Will they be able to develop from small- or medium-sized enterprises to larger ones, even become world-class enterprises? The answer is yet to be revealed.

Case 1: Yeo Hiap Seng: The Collapse of a Family Enterprise over Three Generations

Introduction

Published on the finance front page of *Lian He Zao Bao* on May 2, 1998, a news article described the current situation of Singapore YHS Co Ltd after it was purchased at a high price by Ng Teng Fong, a real estate mogul.

Ng Teng Fong purchased YHS, a beverage and food manufacturer in 1995. At that time, market analysts could not believe that Ng Teng Fong would be interested in the food and beverage industry. Orchard Parade under Ng Teng Fong's control of Far East Organization announced the day before that it sold 12.45% of YHS shares at $100 million to Danone Group, a French food company. This move lent credence to past market speculation.

Through painstaking and fierce competition with his rivals in 1995 Ng Teng Fong purchased 86% of YHS shares at a high price. With 12.45% sold and 73.55% remaining, this left the market wondering if Mr Ng would continue to sell the shares of the century-old company.

Danone was granted share option. If it increased its YHS shares to 51%, it would gain control of the family enterprise. It seemed that Mr Ng intended to fade out of the company. In reality, his goal had been accomplished after he obtained the plot owned by YHS to develop his private real estate business.

In 1995, Ng Teng Fong seized control of YHS from a Malaysian businessman by the name of Quek Leng Chan (Kwek Leng Chang) at a high cost, from which many members of the Yeo's family made their fortune. Then, he sold part of the shares at $5.65 each, a price higher than the purchasing price in that year, bringing $11 million profit for Orchard Parade.

Danone had its own calculated plan to become a shareholder of YHS, which is still a widely known brand in the region. Years ago, YHS suffered significant loss when it purchased Chun King Group, an American food company. Both Chun King Group and YHS sell oriental-style food. The French-food company stood ready to employ the business reputation of YHS and its marketing network.

One of the conditions proposed by Danone was that YHS should focus on food and beverage, and be separated from the real estate business developed by Ng Teng Fong. Failure to do so would result in the sale of shares back to Orchard Parade at the original price.

For YHS, business restructuring was nothing new. YHS had experienced business restructuring after new shareholders stepped in. Far East Organization had planned to reduce the shares of YHS, that were controlled by Orchard Parade, to eventually 22%. Thereafter, Orchard Parade would not be a large shareholder, but it might depend on Danone Group to explore a wider market, making it a worthwhile deal.

It was indeed a worthy deal to find a good buyer for part of YHS shares. But with the depression of the real estate market at that time, Far East Organization had more problems to tackle with: Orchard Parade had to settle the developmental housing project of YHS by investing more funds to expand the real estate department of YHS into a listed company.

The family enterprise YHS, which had started from scratch developed into a holding company and finally evolved into a non-family enterprise. The evolutionary history of the family enterprise is an exemplary case study to explore the multiplication of a family, participation of family members in business, and influence of ownership changes on the lifespan of family enterprises.

History of YHS

Yeo Hiap Seng, an enterprise dealing with sauce industry, was established by Yeo Renliu (Keng Lian) in Zhangzhou, Fujian Province in 1901. Born in Quanzhou, Fujian in 1860, Mr. Yeo followed his father to Zhangzhou, where he converted to

Christianity at the age of 31. He established YHS when he was 41. Mr. Yeo named his sauce factory Yeo Hiap Seng, which has a profound meaning. In Chinese characters, Hiap consists of a "+" which stands for a crucifix, and of three 力 (power). It was Mr. Yeo's wish that the whole family, with the blessing of Jesus, to be of the same mind to achieve great success in their business.

Yeo Renliu has eight children: five boys and three girls. Thian In is his eldest son and Thian Soo, Thian Kiew, Thian Seng and Thian Hwa are the four younger brothers.

In 1935, Yeo Renliu, because of poor health, began to consider the possibility of transferring control right of the factory to the next generation. In the same year, at the celebration of his 60th birthday, Mr. Yeo announced to hand over control of the sauce factory to his eldest son Thian In for management. Thian In was only 22 years old then.

Young as he was, Thian In managed the business with painstaking endeavors under the guidance of his father. And all the efforts paid off. Great progress had been made in the business of his sauce factory. Besides, he sent his younger brothers and sisters to colleges in inland China.

Having suffered greatly from the turbulence of political situations in China then, the brothers decided to move to Singapore for further development. The reason for moving to Singapore was its cultural background and weather. Since most of the Chinese in Singapore came from Fujian, they could communicate with each other freely. The hot weather in Singapore made it easier for soybean to ferment. The low price of salt was another favorable condition to develop the business of sauce making. In February 1937, Thian In, together with his wife and children, moved to Singapore. In autumn of the same year, the two younger brothers, Thian Kiew and Thian Seng arrived in the city in succession. The brothers were determined to start their business from scratch again. They settled down and soon rented a plot of land at Outram Road to build YHS sauce factory in Singapore.

At the beginning, the brothers could hardly adjust themselves to the operational style of sauce-making in Singapore, partly because most of the residents were more accustomed to sauces of the Guangdong style. Besides, factories producing Guangdong-styled sauces were generally equipped with tricycles to hawk around large barrels of sauce. YHS was established for a short period of time and there were only a few helping hands. In addition, they had gotten used to consigning their bottled products to retail stores for sale, as they had done in their hometown.

Thian In decided to return to China in 1941 and asked Thian Kiew to end the sauce business in Singapore. Unwilling to abandon the cause that was established with painstaking efforts, Thian Kiew asked a salt store He Yuan for help. Although YHS had owed a large sum of money to He Yuan, the boss, Zheng Tianyuan, still trusted Thian Kiew. He promised to keep supporting YHS. Soon after Thian In returned from China, the Japanese army invaded Singapore.

17th January 1942 was an unforgettable day for all family members. A bomb was dropped on the YHS sauce workshop and many sauce jars were ruined. Fortunately, some finished sauce products remained intact. Unexpectedly, YHS, through this catastrophe, made unexpected profits. The Japanese army shut down the rest of the sauce factories and forcibly seized their sauce for military use. YHS was not seized because it was bombed. People began to rush for the YHS sauce. It was a turning point for the enterprise. From then on, its business flourished day after day.

After the end of the Second World War, YHS further developed its business and ambitiously planned to enter the Malaysian market. In 1946, in order to facilitate its business, a friend of Thian Kiew who was working in HSBC (Hong Kong Shanghai Banking Corporation) recommended him to buy a plot of land at Bukit Timah Road. With loans from HSBC and Mr Ng Yudai, his father-in-law, YHS possessed its own factory.

In 1951, YHS factory modernized its manufacturing equipments. The use of bottled soymilk patent was invented by their
nephew Chen Chee De, this was another major milestone for
YHS. It began to produce bottled soymilk and other canned
food, marking a new age of product diversification.

Chen Chee De, son of the eldest sister, invented bottled
soymilk, the most well-known product of YHS. The products manufactured by the YHS factory in China also included bean curd and
soymilk. To keep fresh, soymilk must be specially processed. Soon
after Chee De, who had majored in biology and chemistry in college, arrived in Singapore and invented the bottled asepsis soymilk,
making YHS the first company to introduce bottled soymilk.

Establishment of YHS Canned Sauce
Factory Company Limited

In 1956, with the exponential growth in the Yeo's business, the
family decided to develop YHS Sauce Factory into YHS Canned
Sauce Factory Pte Ltd. In the same year, Thian Soo, who was
previously staying in Hong Kong, arrived in Singapore. In order
to reconstruct YHS Sauce Factory, Thian In divided the estate of
YHS into seven portions, one for each of the five brothers, the
eldest grandson Chee Ming, and Chee Kiat. Chee Ming had his
entitlement because of his status as the eldest grandson of the
family, a Chinese traditional way of endowment. Chee Kiat was
given a share because of his remarkable contribution toward the
development of the factory. The signing ceremony of the agreed
division of the estate amongst the seven family members was witnessed by a priest and the seniors.

In accordance with the agreement, Thian In was made the
permanent chairman and concurrently the general manager,
Thian Soo the vice chairman, and Chee Kiat the permanent
finance director. The agreement also stipulated that there shall
be five directors, with an additional two directors in the future

when numbers increase. Moreover, three of Thian In's children and one of Thian Soo's, Thian Kiew's and Thian Hwa's offsprings shall be the successor directors. Should the offsprings of Thian In and Thian Soo be interested in working in the factory, they would be given priority in management positions.

Agreement by Yeo's Family Members in 1956

Extract of a contract between Yeo Thian In and the other members (the contractors) reads as follows:

It was with God's blessing that the Yeo family multiplies in large and thriving numbers. The division and apportion of the family property to each household, was done in the hope that there would be permanent ownership of the family asset.

I. Our father Yeo Renliu, moved from Quanzhou to the city of Zhangzhou to run the sauce business when he was a teenager. It was at Zhangzhou that he converted to Christianity, established a sauce workshop and established a family. As the business of the workshop continued to prosper day after day, Thian In and Thian Soo were asked to quit school to help out in the business. Sadly our beloved father died after suffering from a disease, so Thian In and Thian Soo inherited the business. It was under the guidance and support of Thian In and Thian Soo that the younger brothers and sisters could continue with their college education.

II. Our mother decided to hand the control of YHS sauce workshop in Zhangzhou to Thian Soo and Thian Hwa, and urged Thian In to seek business opportunities abroad. Unfortunately, our mother died before the plans materialized and Thian In returned to Zhangzhou to host the funeral. In February 1937, Thian In, accompanied by his wife and children, arrived in Singapore to scale up the business. In autumn of the same year, Thian Kiew went over to help. Under the well-established brand of Yeo Hiap Seng, the brothers tirelessly ran the business and gradually the products became widely recognized by the Chinese immigrants. Thian Seng quit his job in 1940 and Thian Hwa emigrated from China in 1950 to help run the growing business. It was with hard work and cooperation among the brothers and sisters that the business could prosper.

III. In order to improve the organization, we made plans to restructure YHS sauce workshop into YHS Canned Sauce Factory Co Ltd. It was also an appropriate time to divide all the family assets, including houses, plots, buildings, funds and goods, into seven portions to be shared among the five brothers, the first grandson Chee Ming, and Chee Kiat. Chee Ming received a share because he was the eldest grandson of the family. Chee Kiat received a share because he made the remarkable contribution to the development of the factory. The shares are not to be transferred to people other than the families and never to be divided. The brothers shall support and cooperate with each other to maintain the everlasting cause established by our father.

IV. To honor the contributions of the elder brothers, we hereby recommend Thian In to be permanent chairman and concurrently general manager; Thian Soo to be vice chairman, and Chee Kiat to be permanent finance director. The number of directors shall temporarily be five, and may add two in the future. In addition, three of Thian In's children and one of Thian Soo, Thian Kiew and Thian Hwa's offspring shall be successor director. The offspring of Thian In and Thian Soo, if interested in the work of the factory, shall be given priority in management positions.

V. Offsprings of the Yeo's with different interest may find other jobs but they should never borrow the name or the company or do anything to the detriment of the company's interest. The brand of YHS may be used in establishing a branch company.

VI. In order to groom the Yeo offspring for succession planning, the board of directors shall contribute a certain portion from the bonus towards setting up a scholarship fund with the aim to provide the children with a college education. If needed, the younger members funded by the company shall be encouraged to work in the company after their graduation. If they choose not to work in the company, they would be obliged to contribute 20% of their income to the company during the first four years of their outside employment.

VII. Each family member, of the same flesh and blood, shall work in unity and cooperation with each other and adhere to the Christian faith. All members should carry on the family business with hard work and thrift. Those who may fall into poverty should be assisted and supported by the rest of the family members. The board of directors shall review the outflow of funds in the finances of the company.

VIII. All the facts mentioned above and the division of the shares are made with the consent of Thian In, Thian Kiew, Thian Seng, Thian Hwa and Chee Kiat. Chee Hong represented Thian Soo, who was still a minor then. Thian Kiew should keep the share for Chee Hong and return to him when he grows up. Chee Ming is represented by Chee Heng, who is pursuing his studies. Thian In should temporarily keep his share and return to Chee Heng when he is back.

The contract is hereby executed in seven copies with each member having one copy.

Witness: Fang Han Jing, Gao Jing Ting
Contractors: Yeo Thian In
                   Yeo Thian Kiew
                   Yeo Thian Seng
                   Yeo Thian Hwa
                   Yeo Chee Kiat
August 1, 1956

Alan Yeo, who was pursuing his education in Britain, returned to Singapore and joined his father and uncles in growing and expanding the company business.

The 1960s marked the golden period for the development of YHS. Being the pioneer in venturing internationally, YHS established a network with western Malaysia, eastern Malaysia, Hong Kong, America and European countries.

YHS planned to be listed in 1968. In order to prevent the company from falling into the hands of others, the family members, after some negotiations, decided to establish a holding company jointly controlled by the family members. In 1969, YHS was listed and YHS Holdings owned 49% of share rights of the listed company.

In July 1975, YHS was granted exclusive dealership by Pepsi for the region. YHS was authorized to be Pepsi's bottling manufacturer in Singapore, with the exclusive right to bottle, sell and distribute all beverages under the Pepsi brand.

In 1971, YHS invested in Malaysia to build a factory. Three years later, YHS (Malaysia) Public Company was established and was listed in the Malaysia Stock Exchange in 1975.

Development of the Family Cause

The 1980s was a peak period for the cause of the family, when the company implemented a series of reform and innovations in strategies, product innovation, operation management and organizational structure. By doing so, the listed company performed well and took a leading role in the beverage market.

Products: YHS invested on a lot of scientific research to promote the variety and packaging of beverages. The company developed many popular Asian style products such as iced tea, sugarcane juice and mixed juice. Its profit from beverage production and sale accounted for 70% of the total profit of the company.

In addition to its agreement on bottling and distribution with Pepsi, YHS also reached an agreement with Beecham (Production) Singapore Co Ltd to package and distribute Ribena to retail stores through the direct sales network of YHS.

In 1985, YHS got in touch with Gatorade, a famous American brand, and was licensed the right to produce and distribute of 7-Up, its beverage product.

The right to be the general agent of Evian mineral water in Singapore and Malaysia was also granted to YHS in February 1990, and so was the right of Moo milk a year later.

YHS was also granted the distribution right of two kinds of French wines and Budweiser beer. Significant progress was made in food production. Chili sauce and ketchup made by YHS became daily food for almost every household; canned beef, chicken and curry mutton also found their way into the market.

Focusing on the food and beverage market, YHS became a leader in the market of non-carbonated soft drinks in Singapore. It was also one of the leaders in the condiments and canned food market.

Operational management: To enhance the growth of products and market, the company signed a software contract for S$1.6 million, aimed to foster a computer-assisted management environment for manufacturing.

In addition, the company introduced a bottling production line with a production capability of 1,000 bottles per minute, making it the fastest production speed in Southeast Asia.

The company never stopped in the research and innovation of beverage packaging technology. As early as the 1970s, YHS introduced packaging technology with plastic bottles for Pepsi and Minolta products, becoming the first in Asia to bottle soft drinks with pull-tab cans. The innovations in its product packaging technology had remarkably expanded its beverage and food market.

Strategic planning: The enterprise began to diversify its industry as a growth strategy. In 1987, YHS tried to diversity its business into the prawn-breeding industry, by joining forces with

Flowell in high-tech prawn ponds. However, the pond was forced to shut down in 1992 due to the significant losses it suffered, which culminated to US$10 million.

In 1988, YHS purchased 25.5% of the total shares of Zeng Yu Wang Securities Company, marking its entry into the industry of securities.

YHS began its campaign of exploring overseas markets in the same year. It set up a subsidiary company in Canada and invested $15 million to expand its storage and factory in North America, hoping to increase its production of beverages.

In 1989, the company, in association with Temasek Holdings, purchased the Chun King Group at US$52 million, each owning half of the shares of the affiliated company. YHS suffered investment losses in the Group for successive years. For the first time, a financial deficit of $1.4 million was incurred in 1991.

Organizational structure: As the company business increased and the size expanded, it became an urgent task to adjust the organizational structure. At the beginning of 1994, YHS underwent a major reorganization. The core business was allocated to four exclusive investment subsidiary companies, with YHS still retaining its functions in finance, promotion, technical service, strategic planning and HR, playing a role of an investment holding company.

The four newly established subsidiary companies had their own independent business focus. YHS Manufacturing Pte Ltd focused on food and sauce; YHS Canning Pte Ltd on beverage business; YHS Sales Pte Ltd on sales and distribution; and YHS Exports Pte Ltd on exports.

After the company's reorganization, the main assets of YHS Ltd included the brand and its investment in each subsidiary company.

As Alan Yeo, chairman of YHS Ltd, put it, the internal reorganization and restructuring would surely improve the company in its surveillance and management of the business, affording each subsidiary company its independent finance and operation. In addition, the plan would also consolidate the focus of different business entities, expand import and export trade and intensify its operation and distribution capability.

Internal Family Conflicts

By the 1990s, the Yeo family members were divided in their opinions regarding investment decisions and management. After 1993, although decisions were still made by the majority, it became increasingly difficult to reach a consensus, as the relationship among family members grew increasingly complicated. YHS had an abysmal performance in 1993.

On April 22, 1994, Wing Tai Holding Ltd, a company in real estate and garment manufacturing, proposed to purchase a huge number of ordinary shares of YHS through Citicorp Investment Bank (Singapore). The sum of the shares accounted for 25.5% to 40% of the total issued shares of YHS. Analysts estimated that if Citicorp were to develop the plot of land owned by YHS at Bukit Timah Road, which was worth $100 million, into a commercial or housing project, it could reap $25 million in net profit. Alan Yeo, one of the controlling shareholders of YHS, delivered an announcement in his personal capacity through Citicorp to support the purchase of YHS by Wing Tai Holdings. However, other members of the family, jointly holding 53% of the total shares, did not agree with the purchase. Instead, they demanded a buy-back of the 47% of YHS shares owned by the three family members, including Yeo's. In addition, they asked Alan Yeo, chairman of the company, to resign. The opposing side held the opinion that the listed YHS Ltd should be run by professional managers instead of YHS Holdings. Alan Yeo, in his personal capacity, announced that the three families in support of the purchase would not sell their shares to other shareholders.

It was the right of shareholders, not others, who should decide he stays or resigns. In his opinion, the other six families did not share a common understanding and point of view. Under such condition, the holding company should be dissolved instead of being retained. Only by so doing could each family hold direct shares of YHS and avoid unnecessary dispute in the future. A shareholders' meeting was held the following day and a decision was made to deny the purchase option as proposed by Wing Tai. On May 16, Alan Yeo explained his original intention and position with regard to the Wing Tai's intended purchase of the company to YHS employees the pointed out that he was in support of selling part of the shares to settle the disputes within the family.

On May 17, 1994, Alan Yeo made an application to the court to dissolve YHS Holdings. Once dissolved, all shareholders of the Yeo family will directly hold shares of the listed YHS Company. At the same time, Alan Yeo sought the court's order to prevent YHS Holding Pte Ltd from raising any demand to change the structure of the Board of Directors in the YHS listed company.

YHS Holdings comprised six Yeo families which were then divided into two factions: Alan Yeo, Yeo Chee Heng and Yeo Thian Hwa were in one faction, and Yeo Wei Li, Yeo Chee Wei and another uncle Yeo Thian Seng were in another.

The court hearing started on May 23. Two days later, it ordered YHS Ltd to convene a special shareholders' meeting and put forward the proposal to recall Alan Yeo from the office of chairman and director in the listed company. The high court also pronounced that before the official hearing on the the case concerning Alan Yeo's application for the dissolution of YHS Holding Pte Ltd could begin, YHS Holdings could not employ any action to recall Alan Yeo from his office of chairman and director of the listed YHS Ltd. On June 3, Alan Yeo once again made an application to the high court to dissolve

YHS Holding Pte Ltd. On June 20, the high court began legal proceedings of the case. As Alan Yeo disclosed, at the special shareholders' meeting held in February 1992, Yeo Chee Wei, the ex-director of the company, raised a suggestion to divide the Holding company into six private companies. The suggestion, however, was not accepted as it was prescribed in the agreement made by the brothers that any withdrawal of the shares of the holding company by any family members must first obtain the consent of other shareholders. Alan Yeo also said that YHS Hong Kong had been suffering losses since 1992, and the licensed company with Pepsi suffered deficit at the end of 1991. However, Yeo Wei Yi, manager and concurrently director of the company, left the company which was based in Hong Kong. Family member Yeo Wei Li had always been responsible for two projects of investment and operation in North America, including Chun King Company and a soymilk factory in Canada. In the next few days, Alan Yeo confessed in the high court that the families once discussed how to settle disputes among family members before Wing Tai Holdings raised its proposal for purchase.

In 1992, when the family of Yeo Thian Seng and the family of Yeo Chee Wei decided to sell their parts of shares and right issue of YHS Holdings, Alan Yeo had a word with Keppel Group, urging it to buy the shares held by the two families. After the talks with Keppel, he did not inform the two families of the price, but informed the other families. YHS Holdings decided to sell to Keppel at a high price, making Keppel a shareholder of YHS Holdings after the purchase. The share price paid by the Keppel Group would be used in four areas: YHS Holdings would pay the two families for the shares they sold; repay part of $12 million of bank loan; pay other shareholders as compensation; and the remnant would be kept in YHS Holdings. Although in possession of 46.5 million shares of YHS Ltd, the Holding Company could never make an agreement with the two families in terms of price. Later, Yeo Wei Li expressed his desire to sell his part of shares and right issue. In June of the same year, when the two families got to know that Keppel, the purchaser, was a third party, they gave up their plan to sell both the shares and the right issue. Instead, they decided to sell only the shares in the hope of upholding the position of the whole family in the Holding Company. With the adherence to the decision of the two families and the unacceptable price of $27.2 per share, the plan of selling shares to Keppel fell through. When the plan failed, Alan Yeo lost support from another family member, Yeo Wei Heng.

Yeo Chee Heng's son, Yeo Wei Yi, one of the four family members in support of Alan Yeo, said that business decisions were made in YHS with consensus of shareholders in the years before 1991. Since then, decisions were made by the majorities. The joint testimony of the family members opposing Alan Yeo declared that Timothy Yeo, son of Alan Yeo, was once denied of his proposal to purchase the 140 thousand shares (4.32%) owned by Yeo Wei Heng at $6 million at the end of January 1994. If the purchase had succeeded, Alan Yeo would have increased his share from 47% to 51.5%. His intended move completely disappointed other family members who felt that Alan Yeo had betrayed them. Yeo Chee Chao claimed that Alan Yeo ran the company in an arbitrary way, making a lot of decisions all by himself without asking for opinions of the other directors.

When Yeo Thian Hwa, one of the directors of YHS, was required to testify in court, he confessed that the dissolution of the Holding Company might be the only choice left for the family members since they could not get along well with each other. The 82-year-old Yeo Thian Hwa admitted that the family members of the third generation had grown up and needed their own space for development. He recalled that the shareholders were always in unity while making business decisions during the years from 1969 to 1985 when the deceased Yeo Thian In was the chairman of YHS. In his memory, the directors would get together to discuss business at 5 p.m. every Monday and were free to put forward their own opinion on major issues. Sometimes they might chat with each other in a relaxed atmosphere. To Thian Hwa, that was the appropriate approach to run YHS. As he disclosed, he was once asked to take the office of chairman after Thian In died in 1985, but he declined because of his poor English. Alan Yeo then was appointed chairman of the company.

On the sixth day of hearing, Yeo Chee Feng, daughter of Thian Seng and accounting manager of YHS Holding Company, confessed that her family decided to sell their part of shares of YHS Holdings together with the family of Yeo Chee Wei mainly because her father was asked to resign from director of YHS. What's more, Alan Yeo, the man in real power, was then dissatisfied with her family members, most of whom had quit their jobs in YHS Holdings. She also pointed out that the business of YHS became worse and suffered losses in 1991. Suggestions put forward by her family members were generally not accepted by Alan Yeo. For example, her family, in association with the family of Yeo Chee Wei, once raised a motion for the establishment of an executive committee, but was denied by Alan Yeo. In Chee Feng's understanding, the denial of the suggestion constituted one of the reasons for the family of Yeo Chee Wei to sell their shares. Although Alan Yeo finally compromised and promised to establish the executive committee, the plan was not implemented until February 1992. She was totally disappointed with the delay.

The case of YHS Holding Company entered the stage of court debate on June 29, 1994. The defense lawyer argued that Alan Yeo had discussed with the Keppel Group and Wing Tai Holdings on the purchase of YHS shares, which could jeopardize the control right of the Yeo's family in YHS. Alan Yeo betrayed his family members by trying to sell the shares on two attempts. In addition, the company had been performing poorly. For this reason, family members who opposed him were entitled to dismiss him from his position. Representatives of Alan Yeo argued that when they demanded to dismiss Alan Yeo, the family members of the opposition had interest other than that of the company's. The family of Yeo Wei Li, was asked to quit from the Holding Company because he knew that he would not be able to become a director once Keppel became a major shareholder. The reason for the family of Yeo Thian Seng to quit did not lie in the poor performance of YHS. As Yeo Chee Feng confessed, her family decided to sell the shares because her father and the other three members were asked to leave their positions. As for the family of Yeo Chee Wei, he made the decision to sell his part of the shares because he was dismissed from the position of Executive Director in 1992. It was the break-up of family relations that resulted in the application to dissolve the YHS Holding Company.

Lim Teong Qwee, the judiciary commissioner of the high court hearing the case of YHS, declared on July 1, 1994 that the collective management approach of YHS had no longer adapt to the structure of the listed company. In accordance with the provisions of Justice and Fairness, Article 254 in the Company Ordinance, he adjudicated YHS Holding Pte Ltd to be dissolved. The high court also announced to authorize three accountants from KPMG as liquidators for the Holding Company.

The high court judge, Lim Teong Qwee, agreed with the statements by Alan Yeo's lawyer that the Holding Company was actually run in a manner similar to a partnership. He pointed out that the problem originated from the demand of Yeo Chee Wei to liquidate the Holding Company in February 1992, showing that a new arrangement must be adopted. Decisions of the Holding Company were made with the consensus of shareholders in the years before 1991, which was a unique arrangement;

but since then, the company began to make its decisions by vote, for the shareholders differed in their opinions, which meant the emergence of a new structure.

At the same time, he figured that the break-up of the partnership stemmed from the demands of family members such as Yeo Wei Li to dismiss Alan Yeo from his position in YHS. If the other side of the family members were not satisfied with the performance of Alan Yeo, they could settle the problem by other means. However, the family members of the opposition chose to decide the fate of Alan Yeo by a cast of vote, showing proof that the arrangement in the past had been abandoned. The judge did not believe that the only reason for the opposing family members to dismiss Alan Yeo was because of the poor performance of YHS. He was quoted as saying that family members of the other side should have been fairer in the case. Based on the abovementioned reasons, he agreed that the relationship of trust and dependence among family members was already damaged.

The applicant Alan Yeo, however, was not pleased with the dissolution of YHS Private Holding Limited. It was a sad day. The Yeo family was broken up and 39% of the share control right had to be surrendered. Alan Yeo told his family members that "we won, but all of us should feel sorry about it". Calmly, he told the journalists: anyway this was a good decision. No more family disputes, no more quarrels in the future.

The other side in opposition to the dissolution of YHS Holdings felt equally sorry and disappointed. Yeo Chee Xiang believed that it was a humiliation for YHS, for the property inherited from ancestors would soon fall into the hands of others people. Since the share rights would be divided after the dissolution of YHS Holdings, it would no longer be possible for any individual family to control YHS. Yeo Wei Li said that he would never sell his part of YHS shares even if the Holding Company is dissolved, for that was what he inherited from his father, and he would save it for his son. Mr Ng Lay Hua, mother of Yeo Wei Li, was very sorry and disappointed for not being able to maintain the cause that was painstakingly established by her deceased husband and the several uncles. Yeo Wei Li, having worked in YHS for 22 years, was the general manager from 1998 to 1992 and the senior vice president since 1994. Yeo Wei Heng, who served YHS for 15 years, even shed tears at the judgment. He lived in the US for three years and was the vice president responsible for YHS's business in America.

Epilogue

When members of the Yeo family were engaged in heated disputes, Ng Teng Fong became a major shareholder of YHS and began to play a significant role in the company by purchasing shares of YHS through Orchard Parade, Far East Organization and Sino Land Co Ltd, Hong Kong.

After the dissolution of YHS Holdings, the shares of YHS Ltd owned by members of the Yeo family gradually dispersed. Major changes also took place at the management level of YHS Ltd. Among the many family members who left YHS, Alan Yeo, on February 6, 1995, resigned from the board and from all the positions in the subsidiary companies and allied companies.

On February 8, 1995, First Capital under Quek Leng Chan in association with Sembawang Industry Pte Ltd (affiliated to Sembawang Corporation Ltd), Straits Marine Leasing Pte Ltd (affiliated to Haw Par Brothers International Ltd) and KMP Pte Ltd (under Lim Sioe Liong, a wealthy Indonesian businessman) began to participate in the campaign to buy over YHS. When the shares held by both sides increased, the competition was growing white-hot. On June 26, an extraordinary war for the dominance of share control escalated as First Capital proposed to purchase at $4.70 per share and Ng Teng Fong delivered his plan to purchase at $5 per share. In order to win the share control right, Ng Teng Fong increased his offer to $5.25 and then

$5.35 per share. By September 11, 1995, Ng Teng Fong held 45.62% of the shares of YHS. The following day, the group headed by Quek Leng Chan announced to give up the purchase of YHS and sold its shares to Ng Teng Fong, a deal which rewarded Quek with a profit of $50 million. On September 18, some members of the Yeo family sold their shares to Ng's company.

On the first two days of October, Yeo Wei Li and Yeo Chee Xiang, the last two directors of YHS from the family, resigned from their positions in YHS in succession.

Table 1.1:   The Change of Share Right of YHS

Date	Share Ratio of YHSH (%)	Ng Teng Fong's Share Ratio (%)	Quek Leng Chan's Share Ratio (%)	Closing Price of the Day (dollars)	Price of Warrant of the Day (dollars)
1994.05.13	38.90	6.56		3.68	
1994.05.18		7.85		3.90	
1994.05.19		10.48		3.90	1.41
1994.05.20		14.48		3.92	1.44
1994.05.24		15.78		4.08	1.72
1994.05.27		16.75		4.20	2.02
1994.06.03		17.08		3.85	
1994.06.14		18.08		3.94	
1994.06.20		19.00			
1994.06.28		19.81		3.94	
1994.06.30		20.00			
1994.07.04		20.73		3.88	1.33
1994.07.05		20.82		3.64	
1994.12.09	14.32				
1995.03.08			6.70	4.08	
1995.03.15			9.10	4.10	
1995.03.24			17.03	4.10	
1995.03.27		24.77		4.20	
1995.03.31			19.35	4.20	
1995.04.06	9.76				
1995.04.13			22.86		
1995.06.05	0.07				
1995.06.26			26.27	4.70	
1995.06.27		24.83		4.90	
1995.07.07		24.90			
1995.07.31		27.12	30.37	5.15	
1995.08.11		30.37		5.25	
1995.08.30		42.89		5.35	
1995.09.01		42.93		5.35	
1995.09.04		43.43		5.35	
1995.09.05		43.55		5.35	
1995.09.07		44.50		5.35	
1995.09.08		44.88		5.35	
1995.09.11		45.62		5.35	
1995.09.15		86.89		5.35	
1995.09.28		88.80		5.35	

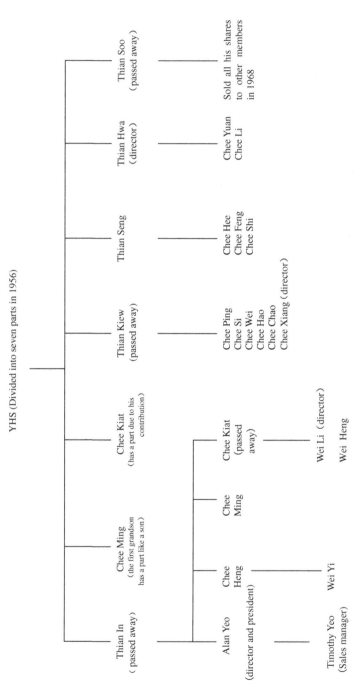

Figure 1.1:   The Earliest Seven Shareholders of YHS and Their Sons and Nephews

2

Family Enterprises in China: The Struggles of the First Generation

In the past 30 years, family enterprises in China have sprung up rapidly since the introduction of the country's economic reform and open-door policy. The rapid pace and size of development won the admiration of many, and at the same time, invited questions such as: Is the old Chinese proverb "wealth does not sustain beyond three generations" still relevant today? Will the centuries-old stories repeat themselves? What can we learn from them?

Modern Chinese family enterprises have yet to prove that they can survive three generations but there are already evidence to show that many cannot even survive beyond the first generation. The development paths of the two well-known family enterprises in this chapter reflect the most obvious problems that these family enterprises encounter, namely, governance structure, and professional management.

Governance Structure in Family Business

The collapse of Delong is a typical example of how poor governance structure will eventually lead to troubles and ruin the company.

In the long run, a vulnerable and irrational governance structure in family enterprises will not only militate against sustainable development of family enterprises, but also exert a negative impact on national security. The financial crisis in 1997 triggered a "Pyramid Conspiracy" that eroded the interests of small and medium-sized shareholders and creditors of family enterprises in East Asia.

The problems behind corporate governance embodied in the crisis can provide lessons for Chinese family enterprises.

Family enterprises in East Asia play a critical role in the economy of the region. We have Formosa Plastics Group owned by Wang Yongqing, Cathay Group owned by Cai Wanlin in Taiwan, Cheung Kong and Hutchison Whampoa owned by Li Kashing in Hong Kong, Kuok Brothers owned by Guo Henian and Lion Group in Malaysia, Guo Fangfeng family enterprise group, United Oversea Chinese Bank Group owned by Wee Chow Yeow and YHS in Singapore, Bangkok Bank Public Company Limited and Charoen Pokphand Group owned by Xie Guomin in Thailand, Salim Group owned by Lin Shaoling and Lippo Group in Indonesia, and Chen Yonzai Group in the Philippines, to name a few. Statistics (Larry Lang *et al.*, 2001) show that the percentage of market capitalization of the listed companies controlled by the top 15 families of East Asian in their GDP are: 84.2% in Hong Kong, 76.2% in Malaysia, 48.3% in Singapore, 46.7% in the Philippines, 39.3% in Thailand, 21.5% in Indonesia, 17% in Taiwan and 12.9% in Korea. It is obvious that family enterprises play a significant role in the economy. At the same time, problems in the governance structure of these enterprises were time-bombs against future healthy development of economies. Since the financial crisis first began in Thailand in 1997, it swept the financial markets of Southeast Asian nations and spread to other parts of East Asia. The far-reaching crisis went beyond people's expectation. Research studies conducted on the financial crisis discovered that the vulnerability of legal systems on corporate governance exerted a significant impact on the collapse of the stock and exchange markets. A corporate governance system that is punctuated with flaws swiftly turned an initial currency crisis into an economic disaster.

Since the legal protection system for the rights of small and medium-sized shareholders in East Asia region have fallen behind that of developed countries, the serious flaws in corporate governance further damaged the confidence of investors and caused the crisis to become a cascading avalanche. The differences in the extent of legal protection in different nations of the region contributed to the differences in the degree of the crisis. Studies conducted by the World Bank governance group found that major separation between ownership and controlling-right remained in family-controlled enterprises and small-sized enterprises of the nine economies in East Asian regions. The phenomenon of the general adoption of a pyramid structure and cross share-holding or special vote amplified the controlling right over bottom companies and enabled families to enjoy a controlling right over the listed companies well beyond their ownership or share-holding. Family enterprises transferred the fortune of the listed companies to the non-listed companies owned by the family, and shifted debts and poor-quality assets to the listed companies so as to exploit small and medium-sized shareholders and creditors thus revealing serious flaws in corporate governance. Once a crisis occurs, holding shareholders invariably would sacrifice the interests of the others to safeguard their own. Professor Larry Lang, a member of the World Bank governance group, together with other scholars, found in a comparative study conducted between family enterprises of Asia and Europe that there were a number of family-owned listed companies of "non-tight-controlling" (the controlling right ranging between 10% to 20%) that small and medium-sized shareholders failed to set eyes on. The kind of "non-tight-controlling" company accounts for 2.94% of the total listed companies in Europe, but the number in Asia reaches as high as 15.44%. Thus, controlling shareholders are not subject to the supervision for abnormal capital and they have the chance to exploit small-sized shareholders, by distributing lower valuated dividends, selling the assets of a controlling listed company to its wholly owned subsidiary at a price lower than its cost, or by purchasing the assets of its wholly owned subsidiary at a price higher than its cost. Moreover, almost all "non-tight-controlling" enterprises in Asia took advantage of related bank loans, but the odds in Europe are quite low, for the financial companies over there generally pay much more attention to the companies at the lower end of the family management pyramid. In listed family enterprises of Europe, the second largest shareholder tends to monitor the "self-interested behavior" of the major shareholder to reduce the risks of exploitation. But in listed family enterprises of Asia, the second largest shareholder tends to conspire with the major shareholder in the exploitation of small and medium-sized shareholders. Prevalence of the interlocking director system in Chinese organizations in Hong Kong and Southeast Asia, for example, easily reminds people of conspiracy beyond strategic interest. When stock markets boom, major shareholders utilize cash to increase their fund and borrow money from financial institutions to expand the credit. The money, however, is not used for the enterprise itself. Instead, they devote the fund to share price and high-risk assets investment (for example, land). Once stock markets get gloomy, pressed by the shrinkage of financial guarantee, they have to maintain high share prices to reduce the pressure from financial institutions for the loan. To maintain high share prices with insufficient funds at hand, they tend to procure the funds of the listed company by way of insider trading to speculate in share markets. As they intensify their support for the shares price, more and more funds are drawn out from the company. Once the stock market crashes and the company is forced to close or withdraw from market, the victims are the ordinary investors. The phenomenon, which had recurred in Delong, China, should be a warning to others.

The existence of many shadow shareholders in Asia makes it hard for external investors to quickly identify the real controller of the enterprise, which seriously impairs the judgment of investors. Thanks to a more restricted regulation on corporate disclosure and a more independent and powerful external judiciary system in Europe, the pyramid structure is rarely adopted in Europe. Therefore, we should draw lessons from the serious consequences incurred by the problem of governance structure in East Asian family enterprises.

From the situations of some family enterprises in the US today, we may find that many of them are top money-makers with long history. Among the well-known multinational enterprises are Ford, DuPont, Kodak, GM, Motorola, Philip Morris and Disney. The contributions they have made to the US economy are as healthy and positive as their own developmental growth. This is closely intertwined with their mature and improved corporate governance structure and the practice of sharing weal or woe with small and medium-sized shareholders. Even in the US where the market-oriented model prevails, the shareholding of family enterprises is gradually diluted, but many families are still the controlling shareholders. With the advanced concept of management, they attach importance to relative controlling and often employ professional managers. Although they generally take their seats behind the scene, shareholder family members will, in times of crisis, promptly get rid of the CEO and take control and action personally. For example, Ford Company, with a history of one hundred years, was listed in 1956 with the Ford family holding 40% of the shares. In November 2001, Jacques Nasser, the former CEO of Ford who was once awarded the best manager, was dismissed from the company, after 33 years of service, for a significant drop in the company's performance. He was subsequently replaced by Bill Ford, great-grandson of Henry Ford, the founder of Ford Company. That was the first time since 1979 that the Ford family returned to the scene and took charge of the overall management of the company. Another example is DuPont with a history of 200 years (listed for 80 years), whose family still controls 24.6% of the company shares. Having gone through ups and downs for many years, the family-controlling companies became public enterprises by diluting their own shareholding and taking in excellent managers. They have a relative degree of control and enjoy advanced concept of management. Moreover, they remised more shares after being listed and accomplished a shared growth of fortune with their own public shareholders. These explain why the enterprises could last for centuries.

At the same time, the overall system of governance structure in the American economic environment is relatively advanced and matured. Generally speaking, family enterprises in the US are integrated listed, so shareholders are shown as individuals. Under sound laws and supervision, less insider trading occurs that threatens the benefits of small and medium-sized shareholders. Hence, for centuries-old enterprises or new high tech giants, the ratio of family controlling is relative. What's more, with a full flow of shares, an active market of controlling and relatively dispersed shareholding rights which invite competition for the controlling right of the corporation controlling shareholders are compelled to serve the benefits of all shareholders. In addition, credit-rating organizations with authorities, together with many professional financial analyzers, observe the every move and action of the company, which makes family controlling shareholders less able, and willing to harm the interests of external shareholders. Even when family enterprises fail as a result of poor management, organizational investors will take the initiative to intervene and actively advocate reform in corporate governance. The proportion of organizational investors will not be low, for the shares owned by them will increase with the expansion of the corporation. When the company declines in performance, selling of shares will cause further decline, which would incur even greater losses for organizational investors. So the investors are compelled to intervene to prevent further decline. By doing so, the phenomenon of going with the flow can be avoided. A large proportion of independent directors in the board of directors in American and European enterprises contribute to the protection of the benefits of small and medium-sized shareholders.

As far as economic development phase is concerned, American family enterprises in traditional industries have generally transformed into public companies. While in new industries, the introduction of venture investment and the NASDAQ market rapidly disperses shareholding rights of high tech companies in the process of expanding. In these companies, absolute shareholding (generally refers to 50% of shareholding rights) is rare. In addition, owing to the restrictions placed by the Investment Management Law on the ratio of Joint Stock Company and long-term separation between banks and trust investment, few holding companies in America adopt the pyramid structure. Instead, they focus on reducing the agent cost of managers and making rational and effective decisions.

Compared with family enterprises in other regions, what are the limits and problems in governance structure of the Chinese family enterprises? Firstly, the single structure of board members in current Chinese family enterprises limits further development of the enterprises. Most of the board members only include the founder and family members. Directors representing fund and technology are often excluded. In fact, it will be a most-rewarding practice for the sustainable development of family enterprises to include industrial experts, financial experts, capital operation experts and managerial experts into the board. At the initial stage, most Chinese family enterprises focus on a "knock-out" product to gain an edge in their industry. However, the problem of strategic product direction still exists even if they develop at a rapid pace. To solve the problem, diversified membership in the board will be able to provide more possibilities in funding, management and strategies for the further development of family enterprises.

Secondly, non-listed family enterprises often encounter financing problems. In order to avoid tax, most of the family enterprises tend to conceal their financial statements and the nature of family enterprises makes this possible. Thus, it becomes difficult for outsiders to learn about the real financial situation. Consequently, family enterprises can hardly obtain external finance (investment or loan). Without support of external capital, it may be extraordinarily difficult for the enterprises to expand through their own accumulation. It is estimated that 70% of the family enterprises will wind down in five years.

The assets of listed family enterprises are rapidly accumulated after being listed. The assets of the newly listed top five family enterprises (often referred to as "Five Riches") increased by three to nine times after the three stages. As for the equity structure, generally speaking, families get more than 50% of controlling rights. The proportion of the second largest shareholder falls far behind that of the controlling family, and most of the shares owned by the former are non-negotiable founders' shares. The ratio of negotiable shares stays right around 25%, the critical point. It is obvious that family shareholders firmly held the controlling right. What's more, the degree of disclosure over ultimate owner differs: founders of some companies are generally corporate bodies instead of natural persons, making it difficult to identify whether the equity structure is also a similar pyramid. To be listed becomes a choice favored by many family enterprises, because of quick accumulation of assets after being listed. In many cases, they try every means to be listed, even though they are not eligible for the conditions of IPO. One of the choices is to arrange for back-door listing, i.e., to acquire the controlling right of a listed company by purchasing non-negotiable shares of the company (most are listed state-owned enterprises). Many companies have adopted this method because of low cost — lower than that of purchasing negotiable shares, high speed (unnecessary to go through reviews by IPO or tutorship period), large quantity of objects for choice and the support from local governments. The effects, however, vary: some family enterprises have achieved size effect by making good use of the fund collected after being listed. Moreover, they have facilitated a stable and continuous growth of profit by way of consecutive allotment finance; other family enterprises, however, manipulated share prices to satisfy their own interests. Their investment in industry fell far behind the increase of the prices. The share prices, which have seriously exceeded performance, will ultimately return to a rational level. Manipulation over share prices is likely to result in collapse of the fund chain and act as a threat for the future. To substantiate these claims consider the Delong case.

The problem of corporate governance has always been a noteworthy topic, for it involves the direction and control system in an enterprise, the distribution of rights and obligations among the board, managers, shareholders and other stakeholders, rules and procedures for corporate decision-making, and the method to realize the aim of a company and the structure to supervise performance (Organization for Economic Cooperation and Development (OECD), 1999). Moreover, governance structure may exert an influence over the management of an enterprise, and even over the security of national economy and finance. Compared with other kinds of enterprises, governance structure in family enterprises is more likely to be controlled. Therefore, the reasonable and rational choice of governance structure constitutes one of the important factors for the healthy and sustainable development of family enterprises.

Case 2: Delong: Corporate Governance

April 14, 2004 is the day that will be deeply imprinted on the mind of Delong. It is on the day that Delong troika, i.e., He Jin Investment (000633), ST Tun He (600737) and Torch Automobile Group (000549), begun to go limit-down, which was a prelude to the collapse of Delong. The total assets, which were valued at more than tens of billion of yuan, rapidly shrunk to near zero within only a month. According to some assumptions, the financial black hole of the whole Delong system is as big as tens of billion yuan.

Till June 30, various financial black holes disclosed by ten Delong-related listed companies, such as ST Zhong Shi, Tian Shan Co Ltd, ST Zhong Yan etc. had reached billions of yuan. The "landmine" began to explode all around. The influence of Delong black hole had extended to a much wider field. A group of financial institutions, which had direct or indirect relationship with Delong, surfaced. Zhong Fu Securities, Jian Qiao Securities, De Heng Securities, and Heng Xin Securities had been exposed one after another to be associated with Delong. Many listed companies which have entrusted their financial business to the above security companies were victims, among which were Chongqing Estate Development Joint-Stock Co Ltd, Shang Gong Co Ltd, and Jiangsu Qiong Hua High-Tech Co Ltd etc. Under the huge pressure of 40 billion debts, Delong was in a hopeless plight. In August 2004, Hua Rong Assets Management Corporation took over the assets of Delong.

On November 3, 2004, the troika of Delong — St Tun He, He Jin Investment and Torch Automobile Group — announced almost at the same time that Hua Rong Assets Management Corporation had successfully taken over the assets of the three companies and begun to engage in the substantial operational work. Till then, Hua Rong had formally taken over control of Delong group. Hua Rong is an asset management company, which is renowned for its better control of non-performing assets.

Thus, the largest Chinese civilian-run enterprise — Delong, which had been established by the four Tang brothers — formally ended.

After taking a deep sigh, Tang Wanli, the director of Delong group, said "This is too dramatic. I can't bear it!". Delong, the corporation that ever had control of the market, had completely died away. Delong, whose total asset was valued at 27 billion yuan, was ranked first in the Chinese family enterprises. There used to be 177 subsidiary companies and 19 financial institutes belonging to Delong, the value of which totally reached some hundreds of billion yuan. Delong had even been regarded as the icon of Chinese civilian-run corporations. In the past 18 years, from a small-sized company originally established in the northwestern border of China, it had developed into a financial and industrial empire, which was valued at over 120 billion yuan. On one hand, Delong expanded largely to purchase hundreds of companies, ranging from cement, auto parts, electric instruments, and heavy truck to ketchup and plant seeds etc. On the other, it also took in Jin Xin Trust, De Heng Securities, Xinjiang Financial Leasing, New Century Financial Leasing and many other commercial banks and financial companies. On January 12, 2005, the committee of Shanghai Pudong People's Congress declared that Tang Wanxin, the representative of the second People's Congress, had been "taken into custody". His rights as a representative had been suspended. In fact, Tang Wanxin was arrested on December 17, 2004, and had since been detained in a prison located in Hubei province. One of the great private entrepreneurs had fallen. Once the model of Chinese stock market makers, he had lost all of the glory and may have to live the rest of his life in the lonely prison. So 2004 could be known as the year of death of Delong.

The Establishment of Delong

Delong was established by seven college students. It is a Chinese family holding company, whose shareholders are the four brothers of Tang family, Tang Wanli, Tang Wanping, Tang Wanchuan and Tang Wanxin. Since taking over control of the three stock-listed companies — He Jin Investment, Torch Automobile and Xinjiang Tun He, Delong successively merged, purchased and integrated hundreds of companies. In Xinjiang province alone, there were a few dozens of companies associated with Delong. The three tall buildings standing in the center of Urumchi — Hongyuan Building, Tun He Building and City Hotel — are regarded as the three-dimensional symbols of Delong. The total sales of Delong and so-called Delong system in the year of 2001 had exceeded 20 billion yuan. And thus 2001 was called the year of Delong, during which any stock associated with Delong experienced a crazy increase.

Delong's success began in 1986. With only 400 yuan in their pockets, 7 young college students headed by Tang Wanxin, who was driven by the desire of making contribution to their country through business, established a color photo development company named "Friends" in Xinjiang region. At that time, the business of color photo development was new and this way especially so in the virgin territory of Xinjiang. Since the photo development was very expensive in Urumchi and Friends Company could not bear the costs of expensive photo development equipment, these college students chose to travel frequently from Urumchi to Guangzhou where they developed the roll films to photos. At that time, there were few competitors in the business of color photo development in Xinjiang, the Friends Company could rapidly accumulate enough capital to buy a second-hand color photo development equipment. Thanks to the comparatively low price, Friends Company held a tight rein on the entire market. Within only one year, revenue generated from color photo development amounted to 10 million yuan. With their first barrel of gold, Tang Wanxin and the other six partners began to explore the wholesale business of clothes, dried noodles and fertilizer, etc.

In 1988, the Xinjiang Technical Committee contracted its subordinated New Products and New Techniques Development Department to the four brothers. Since then, they began to undertake the business of software development. The Urumchi New Products and New Techniques Development Department and the Tian Shan Commodity Trade Company are regarded as the rudiment of Delong. But the businesses they dealt with, such as color photo development, clothes wholesales, food manufacture, computer selling, were not so profitable. Till 1990, the Tang brothers had lost all their 10 million yuan capital, which was an astronomical number. They had also run into serious debts.

In 1990s, they changed their business from software development to computer selling. And the Xinjiang Delong Company was formally registered as a company with collective nature. They rode on the rising tide of the third industry, wading into the fields of entertainment, restaurants and real estate. In 1992, when Delong had earned enough funds, they established Delong Industry Company, whose main businesses focused on real estate and stock operation. In March 1993, Tang Wanxin and the others registered Urumchi Real Estate Development Company, with the capital of 80 million yuan. This company was of the nature of civilian-run collective ownership, which was under the charge of Xinjiang Delong Company.

When Delong was involved in the stock market, its business could be seen as a gamble rather than a trade. In the newborn Chinese stock market, opportunities co-existed with risks. At the time when most people were afraid to engage in the risky originally issued stock, Tang Wanxin, in contrast, firmly believed that stock had the possibility of value increment.

The Development of Delong

By mid-1990s, Delong started its way of multi-dimensional development, giving its priority to investing in a variety of projects.

In 1994, the Xinjiang Delong Agriculture and Livestock Co Ltd, was established, with the registered capital of 100 million yuan. It undertook the agriculture and livestock development in Xinjiang region.

In 1995, after the initial capital accumulation, the Tang brothers commenced their overseas traveling to carry out their field study and research on the industry and capital markets of Western developed countries. Tang Wanxin and other Delong staff thought that there is a basic rule during the course of world industrial structural modification, i.e., the baton of manufacturing is passed from Europe and America to Japan, and then from Japan to Taiwan, Hong Kong and South-eastern Asia. And now it is being passed on to the mainland of China. Tang Wangxin was convinced that this would be a historical opportunity for China and that "manufacturing industry should root itself deeply into the land of China." Then Delong of that day had set down the development objective for the enterprise — embarking on the project investment. Xinjiang Safflower Development Co Ltd, Urumchi Xianghe Industrial Co Ltd and Beijing Wanxinda Electric Appliance Co Ltd sequentially came into being, whose registered capital were 2 million yuan, 1.2 million yuan and 3 million yuan respectively. In addition, they also set up the Xin Zu DeLong Agriculture and Livestock Company, Beijing Zong Fu Properties Co Ltd, Beijing Jiji Disco P. E. Amusement Co Ltd (joint venture with Taiwan capital), Shanghai Xing Te Hao Enterprises Co Ltd (joint venture with Hong Kong capital). These enterprises, together with the two huge buildings — Hongyuan Building and City Hotel — standing right in the center of Urumchi, were considered as the symbols of Delong's second development phase.

In May 1997, based on the "Law of Corporation" Urumchi Delong Real Estate Development Company applied to become a limited corporation, with the registered capital of 30 million yuan. Tang Wanxin took the responsibility of the legal representative. And the corporation founders, Tang Wanli, Tang Wanping and Huang Ping, etc., became main shareholders. And since then, Xinjiang Delong International Industry General Company had also been restructured as Xinjiang Delong (Group) Co Ltd, which indicated that Delong, for the first time, had shaken off the restriction of the collective nature, becoming a traditional Chinese family holding enterprise, whose main stockholders were the four Tang brothers.

Delong's Road of Expansion by Integrating Industry and Finance

Another distinct feature of Delong, however, lies in its operation in capital market, which enables the enterprise to expand at an unimaginably rapid speed. Three major campaigns attributed to its success.

Tun He campaign

In February 1996, Xinjiang Delong, in association with ten other organizations and companies in Xinjiang, including Xinjiang Tun He, contributed 7 million yuan to establish Xinjiang Financial Leasing Co Ltd, marking Delong's formal entry into capital market. Ever since October 1996, when Xinjiang Delong International Industry General Company was assigned 10.18% of the stock shares of Xinjiang Tun He and thus became the third largest shareholder of Xinjiang Tun He, Delong formally began its capital operation. Although its size ranked the second in cement enterprises of Xinjiang region, Xinjiang Tun He faced fierce competition for market share from

Tian Shan Cement, a leading enterprise in the region which located no more than 50 kilometers away. After taking over Xinjiang Tun He, in the form of selling 51% of physical assets to Tian Shan Cement by Xinjiang Tun He, Delong completed an integration of cement market which accounted for 60% of production capability in Xinjiang region. Xinjiang Tun He, getting rid of its formerly gray-coated impression, transferred its major business to the Red Industry, thereby centering on the processing of special local fruits and vegetables such as tomatoes, carrots, safflowers and Chinese boxthorns. Presently, its production capability for ketchup ranks first in Asia and second around the world. In order to penetrate and conquer the international market, Xinjiang Tun He purchased a foreign marketing company with marketing experience for ketchup for more than 20 years. In addition, it consolidated its cooperation with the US Heinz Group. Domestically, Xinjiang Tun He acquired 51% of stock equity of Hui Yuan Group, a well-known enterprise in fruit juice beverage market, enabling the production of ketchup from Tun He to account for 85% of the national market and 6% of the global market. Tun He's export volume for ketchup ranks first in the country.

Delong began to adopt its first step. On the one hand, Delong tried to increase Tun He's competitiveness through investments on technology reform and capacity enlargement; while on the other, Delong purchased some neighboring medium and small-sized cement plants and then gradually undertook technology reform and capacity enlargement in those plants — to invest all the funds raised from former two stock dividends into this field.

After one year, Tun He had developed into the second largest cement enterprise in Xinjiang region, with the annual capacity of over 1 million tons. Under this circumstance, Delong took its second step. In March 2000, Tian Shan Co Ltd and Tun He Co Ltd reached an agreement with the mediation of Delong:

Xinjiang Tun He sold its physical assets, which had the annual capacity of 1 million tons, to Tian Shan Co Ltd. And then they would reorganize a new limited corporation — Xinjiang Tun He Cement Co Ltd — whose registered capital was valued at 350 million yuan. In the new corporation, Tian Shan Co Ltd would buy 51% of stocks with the funds raised during 2000, and Xinjiang Tun He would possess 49% by the form of providing physical assets. The integration had achieved the result of one plus one being more than two. And Delong's third step was underway: the main business of Tun He had transferred from cement to deep processing of agricultural products, such as tomatoes. This market had been developed by Delong for quite a long time, and was comparatively mature. And this transformation was called by Delong staff as transferring from "grey industry" to "red industry". The so-called "red industry" refers to the deep processing of special local products in Xinjiang, including tomatoes, safflowers, carrots, medlars, megranates, red grapes and Chinese dates etc. This industry has prominently expressed the strategic thought of "transferring the resource priority to the economic priority".

Just as expected by Delong staff, the transformation of Tun He was very successful. Its annual production capacity of tomato sauce had reached 240 thousand tons, only 2 tons less than that of the US Heinz Group, whose production capacity was among the first in the world. Tun He mainly exported its products to Europe and the US. Its output had ranked the first in the whole country, which annually increases the foreign exchange of $40 million.

The Campaign of He Jin

In June 1997, Delong put forward its second large step of capital operation. Beijing Zong Fu Properties Co Ltd, which was closely associated with Delong, had been assigned the state-owned stock share of Shenyang He Jin Co, through Shenyang Assets Management Ltd. Thus the quotients of Xinjiang Delong and Beijing Zong Fu in He Jin Co respectively reached to 29.02% and 11%. The two of them became the first and the second largest shareholders of He Jin Co.

The first act that Delong took after mastering He Jin was not in the traditional fields. Together with National Emulation Center, it established a joint venture enterprise named Beijing Titanium Alloy Multidimensional Movies Equipment Development Co Ltd, which focused on the development of "Space Shuttle". "Space Shuttle" is a kind of fashionable and dynamic toy. The moment it was introduced to the market, it rapidly grabbed public attention. The sales continued to increase rapidly for the next two years. But in the third year, orders for the toy took a sudden dive. That was because one space shuttle is sufficient for one theme park. Consequently, He Jin made a prompt decision to transfer the "Space Shuttle" project to others.

This "Space Shuttle" incident further proved the standpoint of Tan Wanxin: that the most promising direction of Chinese enterprises is the traditional industry. Only within this industry could the advantages in the fields of labor and techniques be realized.

Delong carried out studies on Chinese export structure, finding out that the export market for electrical equipment was comparatively small. Only few big enterprises are in this field. However, the overseas market for the electrical equipment was rather big, valued at more than US$10 billion. Furthermore, China's export had continued to increase for the past 10 years at the rate of 20% per year.

From 1998 — the second year that the share right undertook changes, He Jin Holding invested almost all of the funds raised from the capital market into a series of merger, purchase and integration. As a result, He Jin Holding was renamed as He Jin Investment.

Delong adopted the strategy of "coopetition" — cooperating with their main competitor, the globally biggest electrical equipment company (US Murray). A producer of outdoor machinery with a history of more than 70 years, its hand-propelled and sit-type croppers occupy the largest and the second largest shares in the global market.

In the latter half of 2000, He Jin established a strategic partnership with Murray.

According to publicized information, the cooperation mainly included: selling the products of He Jing under the brand and through the marketing channel of Murray; manufacturing Murray's products in the production base of He Jin; jointly developed products which could be sold to Europe and the US; providing support for Murray to stock components in China.

According to Kong Qinghua, the Board chairman of He Jin, the value of this cooperation lies in the connection between Chinese production and US brands, selling channel and after-sales services, and therefore rapidly promoted the increase of market share and profits.

The Campaign of Torch

The third campaign listed in the Delong operation history is the campaign of Torch. On November 6, 1997, Xinjiang Delong was assigned 25 million state-owned stock share of Zhuzhou Torch through the Zhuzhou State-owned Assets Administration Bureau, hence becoming the biggest stockholder of Torch holding 25.72% of its total stock capital. After entering Torch, Delong not only provided 70 million yuan but also introduced the concept of "large scale automobile components", turning a small plant which used to produce only spark plugs into an influential enterprise which had the capability to produce a series of automobile components and other mechanical and electrical products. The amount of exported components of Torch gradually rose to number one in China. Torch subsequently purchased

Zhuzhou Piston Plant, Shanghai He Da Auto Parts Co Ltd, Zhuzhou Torch Real Estate Co Ltd, and Xinjiang Machinery Import and Export General Company etc. It had also been assigned stock shares of Hong Kong Hong Ben. The number of the companies involved in the Torch capital operation and reorganization was more than 20.

With the three major capital operational campaigns being completed, Delong moved its headquarter to Shanghai — the financial center of China. In January 2000, Delong International Strategic Investment Holding Co Ltd was registered, with its headquarter located in the magnificent Securities building Pudong, Shanghai. Its registered capital was 200 million yuan. Both Xinjiang Delong Group and Xinjiang Tun He Group were under the charge of this new corporation. In August 2000, this newly established corporation was renamed as Delong International Strategic Investment Co Ltd. In October of the same year, the corporation increased its registered capital to 500 million yuan. The capital was provided by 33 original members of Delong System. The amount they provided varied from 2.5 million to 68 million yuan. Currently, the "new Delong" refers to the new Xinjiang Delong Group Co Ltd, which had been reorganized by Xinjiang Delong International Industrial Co Ltd. In this new Group, Delong International Strategic Investment Co Ltd possessed 92% stock share, and Tang Wanli held 8% stock shares. Delong had tried to gradually make the concept of "regional" more indistinct. It had walked out of Xinjiang region, stepping into central cities of China, such as Beijing, Shanghai and Guangzhou, etc. Their overseas base was set up in the US.

The Collapse of Delong

Warning — the alarm bell rings

At 9:40 a.m. on October 11, 2001, it was a historical moment. It was at this instant that the stock price of Xinjiang Tun He showed sudden signs of a downward spiral. Within 30 minutes, its price had rapidly dropped from 22.62 yuan to 21 yuan, with a 7% reduction. The stock market took a strong beating, and Delong, the last stronghold of Chinese stock market could no longer sustain and collapsed. Actually, the collapse of every empire begins from its weakest link. Therefore, although Delong's strongest stocks had been "insistently" holding a higher price, the fault of a collapse had already been disclosed.

Barriers to enter ST Zhong Yan

Having been extremely prosperous in the past, Delong would never realize that one day, it would encounter such a tough resistance from one listed company. In retrospect, perhaps the reasons lay in the true strength of Delong: (1) in the course of stock share transferring, Tun He Group had been criticized as "being assigned by way of fraud, and consequently it would not be lawful"; (2) the temporary shareholder meeting was regarded as "illegal"; (3) at the time when the new Board take over, there was nobody in the company building, with the business license and seals had all being taken away by the former Board chairman.

From the point of view of the secondary stock market, after ST Zhong Yan became the member of Delong system, the increase of its stock had only continued for a few days. By the end of July, its price had fallen down from a historic high price of 21 yuan to 14 yuan. In the short span of two months, its stock price had dropped by 33%. This could be seen as the first alarm.

Two limit-downs of Tian Shan Co

Tian Shan Co could be seen as the "outer" member of Delong system. Ever since it purchased 51% net assets of Xinjiang Tun He in October 2000, its stock price rose sharply, from 12 yuan to 28.5 yuan in that same year. Even though its December 2000 stock price had been gradually descending, its mid-year report of 2001 could be seen to have had a close association with Xinjiang Delong: (1) it had superadded 191 million yuan investment to Xinjiang Tun He; (2) its investment to Xiamen United Trust was 30.45 million yuan, accounting for 9.48% of its total investments; (3) the newly added short-term investment (50 million yuan for one year) in the report was consigned to Jin Xin Trust to buy national debts; (4) Xinjiang Financial Leasing Co Ltd, holding 1.5 million stock shares of Tian Shan, was its fourth biggest shareholder.

From the point of view of the secondary market, on October 10 and 11, 2001, Tian Shan Co had continued undergoing two limit-downs (on October 10, ending with limit-down, and on October 11, opening with limit-down). This situation had aroused true market concerns — could the Delong system collapse from the performance of its "outer" members? This could be seen as the second alarm.

The Candle Hammer of Xinjiang Tun He Co

When all the three Zhong Ke system, Yinchuan Guang Xia and East Electronics collapsed, Delong no longer had any competitors in China. Ever since July 2001, the Shanghai stock index had dropped by as much as 25%. The falling of individual stock price had been the general tendency of markets. However under this circumstance, He Jin Investment, Torch and Xinjiang Tun He of Delong system raised their stock price against this tendency to a historical level. This action was quite suspicious and aroused many market concerns. In the morning of July 11, the stock price of Xinjiang Tun He begun to dive, but it rose rapidly again and ended with an increase of 1.63%. A key factor for a strong stock is the support from its stockholders. Once it loses this support, the stock price would have a domino effect. Therefore, the appearance of the Candle Hammer, which had never been shown in the history of the three stocks, had aroused enough concerns. The currency of the three stocks was too valuable — Torch 5.9 billion, He Jin 4.5 billion and Xinjiang Tun He 4.3 billion — and it would be very risky to provide enough funds to support their current price.

Doubts appearing

Since 2002, Xinjiang Tun He had frequently carried out affiliated trading with major shareholders. But behind the affiliated trading, there was a lot of abnormality that needed explaining. For example, in April 2002, Xinjiang Tun He purchased 98.68% stock shares of the Xinjiang Kai Ze Tomato Products Co Ltd from the hand of its major shareholder — Tun He Group. Kai Ze Co, which used to be a subsidiary company to International Industrial Co (000159). Since its setting up in 1998, it had suffered continuous loss. On December 2, 2000, Tun He Group purchased 98.68% stock shares of Kai Ze Co with 96.01 million yuan. After the purchase by Tun He, Kai Ze Co continued losing money in business. In 2001, the total loss had reached 26.06 million yuan.

However, after Xinjiang Tun He had purchased Kai Ze Co, the income of Kai Ze increased astonishingly. In 2002, Kai Ze brought a yield of 22.29 million yuan to Xinjiang Tun He. How could Kai Ze, a corporation with continuous losses, turn loss into gain, after being purchased by Xinjiang Tun He? Did Xinjiang Tun He have some secret formula for success? But it did not seem to be so, when looking at the purchases of Ke Lin Co and Hua Xin Tomao Co which continued losing. In fact, Kai Ze was only one of the miracles of the affiliated trading of Xinjiang Tun He.

On April 30, 2002, from the Tun He Group, Xinjiang Tun He purchased Gu Cheng Co, Wu Gong Co, E Min Cement Co and Bu Erjin Co. During May till December 2002, these four small-sized companies, with an investment of only 10.7251 billion yuan, had actually brought Xinjiang Tun He a profit as high as 27.9 million yuan. However, in 2003, Xinjiang Tun He sold these companies without rhyme or reason.

The suspicious unaffiliated trading

On July 19, 2003, He Jin Investment declared that its intension to purchase 70% stock shares of Wenling Long Jiang Machinery Manufacturing Co Ltd, originally held by Shanghai Chuang Suo Co. He Jin announced that it had no relationship with Shanghai Chuang Suo, but in fact Chuang Suo had bought the stock shares of ST Zhong Yan at an auction in November 2002, becoming its third largest shareholder. ST Zhong Yan was incidentally one of the members of Delong system.

What was more confusing was that the 30% shares of Long Jiang Co held by Shanghai Chuang Suo was transferred by Torch to Chuang Suo in 2003. Why did Torch transfer its stock shares through Shanghai Chuang Suo, to He Jin Investment? The relationship between them was not as simple as what they had declared.

Besides, on January 29, 2003, Xinjiang Tun He announced that they would transfer their shares in Jin Xin Trust to Zhong Ji Holding and Shanxi Heng Ye respectively, both of which, according to Tun He, had no relationship with it. But the fact was that Tun He was closely associated with the two companies. In as early as May 2000, Zhong Ji Holding, together with Torch and Shanghai Ao Shen, had established Zhuzhou Torch Environmental Technology Co Ltd by joint venture.

However, what was more astonishing was that on December 16, 2000, He Jin Investment said that Hai Tong Securities would sell its shares of He Jin to Hua Yue Investment and Zhong Ji Holding respectively. At that time, the price of He Jin stock was more than 30 yuan per share, but the transfer price was only 13.33 yuan. Then after only three months, the transferred stocks had been put onto the market. By so doing, the two companies, closely related to Delong system, had made a big profit of more than 380 million yuan. So it was very suspicious why Hai Tong Securities, a company having a close relationship with Delong, was so generous to those two companies.

Furthermore, the financial status of the companies within Delong system was also worrying. Till March 31, 2003, the total long-term and short-term loans of He Jin Investment, Xinjiang Tun He and Torch had exceeded 7 billion yuan. Their debt-to-asset ratio had reached 65.81%, 72.48% and 70.50% respectively for the three companies. The accounts receivable of the three companies had exceeded 3 billion yuan. And their assurance amounts had exceeded 2 billion yuan.

Stock crash

On December 16, 2003, Delong impawned its 100.2 million corporation stock shares of Torch. This act aroused doubts and concerns from the whole market. Consequently, Delong continued impawning its stocks, which further deepened the concerns. The stock share of Torch, Xinjiang Tun He and He Jin Investment had been successively impawned. And the decline of the stock prices seemed to predict certain nightmares. Delong kept stressing the safety of its capital chain, but market confidence in Delong was rapidly disappearing. As the stock prices underwent a complete reduction, Delong was forced to face the fact that they were encountering severe problems. As such, Delong began to sell its subsidiary companies. ST Zhong Yan was transferred to others.

If the subsidiaries could be limited to the drop of stock prices, then Delong should be able to withstand it. The cracks between

Delong and its subsidiaries or affiliated systems had driven the Delong-shaped industry chain to a drastic breakdown, especially when Delong troika had actively tried to break away from Delong in order to protect themselves from impending damage. The announcement of impawning, assurance and frozen assets came one after another. Since the end of 2003, Delong had impawned many of its stock shares from Torch, He Jin Investment and Xinjiang Tun He. As a result, Delong's remaining shares of Torch were limited to 260 thousand. Almost all the He Jing Investment stock shares belonging to Delong were impawned. The entire Xinjiang Tun He corporation shares originally held in the hands of Xinjiang Delong Group Co Ltd had already been impawned to the banks. The capital black hole of the four listed companies was gradually disclosed. Most of the problems were caused by illegal assurance and embezzlement of the capital by large shareholders and affiliated parties. He Jin Investment pointed out that the current accumulated assurance had reached 718 million yuan, accounting for 136.68% of all the net assets of 2003. Additionally, the assurance announced by Torch and Tian Shan Co had also exceeded the assurance proportion stipulated by "Notice on Regulating the Capital Transferring between Listed Companies and Affiliated Parties and the Assurance of Listed Companies". By April 30, 2004, Torch's holding stockholder Xinjiang Delong and other affiliated enterprises had embezzled a total of 304 million yuan. As evident in the impawning certificates of deposit, Delong International had embezzled 290 million yuan of Xinjiang Tun He. According to Torch's announcement, the 100 million yuan national debt bought by its subsidiary company, Space Torch, had been embezzled by De Heng Securities, which was held by Delong. He Jin Investment holding subsidiary companies had a total 214 million yuan which had been embezzled by both De Heng Securities and Heng Xin Securities. The huge financial black hole ultimately led to a complete collapse of the Delong system.

The Dilemma of Management System for Family Business

Whether to have professional managers who are outsiders in a family business is a struggle of "to be or not to be". The Hamlet dilemma surely puzzles family enterprises like Huanghe Group (see Case 3, p. 72) which are in a phase of rapid development.

To make enterprises bigger and stronger, family business needs to adopt modern management. The employment of professional managers, especially in high-level positions, helps reduce the risks and costs of decision-making and enhances the efficiency of management. The success ratio for finding top managerial talents in a certain closed scope (within the family) may be far lower than that outside the family. For this reason, family enterprises should meet the need of the enterprises for growth and development by introducing professional managers. Modern and advanced enterprise system in accordance with social development should be gradually established, and institutionalized and standardized management be implemented. Institutionalized and standardized management means that enterprises must adhere to certain rules in their management and carry out an internal rule "by law" instead of "by human". As Drucker, the father of modern management, puts it, "a successful enterprise will not be by a single person, but an excellent team of managers. To survive and effectively operate, at least a non-family member is needed at top management, no matter how many family members are there and how outstanding they may be." An important symbol marking professionalized management is that non-family members may get top positions in the company and win trust. Theoretically, the participation of family members in the management does not necessarily exclude professionalized management, and similarly, the introduction of external managers does not necessarily means professionalized management. Nevertheless, from a practical point of view, professionalized management is generally understood as the management by non-family members, because professionalized management is hard to obtain if many family members stay in enterprises.

As they expand, the enterprises will definitely develop more products, carry out more business activities and even get involved in more industries, of which the consequences are a more complicated and changeable environment facing the enterprises. As a result, it requires existing managers to perform more functions and acquire more knowledge and skills. Consequently, if the management, knowledge, and skills of the family members in managerial positions cannot be significantly increased (and that's always the case), the introduction of professional managers will be an inevitable choice for the growth and development of family enterprises.

Studies show that more than 90% of the owners believe that the family-oriented system of employment has obstructed the development of enterprises; 57% of the owners vote against the practice of ensuring the controlling right by appointing their own offspring as bosses. The introduction of professional managerial capability, therefore, has become a key issue in the growth and development of family enterprises.

However, the implementation of professionalized management in family enterprises of the current stage will encounter practical obstacles. From April till July 2000, a research team focusing on "the Studies of Chinese Private-owned Enterprises" carried out an investigation on 3,258 private enterprises in China. The results show that at the end of 2001, 70% of the target enterprises adopted the organizational form of limited liability company, which indicates that reform for family-oriented management has taken place in most of the private-owned enterprises. Nevertheless, the average ratio of the individual capital of the owners in total capital of the enterprises still stands at 76.7%, showing that most of the private-owned enterprises remain as family enterprises. Out of the 96% of the enterprises, the owners are concurrently general managers or directors, which indicate that family-oriented management is still the most common mode of management. To account for their adherence to the family-oriented mode of management, private owners have two reasons: it is difficult to find trustworthy professional managers and ensure the stability of the enterprises. Indeed, the talent pool for professional managers in China is far from mature, so there is a lack in the supply of high-quality managerial resources for family enterprises. From the history of Chinese family enterprises, we find that the managerial talents of family enterprises, at their initial stages, came from state-owned or collectively owned enterprises. A study conducted in 1993 showed that more than 75% of private-enterprise owners worked in state-owned or collectively owned enterprises as cadres, technical workers, or salesmen. Many enterprises fell short of managerial personnel in the latter part of the 1990s, when many enterprises can hardly find high-quality managers in the market, and the training for employees cannot satisfy demands. The following factors worsen the conflict between demand and supply: (1) the tide of establishing enterprises absorbs talents with high entrepreneurial quality, and it is impossible to train a batch of such talents in a short period of time; (2) the enterprises generally adopt the family-oriented style of organization. The patriarchal centralization of power directly results in insufficient authorization for the management at middle or lower levels, especially by non-family members. As a result, the speed of experience and knowledge accumulation slows down; (3) A number of excellent managers are employed by foreign invested enterprises. Although some of them are transferred to family enterprises, the differences in managerial patterns, culture and experience often resulted in conflicts of management style. The family enterprises with a certain scale began to create strong demand for the introduction of external managerial capability. The rapid increase in the number of such enterprises leads to a sharp rise of the demand for managerial capability, but the supply of management talents is limited. Consequently, the supply of management talents cannot effectively satisfy the demand of family enterprises. Moreover, due to the imbalance between the supply and demand, professional managers naturally enjoy the advantages to bargain, which indirectly discourages family enterprises from hiring expensive professional managers.

Another reason that contributes to the refusal of family enterprises to give up the family-oriented system is the possibility of the internal instability. In addition to the changes in the control right of the enterprises, the managerial revolution for profession is also accompanied with the diversity of ownership, innovation of enterprise system, changes of leading and decision-making patterns, and the reform of managerial and employment system. Inevitably, the reforms will result in conflicts between family members who are accustomed to the management by kinship, and the professional managers who urge to enforce systematic and standardized management. As Sun Yingui, president of Bailong Group specifies, "the most difficult thing to do in a family enterprise is the implementation of systematic management. The founders of enterprises are brothers, who in most cases will destroy the systems." That is also the feeling of many founders of family enterprises, some of whom, however, uphold the principle of "no families in management" to facilitate the reform. Unfortunately, internal conflicts may be easily aroused by doing so. As a result, the reform in management can hardly be achieved and the trust and respect among family members might collapse, and even worse, it might lead to the dissolution of the enterprises.

Thirdly, lack of credit under the economic environment in China is an obstacle for family enterprises to introduce professional managers in their management reforms. On one hand, it is difficult for owners to monitor professional managers who have more information of management; on the other hand, many owners, with more financial information, have "two sets of accounts" to avoid tax. By doing so, managers often doubt whether they will be paid in a long run in accordance with the actual accounting profit. Thus, managers tend to care about current income instead of long-term achievements and owners can hardly guarantee managers' service for the long-term interest of the enterprise with salaries. Long-term promotion falls into a dilemma since the owners are afraid of being reported if they release the actual account. At the same time, the loss of confidence of managers in enterprises owners will finally lead to the refusal of long-term promotion, which will ultimately invite betrayal from managers. Moreover, the low trust in managers will reduce the psychological cost for betrayal. As a new social class, professional managers are immature with their ethics. In the eyes of the public and the managers themselves, a job may not be for the long term, but a transitional one. The short-term concept hinders the formation of professional ethics and standards, and constitutes a psychological and social basis for the short-term behaviors of the managers. Besides, with a weak external restriction and void internal governance mechanism, failure of managers to realize their words can neither be held as evidence nor punished with detailed legal provisions. So it may be unimaginable for the founders of family enterprises to hand over their property, accumulated with painstaking efforts, to be managed by others.

There are obviously many reasons to explain why family enterprises may encounter many obstacles in their process of enforcing professionalized management: the introduction of professional managers into the enterprises indicates that the pattern of "only one man's words count" will be broken. It is a challenge for both the owners and the managers to agree on a consensus. Should the owners grant the professional managers authority to do anything? Will delegation exceed the risk? How can the owners both stimulate and control the professional managers? In fact, authorization to managers is a process of sharing confidential resources and information. Can the professional managers wholeheartedly serve the enterprises after they possess the confidential resources and information of the enterprises? How should one guard against unethical behavior of managers? How should such behaviors be punished? It matters much whether the social credit system, especially professional managers system is perfect. It may throw family enterprises into major risks if they hurry to introduce the managerial pattern of professional managers under a less improved system environment. The series of problems restrict the introduction of professional managers, and at the same time create a major obstacle for the professionalized management. Chinese family enterprises are hesitant at such a crossroad: turning left — return to family-oriented management, a road with less risk but would not get very far; turning right — completely introduce professionalized management, with risks and an unexpected future. The Huanghe case is a typical example.

Case 3: Huanghe: Familial Management Versus Professional Management

Introduction

Huanghe Enterprise Group, located on the northwest of China, is currently the largest beer production corporation in the region and the only township enterprise among China's top ten beer corporations. The Corporation was founded by Yang Jiqiang, a peasant entrepreneur, with 4000 yuan as original capital. In less than two decades, Huanghe witnessed a rapid development in scale — from founding of Huanghe Beer Plant in 1985 to forming a business group in December 1993; setting up Lanzhou Huanghe Enterprise Co Ltd which went public on Shenzhen Stock Exchange on June 23, 1999; and becoming the only township enterprise among China's top ten beer corporations.

Huanghe Group, which is under the absolute control of Yang family, is a typical family business. Yang Jiqiang, also the head of the family, assumed the position of board chairman. The eldest son, Yang Shijiang, serves as vice board chairman and general manager. The second son, Yang Shiqin, was the manager of a printing company. The third son, Yang Shiwen, took the post of manager in the beer company. The fourth son was the sales manager. As for the daughters-in-law, the eldest one was the service manager, the second as the head of capital returning department, the third one was the head of finance department, and the youngest daughter-in-law was the manager of the drinks company. Most of the relatives of the family also occupied in important positions.

Expansion in scale required more professional management and technology talents. Insufficient human resources set limitations on business development. Therefore, Huanghe began to explore in the field of professional management and made experiments to recruit non-family talents. Both successes and failures were present in this exploration and experimentation process.

A successful recruitment was the hiring of a brewing expert Bai Xianzhong, the assistant director of Lanzhou Brewing Factory to Huanghe Beer Plant. Bai helped to solve technical problems, making great contribution to further business development. Yet, in later recruitments, Huanghe suffered two major setbacks. The first setback was in May 1999 when Huanghe offered high salaries for professional managers. Zhou Yan, an associate professor from Yanshan University, was recruited as general manager. Another seven people were recruited as high-rank management staff. The two sides signed an agreement in which the employees promised to double the yearly output from 200,000 tons to 400,000 tons within one year, and Huanghe Group would pay them a yearly salary of 360,000 and 240,000 yuan respectivly. But it turned out that Zhou Yan and the seven people failed to actualize the goal. During the Spring Festival period, the supply of Huanghe beer was not enough to meet the market demand. In May 1999, Zhou Yan, together with three vice general managers, left Huanghe, taking only four or five thousand yuan as salary. Afterwards, a bigger failure came when Huanghe recruited Wang Yanyuan, who was a lingering nightmare for the Yang family. While being trusted by Yang Jiqiang, Wan Yanyuan secretly transferred huge amount of Huanghe stocks at a low price. By so doing, she soon became the second largest shareholder — holding only 0.41% less than the largest shareholder — greatly threatening the status of Huanghe. In addition, in the name of business or financial consultant fees, Wan Yanyuan transferred 10 million and 2.92 million yuan on two occasions, to another company whose legal representative was her own son. Wan herself summoned the board meeting, openly challenging the authority of Yang Jiqiang. On November 6, 1999, Wan held a board meeting in Beijing while Yang Jiqiang was having another board meeting in Lanzhou. Later, Wan Yanyuan was arrested for committing economic crime, and therefore a temporary shareholder meeting for Lanzhou

Huanghe Stock Co Ltd was held to remove all the directors and supervisors of the 3rd generation, and to elect new directors and supervisors (Yang Jiqiang was elected board chairman and Yang Shijiang vice board chairman) to replace all the top management. The company resumed its former familial management mode. As to the question of how to reform managerial system to ensure further business development, the Yang family was faced with a dilemma.

The History of Huanghe Group

Huanghe Group, located in an important industrial city in northwest China — Lanzhou — was established by Yang Jiqiang. Having worked as a woodworker, lathe operator and driver, Yang Jiqiang grasped the opportunity when the country began to encourage the development of village and town-owned enterprises. In 1982, Yang Jiqiang, together with his partners, signed a contract to take over the village's farming machinery factory. Yang invested in all his money — 4000 yuan. Three years later, due to environmental problems, the factory stopped production. At that time Yang Jiqiang had already earned 800,000 yuan. Soon after the closedown of the farming machinery factory, Yang Jiqiang, together with his sons, began to seek new business opportunities. After a careful market survey Yang Jiqiang discovered a great market potential in beer industry and decided to invest in it. With 1,170,000 yuan raised from the village and 5,000,000 yuan bank loan, Yang Jiqiang and his four sons founded Lanzhou Huanghe Beer Corporation. With crude facilities of brewing kettle, rice-paste kettle, cooking kettle, and filter tank, the annual production of the corporation reached 10,000 tons. Such a production scale made Lanzhou Huanghe Beer Company a rather big township enterprise at the time. From the very beginning, the company put in use advanced technology, skills, and facilities, thus accumulating a great amount of funds for snowballed development.

Under the leadership of Yang Jiqiang, secretary of party committee and board chairman, the Group grew rapidly for over a decade. Originally, the total assets of the corporation were 6.17 million yuan. It became a big corporation with 1.5 billion yuan in total assets, 1.815 billion yuan in immaterial capital, 31 economic entities, 12,000 employees, and a yearly output capacity of 450,000 tons in 2002. On May 13, 1999, Lanzhou Huanghe Enterprise Group issued "Huanghe" stock over the Internet and became the 6th listed company in the country's beer industry. The brand of "Huanghe" was honored by the National Statistical Institute and other bureaus and institutions with accolades like "China's Most Competitive National Brand", "First-class Native Goods", "Top Ten Popular Brands", "Four Important Development Brands in Beer Industry", "Excellent Brand" and "Famous Brand" in the province, etc. "Huanghe" beer was specially appointed for use in national banquets. In April 1999, the National Industrial & Commercial Administration Bureau selected Nation's key protective brands, and "Huanghe" was included. During the four years from 1995 to 1998, "Huanghe" beer successively passed the sample tests conducted by the State Technology Supervision Bureau. Huanghe beer obtained the sanitation registration for export, and passed the inspection and got the approval of ISO9002 and in product quality. In northwestern China, "Huanghe" beer was the only one to get the two quality attestations.

Converging at Huanghe — Talents recruitment

With expansion in scale, Huanghe felt pressured by the lack of professional management. Further business expansion had pushed it to go beyond the family boundary and attract outside resources. This typical China family business began to step on the road of professional management and talent recruitment.

Lanzhou Huanghe Co Group had a slogan — "Converging at Huanghe" — which means outstanding people are gathered in

Huanghe Group, pushing Huanghe forward. Since the founding of "Huanghe", many people had been attracted to the corporation and stayed there. Take vice board chairman Bai Chengzhong, for example. He was a beer brewing expert from another beer corporation. Without Bai Chengzhong, Huanghe Group would never have attained today's accomplishment.

Success usually does not come easily, and Huanghe was no exception. In recruiting management staff, Yang Jiqiang is broad-minded. He maintained that valuable personnel resources are essential for the development of the corporation. In terms of blood relations, qualification and experience, the four sons of Yang Jiqiang, who had been assisting him in pioneering Huanghe Group, should be the primary considerations. However, with due respect for knowledge, Yang Jiqiang decided to employ people with professional management knowledge. Unfortunately, the two influential recruitments of Huanghe Group proved unsuccessful, contrary to Yang's expectation to engage professional managers in managing the corporation.

First Failure (1985–1997)

The first recruitment of Huanghe Group started with Wang Yanyuan. At that time, Wang was a reporter and the vice chairman and secretary-general of the Township Enterprise Association in Gansu province. Wang Yanyuan grasped a chance to showcase her capability to Yang Jiqiang while she was covering the story of Huanghe Group. Wang edited a collection of papers on township enterprise mechanism for Huanghe, which reinforced Yang's favorable opinion of her. At the time, Yang was considering coming into the market with some of the best assets and he believed that Wang would be of great help because she had some connections with famous scholars in Beijing. Yang wanted Wang to join the Group. In September 1997, Wang entered Huanghe Group as the Vice General Manager, responsible for the listing of the company and promotional activities. Her excellent social and interpersonal skills was a big help to Huanghe Group. Over time, Wang did all the planning work and formed the first directorate of the Huanghe Group, in which Yang was the chairman. Three shareholders and eight non-shareholders were included in the 11-member board. Besides, there were also two independent directors. Wang herself assumed the position of the Vice Chairman and General Manager.

Unexpectedly, upon joining the Huanghe Group, Wang secretly strengthened her family power and sought benefits for her own family enterprise. In 1997, Huaxia Pearl Science and Trade Co Ltd was set up in Beijing — only one month after Wang entry into Huanghe Group. The legal representative of this company was Meng Xiangkui, the son of Wang. In 1998, Wang received 10 million yuan business fees from Yang for listing Huanghe. Instead, Wang transferred the money to Huaxia Pearl Science and Trade Co Ltd. In July 1999, the major bracket of Lanzhou Huanghe stock, in the name of the company's financial consultant transferred 2,920,000 yuan to Huaxia Pearl Science and Trade Co Ltd.

In May 1999, Lanzhou Huanghe Enterprise Co Ltd launched its IPO. And in June, the company went public on the Shenzhen Stock Exchange. The largest shareholder was Lanzhou Huanghe Co Group who held 40,000,000 shares, 40.73% stock right of the listed company. Yang Jiqiang held 180,000 shares, and Yang Shijiang — the second son of Yang Jiqiang — held 20,000 shares. Both the two could not rank among the top ten largest stock holders. On July 22, 1999, the listed HuangHe Stock Co Ltd issued an announcement, stating that Huanghe Group agreed to transfer 19,800,000 shares to Beijing Rongyuanxiang Technology Co Ltd — this company had just registered on the same day — at the price of 1.2 yuan per share. But at that time, the net asset value of each Huanghe share was 5.05 yuan. The fund-providers of Beijing Rongyuanxiang Technology Co Ltd were Wang's parents, and the legal representative was Meng Xiaokui. As for this stock transfer, Yang Jiqiang claimed that he was totally cheated — he signed the documment, not knowing what was on it, and the agreement was a falsified document, with some pages taken out or replaced.

In the later half of October 1999, the conflict between the two families deteriorated. On November 6, 1999, Lanzhou Huanghe Co Group was holding two board meetings simultaneously in Beijing and Lanzhou — something unheard of before in China. Only three board members attended the Lanzhou meeting which was headed by board chairman Yang Jiqiang. But in the Beijing meeting assembled by Wang, more than two-thirds of the board members were present. Dramatically, the Beijing meeting was interrupted by policemen, for Wang was accused of abusing power to transfer Huanghe stock illegally.

In December 1999, some stockholders and the board of supervisors assembled an urgent shareholder meeting for Lanzhou Huanghe Stock Co Ltd. This meeting modified the company's constitution, removed all the directors and supervisors of the 3rd generation, elected new directors and supervisors (Yang Jiqiang was elected board chairman and Yang Shijiang vice board chairman), replaced all the top management with new people — Yang Shijiang as general manager, and appointed new board secretary and chief financial officer. Although the Yang family succeeded in protecting Huanghe, the damage caused to the company could not be underestimated. By mid-2001, the Group was operating at a loss.

After this incident, Huanghe resumed a traditional management style. Only three directors from the last board remained in the new board. The new board contained much fewer none shareholders, and no independent directors. Three members from the Yang family were on the new board. The Yang family also occupied the positions of board chairman, vice board chairman and general manager.

Second Failure (1999)

Another failure in professional management recruitment came in 1999 when Yang Jiqiang offered high salary for general managers. In May 1998, Huanghe Group put advertisements in newspapers like *Economic Daily* and *Huaxia Alcohol*, offering a monthly salary of 30,000 yuan for one general manager, and a monthly salary of 20,000 yuan for ten vice general managers. Altogether, 327 people throughout the nation applied for the posts. After careful screening, the Group selected 132 for interviews. Having been screened and interviewed for 14 times, finally 8 persons were recruited — one as general manager, six as vice general managers, and one for some other position. Zhou Yan, an associate professor from Yanshan University, took the position of general manager. The eight persons promised to double the yearly output from 200,000 tons to 400,000 tons within one year, and Huanghe Group would pay them a yearly salary of 360,000, and 240,000 yuan respectively. Yang Jiqiang excluded his own sons, despite their experiences and qualifications, from the appointments for general managers, which fully demonstrated his sincerity and determination in recruiting non-family talents.

Unfortunately, it turned out that the professional managers failed to live up to Yang's expectation. Zhou Yan did not actualize the target monthly output. During the Spring Festival period, the supply of Huanghe beer was not enough to meet the demand in market. According to routine practice, extra amount of products should be produced and stocked in January to ensure sales in the coming holidays. But Zhou failed to have this prepared. The vice general manager of the Group Cheng Long maintained that Zhou cannot quickly adapt himself to his position in Huanghe. He was not capable of managing the township enterprise despite his professional knowledge.

Two months into the job at Huanghe, Zhou had invited dis-
satisfaction from Yang Jiqiang. Yang Jiqiang once said in a meeting that "the person in charge of production knows nothing
about it. Problems abounds. We cannot rely on stock listing.
Only those who make money have the right to spend money."
Yang Jiqiang lived up to his words. Zhou Yan and other people
did not get their full salary for failing to complete their assignment. One manager who received only two to three thousand
yuan of salary asked Cheng Long for an explanation, to which
Cheng replied "You deserve it because you failed to do what you
had promised." According to Yang Jiqiang, the pay should be
tied to work performance. If the general manager could not fulfill his duty, he should make compensation out of his own
money; for the position of general manager can also been considered as "opportunity cost". Zhou Yan, at that time, was considering taking power away from Yang Jiqiang, commenting that
"he (Yang) is such an old man. We'd better kick him out."
Unable to tolerate Zhou Yan and his people, Yang Jiqiang made
announcement in April 1999 that "the performance in the first
three months is far from the goal we set before. All of the eight
sub-companies should shoulder the responsibility for this. From
an analytical and objective point of view, the problem could be
partly explained by inadequate adjustment and adaptation
among the different branches. And at the subjective level, the
primary reason was a lack of effort. Over the past year, I sat back
and watched other people taking charge. But the reality proved
me wrong. It is time for reform. Those who cannot catch up
within three months should be removed. It is the enterprise that
should be saved, not the people." It is hard to tell whether Zhou
Yan was wronged by Yang or he faulted for challenging Yang. In
any event, Zhou Yan, together with three vice general managers,
left Huanghe in May 1999. At the time of departure, they each
received 4,000–5,000 yuan — only one-sixth of the full salary.

Earlier in February, a vice general manager had also left. Among the initial eight people hired, only two stayed beyond five months.

From familial operation to professional management recruitment, and back to familial operation, Huanghe Group, after launching out on its journey, sailed back to its original position. Yang Jiqiang was courageous enough to take the first step. But because of various reasons, Huanghe suffered greatly. Even his own sons complained. Seeing that good intention and great efforts resulted in huge damage to business, those who wanted to follow Huanghe hesitated. Professional managers or familial operation? A left turn or a right turn? — a dilemma emerged.

The failure of infusing talents into the company is caused by manifold reasons:

The first reason lies in the narrow-minded management concept of Yang Jiqiang. Knowing the importance of infusing talents into the company, he was afraid of being elbowed out by these new managers. Therefore, the moment he sensed his position was being threatened, Yang would get rid of the managers and replace them with his own sons. In his interview with a journalist, he showed this kind of tendency. As he put it, "they've got the wrong guy. Can Zhou Yan challenge me? Absolutely not! He is not daring to do that!"

The second reason lies in the inefficiency of the current governance structure of the company. Although a limited joint stock company established in 1993, a standard corporate governance system had yet to be established when the control right was in the hands of the Yang's family and with the board of directors as rubber stamp. The lack of proper governance gave an opportunity for Wang Yanyuan to easily abuse her power and made illegal stock transfer to her own account, thus incurring losses for the company.

Thirdly, the lack of the knowledge in capital market operation had exerted a negative influence on his role in the process of listing the company. Yang once confessed that due to the lack of the knowledge of corporate listing, he entrusted almost everything regarding the corporate listing to Wang Yanyuan, and that, to some extent, had contributed to her immoral behavior.

Return to Family-Oriented Governance (1999–2003)

In May 1999 after the departure of Zhou Yan and the six managers, vice general manager Yang Shijiang took the post of the general manager of the group and concurrently vice chairman and general manager of the company. At the end of 2001, Yang Shijiang replaced his father to become the chairman and general manager of the company. In the fifth board of directors of the listed company held at the end of 2002, Yang Jiqiang and Yang Shifen were elected to be directors and Yang Shijiang was elected to be chairman of the fifth board of directors. Niu Manjiang, another professional, took the office of general manager. Yang Shiyi was elected to be supervisor of the fifth Supervisory Committee. The shares owned by Yang Jizhong of the listed company increased from 180 thousand shares to 252 thousand shares, and that of Yang Shijiang increased from 24 thousand shares to 33.6 thousand shares. In Huanghe Group, the shareholder of the listed company, Yang Jiqiang held the post of chairman of the board of directors, Yang Shijiang held the post of director and concurrently general manager, and Yang Shiyi held the post of executive director and manager of another company.

Till then, the residual distribution of the group company was in the control right of the group by the father and sons of the Yang family. In light of their relations, and in order to differentiate the control of the residual claim right by their shares is of minor significance, we may view their claim rights in the listed company and the whole group as integrated.

Section II

FAMILY ENTERPRISES AROUND THE WORLD

3

Development of Family Enterprises
in Europe and the US

While family businesses are understandably and usually small & medium-sized enterprises, it is interesting that some of the large enterprises today are still family-owned. Among the Fortune 500 companies, 175 are family enterprises. In fact, 40% of the listed companies in the US are controlled by families, such as DuPont and Motorola. At present, family enterprises are developing at different rates in different areas of the world. In countries like the US and Japan, family enterprises have reached the stage of separation of ownership and management. That is, the family enterprises have developed beyond the boundary of family. But in other countries like Italy, family enterprises are still very much family-oriented. Family enterprises in different countries have their own unique characteristics. An analysis of their experiences and lessons would be of great significance to family businesses in China.

To some extent, the history of market economy in Europe and US can be viewed as the history of the family enterprises. Initially, they took the form of workshops. Some of the workshops developed into companies owned and managed by families, and some evolved into enterprises of other types. Before 1840, corporations were exclusively family-owned. In Britain, the birth place of the Industrial Revolution, family workshops were common. Different from workshops in China whose products were mainly for family consumption, workshops in Britain were organized by merchants and the products were intended for trade. At that time, family-owned enterprises were the only model in both trade and finance industry. During that period, honesty and reliability weighed more than professional knowledge in doing business. A large and professional management was not necessary in small-sized enterprise, therefore, family management became a popular practice.

After 1840, innovation in technology and system brought about great changes in traditional family enterprises. These changes were taking place in the organizational structures within the corporations. On the one hand, as a result of innovation in technology and business system, economic activities were going beyond the control of family enterprises. More and more non-family members entered family businesses. On the other hand, innovations multiplied the resources controlled by family. In pursuit of greater profit, family enterprises embraced the idea of competition, and formed alignment to gain the power to establish prices. As a result, monopoly came into being. With changes in organizational structure, traditional family enterprises evolved into managerial enterprises, or modern family enterprises. Typical managerial enterprises include General Electric, Standard Oil Company and typical modern family enterprises are Zinc Manufacturing Co Ltd, American Tobacco Company of the Duke family, McCormick Harvesting Machine Co etc. Within the realm of family enterprises, diverse types emerged. There are enterprises partly or wholly owned by a family (such as the largest jeans producer in the world — Levi Strauss & Co); enterprises that are co-owned by several families (e.g., Burroughs Corporation); and enterprises that are bought and developed by one family (Coca-Cola Company).

Characteristics of American Family Enterprises

Professional Manager Revolution in the Tide of Annexation

At present, a large proportion of companies in the US are family-owned. It is a common practice to employ professional managers to run the enterprises. This phenomenon can be traced back to the so-called "manager revolution" during the period from the mid-19th century to early 20th century when fierce market competition brought about large-scale annexation of companies. Market competition resulted in the concentration of production and the expansion of enterprises, thus calling for sharp increase in capital, and finally leading to decentralization of ownership. It was rare that the family occupied majority of the voting stocks. Non-family members played a bigger role in the enterprise. Management in such enterprises was more complicated, and so the emergence of professional managers was natural. Professional managers first appeared in the railroad industry, the early beginning of privatization. Railroad industry needs large amount of capital, which was usually beyond a single investor. Therefore, bank loans and collaboration of several enterprises were necessary. Correspondingly, banks also had a voice in the decision-making process. Moreover, the railroad industry also set a high demand on technology, and thus professional talents had to be included in the industry. Considering all the factors, manager revolution was an inevitable trend at the time. With the outbreak of WWI in the 20th century, manager revolution had been accomplished in large enterprises in the US. With the separation of ownership and management, private-owned or family-owned enterprises were gradually converted to stock companies operated by professional management. On the surface, complexity in management which was brought about by expansion of market and application of technology, contributed to the necessity of professional management. But social trust was the root cause for the rise of professional management. This transition also witnessed the loss of trust in the American society. Due to population fluidity and immigration, opportunism and immorality prevailed in the society. The owners lacked sufficient trust in hired managers. They preferred to hire people whom they knew well or who were blood-related. But this was only a temporary phenomenon, for the American society has a long tradition for social credit and contract system. Furthermore, the government strengthened qualification system and various regulations and legislations. And a large number of agents were soundly developed. All the factors constituted important external elements which facilitated family enterprises' transition to modern corporations.

Over hundreds of years, America's family enterprises, growing on the fertile ground of American society, have been evolving together with the market and have developed the following characteristics:

1.   Larger, stronger, and more enduring

Stability resulted from long-term control by one or several generations within the family. Take JP Morgan & Co, for example. The company was run by the senior and junior Morgan for more than 50 years. Both the father and the son are notable figures and knowledgeable on banking. Another case in point is DuPont. In its 200 years' history, DuPont went through the hands of several family members. The "three young DuPont cousins" deserved special mention. With their effective and drastic reform measures, they not only made a fortune for the family, but also created a model company of modern enterprises. Other famous family corporations include the Ford Motor Co, IBM Company, etc. These companies have a history that spans nearly 100 years. Family control ensures stability, which is advantageous for long-term development strategy, including talent cultivation, technology exploitation, and brand development.

2.   Clear boundary of property right

Generally, family enterprises in the US have achieved separation of ownership and control, with majority ownership in the hands of the family. Clear property rights are present within the enterprise, between family and non-family shareholder, and within the family (family members can exert control through control stock). Throughout the world, the US, with sound capital market and talent market, is leading in the market economy. Therefore, stock is a reliable indicator for measuring the value of the corporation and performance of the professional managers. Families usually exert control over the enterprises by means of holding control stock, while leaving routine managing work to professional managers. The DuPont enterprise was founded in 1802. 100 years later, in 1902, the company was handed over to the three young DuPont cousins.

In the following half-century, the DuPont family shouldered the primary responsibility in managing the company. It was not until 1970s that DuPont appointed a trusted person to the position of general manager. Currently, the DuPont family is holding 44% of the company stock.

3.   Advantage in number, creating jobs for society

Despite sound modern corporation systems, family enterprises account for more than 90% of all the corporations in the US, and more than half of the GDP. Each year, 78% of the new job opportunities are provided by family enterprises, and 65% of the working population are employed by them. Some big enterprises have a large employment ranging from tens of thousands to hundreds of thousands. For example, Wal-Mart has nearly 30,000 employees; DuPont has 97,000; Ford Motor Co has several hundred thousand. With adjustments in ownership structure, the companies become more and more public-owned. Nevertheless, the family can also exercise control over the enterprise through its role as majority shareholders. If the family holds insufficient stock, its influence can be exerted with preferred stock. Take Ford Motor Co, for example. Although the Ford family owns limited stocks, they still have a say in the decision-making process through "preferred stock".

4.   Strong establishment

America's family enterprises are noted not only for their quantity but also for quality. Famous family enterprises include Ford Motor Company (one of the top 5 in the world's auto industry), Boeing Company (the world's leading aerospace company), DuPont (multinational chemicals and health care company) and IBM ("blue giant" in computer industry). Wal-Mart ranked number one in the 2003 Fortune 500, with $263 billion of business revenue and $9 billion of profit. Exxon Mobil Chemical Company ranked third with $223 billion of business revenue and $21.5 billion of profit. Ford Motor ranked 6th, with $167 billion of business revenue. Family enterprises — Wal-Mart, Rockefeller, DuPont, Ford, and Boeing — occupy a majority of traditional industries such as retail, oil, chemicals, automobile, etc.

5.   Contribution to productivity, modernization, economic and cultural development

Family enterprises, especially large ones, have made great contribution to the increase in production efficiency. They developed advanced management methods, which greatly improved productivity. In 1913, Taylor's management theory was adopted by Ford Motor Company, and was put to use in the assembly lines. This so-called "Fordism" is mass production characterized by a high degree of job specialization. The Fordist model of production is based on three basic principles: (I) Specific tasks and goals for intellectual workers and manual workers. Management staff are responsible for running the enterprise and manual workers only have to do highly specialized tasks routinely; (II) Application of Taylor's management theory. The assembly line was characterized by high degree of specialization; (III) Seeking optimum solution in production to improve efficiency and to lower cost. Specialization of task increased work intensity and productivity, and helped reduce cost. Increase in profit resulted in higher wages for workers, and thus workers were more motivated to work. Ford was a pioneer in applying Taylor's theory and he achieved huge success in the 1920s. Aside from increased productivity, the Fordist model of production also boosted the standardization of production methods and product quality, laying foundation for mass production and public consumption. As more and more companies followed Ford's example, America strengthened its competitiveness in the world's industry.

6.   Innovation in management model

The management model of DuPont turned out to be a great success in improving managerial efficiency. In 1903, DuPont formed an executive committee — initiating the use of a group to replace individual in decision-making. Power decentralization worked very well in practice. The growth of the corporation called for more professional knowledge and experience in management, which is usually beyond the ability of the individual family. The DuPont model is characterized by centralization in finance and a combination of centralization and decentralization in management. The company also devises a means of calculating "return on investment" to measure organizational performance. Under such a model, the branch divisions were more motivated to work. The idea to combine centralization and decentralization in management does not involve abstract theories, but it has been proven to be effective in raising productivity. In the last several decades, DuPont's multi-divisional structure became the model for the modern corporation both inside and outside America.

7. A big boost in research centers

Many family enterprises set up their own research centers, which not only benefit the enterprises, but also the country at large. For example, Boeing Company best represents the history of aeronautical technology in America. The US Congress spoke highly of Boeing: without Boeing, America would have been different and there would not be a free world. There is no denying that Boeing has contributed a lot to the corporate modernization in the US IBM — a "blue giant" in the world's computer industry — attaches great importance to scientific research. In 1954, IBM had 1,440 researchers working in the company. In 1958, Junior Watson established Thomas J. Watson Research Center with experts in diverse areas such as mathematics, physics, chemistry, electric engineering, and computer. Physicist and former Navy chief scientist Dr. Pierre headed the center. Watson Center benefited a lot from the abundant experience and outstanding ability of Dr. Pierre. At that time, the center attracted almost all the notable computer experts throughout the US. The company made a huge investment in the center. During the four years when the center was developing the IBM360 system, the company reaped $5 billion. At present, there are more than 3,000 researchers at IBM, including five Nobel Prize winners. More than 2,000 researchers have PhD qualifications. The Center's current focus is on information technology. The research goal is the development of large, medium, and small computers, and computer network. With sufficient financial and technological support, Watson Center is also making great contribution to America's technological advancement.

8.   Setting up various funds

In addition, family enterprises set up a large number of funds to provide financial support for various social and cultural activities. Andrew Carnegie, known as "the King of Steel", and John D. Rockefeller were among the most active ones in establishing funds. Andrew Carnegie went to the US with his family in 1948 and later made a name for himself in the steel industry. Since 1901, he donated to more than 200 libraries, and set up the Carnegie Institution of Washington, the Carnegie Hero Fund, Carnegie Trust for the universities in Scotland, and the Carnegie Fund for Peace. In 1915, he established the Carnegie Corporation of New York, the largest and best philanthropic foundation at the time. Carnegie donated most of his estate to charity. To Andrew Carnegie, to die with wealth is to die in shame.

In early 1872, Rockefeller helped to form the South Improvement Company, an association that unified many oil refiners in Cleveland with the Standard Oil Company. Within ten years, the company monopolized the oil industry in the US. Rockefeller owned an estate worth $70 million. In 1972, Rockefeller began his charity work, education and religion. He established the General Education Board, Rockefeller Fund, etc. The funds set up by family enterprises also made huge contributions to science and technology, especially in basic science such as biology, physics, astronomy and medicine. America's rapid developments in science, culture, and economics owe a lot to various funds set up by family enterprises.

Case 4: Ford Motor Company — Wealth Beyond Fifth Generation

Introduction

In the current commercial environment of intensified competition, it is not an easy thing for an enterprise to be able to celebrate its 100th anniversary; and if the chairman and CEO are still the offspring of the founders of the company, it is a miracle. The Ford family, however, is the creator of such a miracle, one that established The Ford Motor Company. The years from 1903 to 2003 witnessed a story of painstaking efforts and struggles in the century-old company, led by its renowned founder-owner. This is the story of a family who fought and struggled hard for their cherished value, tradition and honor.

In 1903, Henry Ford established The Ford Motor Company in Dearborn, Michigan, in the US. By pushing forward the manufacturing industry, the motors made by the company drove the whole world forward, and he realized his dream of changing the lives through technology.

In 1919, when he was at the age of 25, Edsel, the only son of Henry Ford, was designated by his father to be the new president of the company and to take charge of the $250 million enterprise. Although Edsel, unceasingly pursuing perfection in his life, had made great contributions to the design of new products and the long-term development of the company, his introverted disposition led to his failure in the power struggles in the company's management. Edsel was unable to gain the full trust from Henry Ford and later died of illness.

The death of Edsel Ford forced Henry Ford Sr. to use Harry Bennet, an employee outside the Ford family, to manage the company. However, Bennet's ambitious desire for power alerted the members of the Ford family. With unprecedented unity, they finally took the power back and entrusted it to Henry Ford II, the third generation of the Ford family. By adopting a series of innovative measures and making vigorous efforts, Henry Ford II saved the Ford Company from the recession after the war. During the years from 1945 to 1953, the company was revived and when celebrating its 50th anniversary, the company was still one of the largest industrial enterprises in the US and was controlled by the family members.

During his term of office, Henry Ford II had employed outstanding managerial talents to run the company, which include Ernest Bridge, Bunkie Knudsen, Lee Iacocca, Philippe Caldwell, Donald Petersen and Red Poling. After a series of training arrangements, Bill Ford Jr., the fourth generation of the family, safely took over the baton.

After he assumed office, Bill Ford Jr. upheld the spirit of enterprise and innovation that had long been valued by the family and saved the company from the mire caused by the investment in the Internet. By taking a series of innovative measures, the company revived and the price of its shares rose again when the company was celebrated its second centennial. On December 22, 2003, the share price of the company once reached $16.79 per share, marking the highest in the past 52 weeks.

In the history of North America, no other family with an industrial background has ever been so influential as the Ford family; from Henry Ford to his sons and grandsons, the leading talents, philosophy of life and traditions of the family exert an impact on the whole world through its Ford motors and products. From Henry Ford, Edsel Ford, Henry Ford II, William Ford and Edsel Ford II to Bill Ford Jr., the family has been striving for their cause. The tradition of being hardworking and enduring struggles has been passed from one generation to another.

For such a modern family enterprise whose wealth lasts for four generations, where does the source of energy for sustainable development stem from? What is the key for the masters of the Ford family to perfectly handle the difficulties once and again and take control and management rights of the company in their hands all along? How can the family members of the fifth generation lead the Ford Company to continue the history into the second century?

Pioneer of Motor Industry: Henry Ford I

Very few people, if any, can challenge the position of Henry Ford in the industrial history of the US. He initiated the motor industry in America and commenced the manufacturing technology of assembly line. The motors made by him became a necessity for millions of Americans, thus profoundly influencing the lives of people and rapidly turning the nation into a kingdom on wheels. For this reason, he was recognized as the pioneer of the American industry. In 1910, he established a wage system of five dollars per day, which opened a new chapter in the labor-capital relationship. Also a pioneer in public relations, Henry Ford, aware of the power of brand recognition, was capable of using all kinds of marketing strategies to promote the image of the company and the products, such as through movies. He was never afraid of failure or bankruptcy, believing that there would always be a way out. This business concept has been influencing his successors for generations. Henry Ford was a pioneer, a founding father, and a symbol of the American dream.

Henry Ford was born in a peasant family in Greenfield, Michigan on July 30, 1863. His father, William Ford, a hardworking and frugal Irish farm owner, had a dream to emigrate and buy enough land, creating a comfortable family for his children, However, Henry Ford, the eldest son in the family, was not interested in running a farm. With books, toys and all kinds of equipments given by his parents, Henry Ford was provided with ample space to do his favorite things. Despite his father's urging, Henry Ford never wanted to become a farmer. William Ford described how Henry was so interested in the steam engine presented at the Philadelphia Exhibition, that the 15-year-old

Henry left school for good then. He arrived in Detroit, where he began to pursue his dreams. Through self-study, Henry became a steam machine engineer. In 1887, he became an engineer/technician, his dream job, at the Edison Electric Light Company in Detroit. And soon he was designated as chief engineer. Although it was a full-time job, Henry Ford was able to make time for his own minor projects using the equipments at the Edison Company. He concentrated on the design of motor and in 1896, he trial-produced a double-cylinder air-cooled four-engine motor. At that time, the motor industry was emerging in Detroit. As Henry Ford was constantly working on reinventing his motors, the desire of establishing a company of his own became increasingly strong. After eight years at the Edison Electric Light Company, Henry decided to give up his well-paid job to establish his very own Detroit Motor Company. Starting from scratch, Henry had to move to a cheaper house in order to save as much money as possible.

However, since the performance of the company could hardly affect Henry's personal interests, this motor lover was not fully motivated to run the company. He was more enthused and immersed in improving motors instead of seeking profit from selling his products. In 1900, the company went bankrupt due to the limited production scale. Despite Henry Ford's failure in his first business venture, some of the shareholders remained confident in him. They rented part of a formerly liquidated factory and invited Henry to continue his research. Based on the foundation laid during his stay in the Detroit Company, Henry's efforts finally brought about the development of a racing car, which later claimed victory at a speed car rally. The success promptly led to the formation of the Henry Ford Company in 1902, named after its chief engineer. Henry owned one-sixth of the shares. Soon after, a conflict in business notion arose between Henry and the company's investors. In the investors' eyes, the new company should aim at producing light, simple and popular motors at the cost of about $1,000 each, while Henry believed that it would be more sensible and perfect to manufacture faster four-cylinder cars with huge engines. In Henry's mind, the only way to make profit was to expand his reputation by producing racing cars. Sticking to his own ideas, Henry remained disinterested and unaffected. He was forced to resign after only four months in the new company. Soon, Henry found Malcolmson, another partner. This time they designed a favorable interest distribution method. According to the partnership agreement, Malcolmson would invest in the manufacture of a sample car which would take part in exhibition, in the hope that the sample car could attract investment in setting up of a new company. The new company would issue shares of $100,000 in value. The stock jointly held by the two original partners would be 51%, with each having half. Both of them would sit on the board of directors. Malcolmson was responsible for finance and management, and Ford was in control of technology and production. The company was named Ford Motor Company.

Henry introduced mass production based on assembly line. In 1903, ten years after the beginning of mass production at the factory in Highland Park, annual production doubled at the Ford Motor Company, while the price of T-type car gradually dropped by two-thirds. It was the use of the assembly line that greatly increased the productivity and started an era that regarded efficiency as a priority. The practice of $5 daily wage (the average daily wage of workers then was $2.34) not only promoted work efficiency, but also contributed to the cultivation of the middle class in the US. It was the bravest commercial innovation and a real trump card. When other motor manufacturers were troubled by labor movements, Ford embraced his employees as a big family, where staff suddenly became willing workers for the company. The practice of Ford Company revealed a profound truth: if a company was willing to adopt brave and innovative policies, social problems would be changed into economic opportunities. As Peter Drucker puts it, "the practice of Ford changed the American industrial society, turning the American labors into basic middle class." The appraisal was enough to make Ford Motor Company the most attractive and attention-worthy enterprise in the US.

Edsel Ford: Talented but Short-lived

As the only son of Henry Ford, it was naturally assumed and expected that Edsel Ford would inherit his father's business. In 1919 when Edsel was at the age 25, he was designated by his father to be the new president of the company and to take charge of the $250 million enterprise. However, the appointment was more nominal than substantial. After his designation, Edsel Ford spent a long time trying to establish his own power base. His autocratic and stubborn father, however, never seemed willing to transfer power to his son even though he had announced his resignation as early as in 1918. In the father's eyes, the son never seemed to be strong and tough.

Unlike his father Henry Ford, Edsel Ford was sensitive, introverted, modest, polite and elegant, and had a unique taste for the arts. It was Edsel who designed the luxurious Lincoln car model, comparable to the Cadillac manufactured by GM. Although Henry Ford loved his son, he did not show enough respect for Edsel. Edsel did not have real power in the company as his father restricted his power in the most open way. Sorensen and Harry Bennet, both trusted followers of Henry Ford, tried every means to impair junior Ford's influence in the company. Edsel was moderate and imaginative, but in the father's eyes, he was weak and frivolous. Henry Ford had always dreamt of cultivating his introverted son into a strong and resilient person. However, Edsel always refused to turn himself into the perfect son that his father wanted.

Although Edsel was always on the leeward in the struggle for power at the management level of Ford Motor Company, his contributions to the company was indelible. His professional experience in the 1930s also marked the success of Ford Motor. He was involved in almost all the positive, progressive and remarkable events of the company, such as the renaissance of the brand Lincoln, the establishment of Mercury department and The Ford Foundation. Moreover, Edsel led the work in body-work design in the Y-type model, which revived the European market of Ford Motor Company. By developing the Y-type car, Edsel inevitably established the bodywork design department for the company. Having no regard for Edsel's dignity, Henry Ford often overturned his decisions, even in public. Inside the company, Edsel felt pressured by his colleagues, Bennet and Sorensen. Being in such a difficult position, Edsel did not choose to quit, but was able to, within his sphere of control, make his own contributions to the company. He spared no effort in bringing the company to the forefront of the industry by promoting body design management and that protected the company from being ruined. Edsel had made enough unique contributions to The Ford Motor Company to become an all-field motor manufacturer. Edsel tried to cultivate in his four children a sense of pride for the Ford family, making them realize that Ford Company was the reason for their good lifestyle and privileges, and that someday in the future they might be needed to run the family enterprise. The business vision of the company was instilled in the minds of the Ford's offspring. Edsel, also enthused by the vision, never doubted or quit despite encountering difficulties during his presidency. It was loyalty to the enterprise that kept him in the company. However, those stressful working years at Ford had seriously affected Edsel's health. He suffered from gastric ulcer and the condition soon deteriorated. In 1942, he was diagnosed with gastric cancer. On May 26 of that year, Edsel died at home.

Henry Ford II: Doing His Utmost to Turn the Tide

After the death of Edsel, Henry Ford had to take over the company once again. But as an old man, his physical and mental conditions did not allow him to stay on the job for long. Handing over the power and control of the company became inevitable. It seemed obvious that Henry Ford II, the eldest son of Edsel and eldest grandson of Henry Ford, should take over the enterprise. However, the handover was a process of fierce struggles. At that time, Harry Bennet, who gained the trust of Henry, was the person in power and control of the company. In reality, Henry Ford had signed a testament stipulating that the position of presidency should be vacant for ten years after his death, and the board of directors, with Harry Bennet as its secretary, should take charge in the management of the company. There was a possibility that Harry might usurp the presidency at any time. The unity of the Ford family, however, was represented in the event. It was said that two ladies played an important role in the power transfer. Senior Mrs. Henry Ford and Mrs. Edsel Ford together controlled almost one-third of the shares of the company. If Henry Ford II did not assume the presidency, then both ladies would sell their shares in Wall Street. With the strong support of the whole family, Henry II ultimately assumed the post of president of the board of directors. Immediately after, Harry Bennet left the company.

In the first month after his appointment as president, Henry Ford II went about making a lot of changes in the company. First of all, he personally fired every assistant of Harry Bennet, who had more interest in working for Harry than for the company.

Then he carried out a series of reforms. The end of WWII also saw the end of lucrative profits from huge government wartime military contracts. Ford Motor Company had to reenter the competition for private civilian cars. Though the considerable profit from the wartime contracts had made Ford a powerful and rich company; in the long run, it was not a reason for optimism. The motor industry featured cyclical patterns and was constantly changing over the passage of time. For that reason, Henry Ford II began to prepare for the decline of car sales at the end of the WWII. Firstly, he consolidated its sales force and sales network. If the dealers were taken away by the competitors, Ford would find itself in a passive position. Therefore, from 1945 to 1946, Henry Ford II frequently traveled to visit the Ford dealers around the nation. He personally met the dealers, visited their showrooms, tried to understand their concerns and promise the availability of new cars. By doing so, Henry II ensured a positive attitude of Ford marketing network for the future, which was a great contribution to the development of the company. The second problem was labor. During the wartime when labor and capital relations were intense, the strikes in Ford Company had seriously hindered the production. Senior Henry Ford was very resilient towards trade union. When it came to Henry Ford II, however, the new boss showed his support for labor-and-capital negotiations and willingness to cooperate with the trade union. He dealt with labor problems in an honest and cooperative manner, unlike his grandfather's hostile and tense approach. As a result, Ford Motor Company became the first major company in America to agree to pay pension for its employees, marking a turning point in the history of labor-and-capital relations in the US. Within the company, Henry Ford II immediately implemented a policy of reform by reorganizing organizational atmosphere, asking managers to respect their subordinates and trying to be more open and honest to the outside world. By doing so, the morale of the employees of the company was greatly uplifted and the number of resignations was significantly reduced. In the Ford Motor Company, under the leadership of Henry Ford II, blue-collar workers were given equal respect as the white collars and even managers. Senior Henry thought of the employees as gears in mass production machinery; but Henry II regarded them as individuals with the right to speak up and the opportunities for professional development. Among all the measures taken by Henry II, the key one was the choice of a good top management team and the establishment of an organization adaptable to the changing needs of the company.

As early as 1956, Ford Motor Company was listed and public participation of the company reached to a certain extent. However, gathering funds from the market was not the reason for listing. Rather, The Ford Foundation, one of the shareholders, sold its shares to realize investment diversification. The Ford family had established The Ford Foundation in order to avoid the high inheritance tax, or rather, to donate part of their shares, out of generosity, to philanthropy. As a charity organization, the foundation annually paid a lot of money to support public causes such as education and medical services. The foundation relied on the dividend of the shares to fund the charity. However, since the performance of the motor industry was a cyclical pattern, that was deemed insufficient. Thinking that it needed more stable and higher investment return, the foundation decided to sell part of its Ford shares to diversify the investment. At the beginning of 1956, after Ford Foundation sold 22% of its Ford shares, more than 350,000 persons held Ford shares, thus expanding public participation to a large extent. However, the control right of the Ford family over the company was not lost, for they still kept 40% of the votes.

When the historical moment came for Henry II to quit and retire from the company, the need to invite competent managers to run the company became an important and difficult task. Fortunately, Henry II was always capable of finding eligible candidates when he needed them. In 1980 when Henry II retired, he made one of his most significant and correct decisions by choosing Philip Caldwell and Donald Petersen as his successors. Their promotions were not based on their personal relations with Henry II; neither were they members of the friendship network of any of the Ford family members. They came from the same working class of ordinary families with traditionally good work ethics and integrity. By designating the two managers, Henry II reaffirmed his unswerving policy of saying no to appoint people by favoritism. The appointment created history, for it was the first time that no family members of the Ford was involved in the top decision-making process of the company. As vice chairman, William Ford could have provided consultative opinions, but he and his brother Henry II left the affairs of the company completely to Caldwell. Philip Caldwell and Donald Petersen proved themselves to be outstanding professional managers with excellent performance. Throughout the 1980s, Ford Motor Company witnessed the greatest revival in the history of business. The company that once registered a record loss in corporate earnings in America had increased its earnings to a level higher than all of the other motor companies throughout the world. In 1986, Ford made a record-breaking profit of $3.29 billion. The stock of the company became a favorite in the Wall Street, whose price rose by as much as 13 times during the 10 years from 1980 to 1989. Business media chipped in to add compliments to the leaders at Ford Company.

This, however, did not deviate from the design that Henry II had for the company: having talented managers to run the company until somebody in the family was competent to replace. Although Peterson was promoted by Henry II to be the chairman, he neglected the person who, for the past several years, had been the leading figure of the Ford family. Moreover, Peterson obstructed Edsel II and Bill Ford Jr., the ambitious fourth generation of the family, to take on influential positions in the company and on the board. As a result, the Ford family could no longer support him and he had to retire, no matter how successful the company had become. Peterson was soon replaced by Red Poling, who worked together with Peterson for many years.

When Poling formally retired in 1993, Trotman was appointed to be chairman of Ford Motor Company. He created Ford 2000, drastically changing the development approach of the Ford motor. In addition, he made Ford Company an international and well developed company at the time of globalization by way of integrating resources and purchasing other brands. However, when faced with the problem of succession, Ford Motor Company was seen to be less globalized. At its centennial, the fourth generation of the Ford family once again succeeded in taking over the helm of the company displaying the capability of the family to cultivate outstanding successors.

From a Boy Born with a Silver Spoon to Leader of the Fourth Generation: Bill Ford Junior

Bill Ford Jr. did not become the steersman of Ford Company because of his birthright. Family edification and childhood education and the experience in the company played a decisive role. His road to promotion at Ford Company was quite lengthy. He worked in 15 posts and changed his post on average every 10 to 12 months (such was the company tradition to cultivate leaders by having them work from financial to marketing and on to the business development department). When he graduated from Princeton University in 1979 and entered Ford Motor Company, Bill was the most junior product planner. Having gained the experience in the various departments, he was promoted to be chairman of the board. Bill Ford was born with a silver spoon in his mouth. However, he was not brought up like the other princes of the Ford kingdom. His life was full of hardships and trials. Bill Ford Sr., his father, had hoped that when the children worked, they should also participate enthusiastically in any kind of competition. Any game played by Bill Ford Jr. and his three sisters was invariably competitive, be it playing cards, after-dinner games or even conversations.

They would never give up their success for politeness, nor admit their failure for kindness. Bill Ford Jr. was not only an A student in academic excellence, but was also very strong in sports. He spent most of his spare time in sports and was the member of the school's football and ice hockey teams. It was his keen participation in sports that had fostered his physical strength, toughened his character and increased his desire for victory.

His mother spent a lot of care in cultivating her son. To prevent him from being spoiled, she had Bill Ford signed up for a youth ice hockey team in St. Clair town near his family. Although the team members were mostly kids from working-class families, Bill Ford would play ice hockey with them every weekend, totally unaware of their family backgrounds. He was neither protected by a bodyguard nor escorted by a driver. He was received by his mother at the gate of the school after the class was over, just like mothers of the other kids would do. Even though Bill Ford knew nothing about fishing, the family believed that it was a good thing for the boy to make contact with the outside world and get to enjoy the beautiful nature. When Bill Ford Jr. was only five or six years old, they took him to a private fishing club located in the northern part of Michigan State. The boy fell in love with the place instantaneously. From then on, outing and fishing became his favorites for his birthday celebrations. These were the sorts of activities that cultivated his love for nature and care of the environment and that influenced his concept of running the company in the future. It was later that Bill Ford Jr. called himself an "environmental protectionist entrepreneur", determined to lead his company and the whole motor industry in a new direction; and responding to criticism that the industry was the cause of environmental problems.

Ever since his childhood, Bill Ford Jr. was taught to be independent. He received little pocket money from his parents and had to work during summer holidays to earn some money.

One of his summer jobs was a gardener, where he had to toil day after day just like the other workers, but with the lowest salary. Once, the boss asked him to fertilize the farmland by dissolving all fertilizers in the water using a blue coloring substance. A gusty wind caused Bill Ford Jr. to stain the white skirt of a lady passing by, which he had to use almost all of his salary to pay for the skirt. Bill Ford went to Princeton University, majoring in history instead of enterprise management or anything related to motor. While in college, Bill Ford learned a lot from the stories of many great leaders in history. The enthusiastic devotion of great leaders in the pursuit of their causes was to have a strong influence on Bill's leadership style in the future. Having an interest in philosophy, Bill Ford Jr. thoroughly studied philosophical issues and began to ponder over social responsibility. In the final years of his college life, Bill Ford Jr. began his practice in social activities by serving as chairman of the Ivy Club. When he was young, Bill Ford Jr. did not care about Ford Motor. Like all other children, all Bill cared about was his fellow friends and the football team. When Bill Ford Jr. was about to graduate from college and started thinking about getting a job, he contacted The Ford Motor Company. In his dissertation "*Reevaluating Henry Ford and Labor Force*", Bill Ford Jr. began to seriously think about issues related to Ford Motor. The Ford family did not exert any influence over his choice of a career. The only advice from his father was that "one has to put in a 100% effort once a decision has been made and to make sure one wants it, and devote oneself to it".

One could say that as a member of the Ford family, motor was in Bill's blood. In 1979 after his graduation from college, Bill Ford Jr. decided to formally join Ford Motor. After 20 years of painstaking efforts, Bill rose to take the office of chairman of the board. When he first started out at Ford, Bill's status (as a member of the Ford family) made it difficult for him to work.

Many superiors were hesitant to coach or guide him, give him meaningful feedback, let alone scold him. He had to overcome his shortcomings by self-communion. What was more, he had to work harder to avoid all the rumors about him abusing his privileges. Years later, with his working experiences in Department of Commercial Truck Engine, Switzerland Branch of Ford Motor Company and Financial Committee of the company under his belt, the time finally came for Bill to take control of the company. In January 1999, 19 years after Henry II retired from the company and after four chairmen who came and gone, Bill Ford Jr., a fourth generation member of the Ford family took control of Ford Company as chairman of the board.

As for his responsibilities in the post, Bill explained, "I am quite aware of my own situation. All the things in my life come from the company and the things that Henry and his offspring did for me and my family. Of course I am very clear about the things that they've done in the post. However, I also know that I am different from them, because the time is different."

At the beginning of his rule, and in order to save Ford Motor Company, Bill Ford Jr. hired some experienced managers in the motor industry. Some high-level managers with successful marketing experience in Europe were put in important positions. For example, Nicholas Scheele, who created a miracle by reviving Jaguar in the 1990s, was designated to be COO, the second in command of the company. David Thersfield, an Englishman and the former CEO of Ford Europe, was appointed to be vice president for international business. In an attempt to arrest the problem of rapid erosion of the company's profit margin and losses suffered from stock decline in 2001, financial experts, including Carl Lacarte, former chairman of Wells Fargo were brought in by Bill and put in important positions. Under the leadership of Bill Ford Jr., Ford Motor returned to its basic business. Almost immediately, he cancelled the service-oriented and Internet-oriented enterprises, abolished the 10-80-10 evaluation plan that seriously affected the morale of the employees, and prescribed that except for stock options, high-level managers must not be paid for any salary or incentive subsidy. By doing so, Bill got closer to the ordinary employees. At the same time, Bill Ford Jr. was carrying out his motor environmental protection plan, hoping to rebuild the long-lasting field-sight-seeing motors into clean fuel cars. Of course, Bill Ford Jr. did not forget to use his own name to publicize the company. Although at the beginning, Bill Ford Jr. was publicity-shy and wanted to maintain a low profile about his family connections, he has since changed his mind and began to appear at commercials advised by marketing officers on how important the tradition of the family meant to the company. In June 2003, the public event celebrating the centennial of the company further deepened the impression and reinforced the confidence of consumers and employees: Ford Company was an enterprise with great traditions. Even though the company had its moments of hardship and difficulty, it was able to claw its way out of each trouble with reinventions and innovations, marching forward from failure toward success.

At the end of 2003, after all the hard work and endeavors, Ford Motor Company was back on the right track and became successful again. Ford F150 truck was awarded "Truck of the Year 2004". Ford, UAW and Visteon, Ford's largest supplier reached an understanding on supply cost and labor. In addition, the price of Ford stock picked up again on December 22, 2003 at $16.79 per share.

Family Traditions

Since the establishment of Ford Motor Company by Henry I, the Ford family has gone on to its fifth generation and they are still a cohesive family. What binds them together is, to a large extent, the enterprise and in particular, the traditions that have been reinforced by the enterprise. In order to maintain internal cohesiveness and external coherence, members of the Ford family would get together annually to hold meetings on the business of the company. The young generation of the family is required to fully understand the legendary stories of the company and the painstaking efforts of the older generations. The family does not force the young members to join The Ford Company, but they are encouraged to integrate with the company. As Bill Ford Jr. once put it, "I don't want my children and the offspring [to] feel [that] it's a pressure to work for Ford Motor Company. I hope that they take pride, instead of burden, in the history of the family."

Members of the Ford family firmly believe that the control of the company by the family members will guarantee strategic vision and long-term perspective in the protection and development of the company in the most feasible way. It has been the case. The premise, however, is that the family is capable of cultivating competent members. In this regard, the Ford family has performed well. Although it experienced ups and downs in the past several decades, and even occasional quarrels, the great Ford family has always been enjoying a centripetal force, even though it owns so much wealth and power. The reason lies in the choice, with special care, of family leaders. They try to avoid internal disputes as much as possible. Each generation of the family devote themselves to the company, firmly believing that working for the company is an honorable and proud thing to do. At the same time, the Ford family "permanently" owns the company by controlling Class B shares of Ford Motor Company.

Under the leadership of the family, the past 100 years have been a century of pride. When it enters its second century, the new challenge the family is facing is how to pass on the torch from one generation to another when motor industry is at the crossroads of development. Members of the Ford family are already making plans to uphold the business reputation and tradition of Ford Motor Company in the next century.

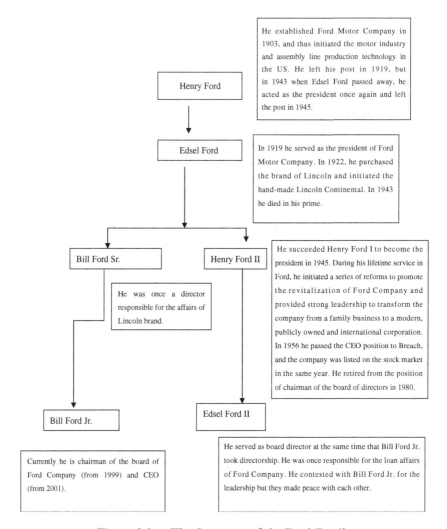

Henry Ford

He established Ford Motor Company in 1903, and thus initiated the motor industry and assembly line production technology in the US. He left his post in 1919, but in 1943 when Edsel Ford passed away, he acted as the president once again and left the post in 1945.

Edsel Ford

In 1919 he served as the president of Ford Motor Company. In 1922, he purchased the brand of Lincoln and initiated the hand-made Lincoln Continental. In 1943 he died in his prime.

Bill Ford Sr.

He was once a director responsible for the affairs of Lincoln brand.

Henry Ford II

He succeeded Henry Ford I to become the president in 1945. During his lifetime service in Ford, he initiated a series of reforms to promote the revitalization of Ford Company and provided strong leadership to transform the company from a family business to a modern, publicly owned and international corporation. In 1956 he passed the CEO position to Breach, and the company was listed on the stock market in the same year. He retired from the position of chairman of the board of directors in 1980.

Bill Ford Jr.

Currently he is chairman of the board of Ford Company (from 1999) and CEO (from 2001).

Edsel Ford II

He served as board director at the same time that Bill Ford Jr. took directorship. He was once responsible for the loan affairs of Ford Company. He contested with Bill Ford Jr. for the leadership but they made peace with each other.

Figure 3.1:   The Structure of the Ford Family

Characteristics of European Family Enterprises

Contrary to their American counterparts, family enterprises in Europe are less open. Relatively speaking, the cooperative relationship between family and non-family members is more difficult to establish and maintain, which is especially true in Europe, for in many European regions such as France and southern Italy, a low degree of trust prevails in the culture. Lack of social trust makes familial cohesion all the more important in family enterprises. In addition, the long history of Europe should establish enduring corporations. It is an innate desire to control more that motivates owners to seek further development for their enterprises. If they have to choose between being in control or further development for their enterprise, a majority of the owners will not hesitate to hold the ownership tight in hand. In Europe, there are various family enterprise clubs, which only allows enterprises that have a history of more than 200 years to join. The members gather together to exchange ideas and establish development strategies. They even send their own successors to each other's companies to gain different business experience.

Therefore, in terms of property right, family enterprises in Europe are featured with concentration of stock right. By holding more than 10% of the stock right, the family contributes to the stability of stock equity structure. Moreover, in Europe, large shareholders can directly take part in the management. All these factors help to establish the European power transfer pattern — "strong inside and weak outside" — that is, outside interference is hindered. Although some European family enterprises have also gone through the transformation from family-owned to public-owned, just like their American counterparts, a number of European family enterprises are exercising a higher degree of familial control. A recent survey on French corporations shows that two-thirds of the large corporations in France are partly or wholly owned by the family, among which a quarter are under direct control of one or several family members. It is obvious that family power is a crucial factor in ownership or even in management transfer.

Family Enterprises in France

90% of the French enterprises with 10–500 employees are family-owned. The turnover of family enterprises takes up half of the total turnover of French corporations as a whole. Family enterprises also account for 63% of the enterprises whose turnover is between 50 million to 2 billion franc. The recent 15 to 20 years has witnessed a drastic increase in economic powers of family businesses. 58.6% of top 500 French enterprises are family enterprises (John Allouche, Brewno Aman). In 2003, the first issue of the American quarterly *Family Business* released the list of top 200 global family enterprises, in which 17 French corporations were included — only second to America. French family enterprises are outstanding not only in quantity, but also in quality. Their contribution to the world economy cannot be underestimated. Large family enterprises in France concentrate on the areas such as retail, food, luxuries, automobiles, and other daily consumption goods.

Unique social, economic, and psychological factors contribute to the rapid development of French family enterprises. In terms of the country's economic development, modern France finds it difficult to carry out large-scale social production due to the lack of capital and technology. Without advanced machinery, the production scale remains limited, which results in limitation in labor force. Therefore, the production tends to be restrained within the family. What make things worse are inconvenient transportation and an underdeveloped market system. Due to inconvenience in transportation, the internal market cannot achieve standardization in pricing. It is likely that corporation owners can gain high profit without advanced technology or renewed products. For a lack of outside competition, they do not have to expand production scale. High profit can be achieved only by an increase in capital investment. The man-made obstacles in standardized pricing system deviate from value law but contribute to the existence of family enterprises. Moreover, modern France has experienced a slow adjustment in industrial structure. The industry of consumption commodities has always been taking up a large percentage. Under this peculiar industry structure, French corporations concentrate on textile or food processing — such industries put a high requirement on quality and craftwork, in which familial workshops are the most suitable pattern of production. In addition, the complexity in manufacturing demands skilled workers in production. Therefore, small-scale production within the family is preferred over social production with mass unskilled workers.

1. The culture of individualism

The long-term existence of family enterprises in France owes a lot to the unique consumption habits of the country. France is a nation of fashion, and its people favor luxury commodities, which, to a large extent, explains the prosperity of luxury commodities industry in the country. Therefore, familial production pattern prospers. In terms of the national culture, France is the country where individualism and the contract spirit prevail. Individualism advocates the idea that one should actualize his life value and earn wealth through his own efforts or with the help from his own family. It is with this notion that gives rise to the family enterprises in France. Additionally, due to insufficiency in social credit, the French tend to depend more on family members financially. It is difficult for them to establish cooperation with people outside their family, which also accounts for the prosperity of family enterprises in France.

2. Socialization and diversification of property right

Besides a large quantity, French family enterprises are also noted for their dimensions and long history, which is closely related to the property right system, management system and structure. Large family enterprises in France have gone through the socialization and diversification process — a breakthrough in property right reform. The shareholder structure takes on different forms, such as mutual stock holding among different corporations, shareholding by employees, and stockholding by both domestic and overseas shareholders. The decentralization of property right facilitates quick fund-raising — a prerequisite for further expansion for the enterprise. Employee shareholding accounts for a large percentage in total stock-holding, which, undoubtedly, is the best incentive for employees. As the result, cohesion and competitiveness of the enterprise get strengthened. Despite socialized property right and diverse shareholders, the family still secured its position by holding about 20% of the stock right. The enterprise will not lose its familial characteristics.

3.   Management — "two boards" decision making structure

In respect of the management structure, it is a common practice for large family enterprises in France to adopt a dual-decision model — "two boards" system. Besides the board of directors, there are special committees, such as compensation committee, finance and budget committee, business investment committee, director nomination committee, etc. The advantage with this management pattern is clear responsibility, and check-and-balance on each other. The board of directors is responsible for formulating overall policies and strategies. They learn the latest enterprise information by regularly reading accounting reports, and then making analysis and forecasts on business. The general manager, who is in charge of specific operation and managerial works, will implement the policies made by board of directors. The relationship between board of directors and the general manager is that of trust and agency. On the other hand, the board of supervisors monitors the work done by the board of directors and the general manager. They can also supervise the enterprise's financial and investing behaviors. In short, with definite rights and responsibilities, the combination of decision-making, implementation, and supervision helps to avoid power abuse. The existence of special committees ensures that the board of directors and managers can get accurate information on time, therefore improving judgment and decision, and avoiding decision-making mistakes.

4.   People-centered management with emphasis on employee interest and participation

Special committees also share the managerial work and help to organize and coordinate routine activities. Large family enterprises in France attach great importance to employees' interests and they encourage participation from them. In some family enterprises, the employees hold up to 10% of the company's stock right. In this way, employees can elect their representatives to be high-level officials so as to protect their own interests. This practice best demonstrates the advanced participation system and people-centered management notion in French family enterprises. Nevertheless, family members are still significant in the enterprise. They usually take the positions of CEO, general manager or director. Familial control continues to exert great influence in the enterprise.

In the aspect of management system, large French family enterprises cultivate people-centered corporate cultures. They hold the notion that the employees are the primary value of the enterprise, and adopt relevant human resource management practices, which cover forecasting changes, screening talents, admitting competence, strengthening communication, and respecting individuals, etc. They emphasize talent-cultivating, potential-exploring, and cultivation of company culture. As part of job evaluation of the employees, the manager will talk to each employee every year to find out their job performance and to help them set future goals; in employer-employee relations, communication is valued. The ability to listen and talk is needed; in terms of skill-training, some enterprises have signed the European social contract with the European Trade Union to ensure protection for their employees. The protections cover a wide range including ensuring life safety, indiscrimination regarding job offer and promotion, providing training programs, and respecting union's work, etc. Large family enterprises in France usually provide different and specific training programs for their employees. In 2003, the training expenditure of some enterprises reached 71 million euros, 3.7% of the total salary expenditure, which is far beyond the percentage — 1.5% — set by law. Conclusively, the management in these enterprises is centered on people, around which all business operation and production activities revolve. The combination of "hard" management with "soft" management facilitates the coordination at material, spirit, and regulation levels, which in turn helps to achieve optimization in enterprise management.

Family Enterprises in Germany

It is universally acknowledged that Germany provides model family enterprises for the world, for they are most successful in integrating modern management concepts into their family enterprises. Through different forms (going listed, transferring part of the stock right, appointing professional managerial staff, and offspring inheritance), German family enterprises have created many famous brands and high-quality products. In Germany, family business occupies the leading position in the national economy. Family enterprises take up a large percentage and cover a wide range of businesses in the country. As seen from statistics, family business is dominant and enduring: 80% of German corporations are family-owned or under familial management; for those with a history of more than a century, 70% are family enterprises; 48% of the largest 150 companies in Germany are family business. A bigger number of small and medium enterprises are controlled by families. At present, family enterprises account for 53% of the German GDP, and 68% of the overall employment. Large family enterprises are powerful. For example, the Daimler Motor Company, founded in 1926 and famous for its Mercedes Benz, is the largest motor company in Germany and the 4th largest in the world. It is a cross-national group combining diverse business areas such as auto- producing, electricity, metro, finance, and counseling service. For years, Daimler Motor Company has always been ranked high in Germany and in the world's top companies. In 2004, Daimler Motor Company was ranked 7th in the Fortune 500 companies, with gross earnings of US$156.6 trillion, and $507 million profit. Moreover, German family businesses are also noted for their rapid development. In the past decade, their development index rose by 206% while that of non-family enterprises increased only by 47%. Family enterprises, especially those large ones, often surprise people with an astonishing speed of development.

1. Governmental support

The expansion of family enterprises cannot be achieved without support from the authorities in Germany. The former board chairman of Siemens Ltd used to be a member in the Germany Atomic Energy Commission. Peter von Siemens, chairman of the supervisory board, was a close friend of Schmidt, the former German Federal Chancellor. For a long time Siemens had its own representatives in the German Parliament. The board chairman of Siemens also took the post of chairman of the German Asia-Pacific Economic Commission.

2. Strictness in successor selection

In Germany, on one hand, only 14% of the family enterprises can last to the third generation, on the other hand, a number of family businesses have been enduring for more than one century, even two centuries. For example, the largest pottery manufacturer in the world — Villeroy & Boch Group — has a history of 258 years, going through eight generations within the family. To a large extent, long-term continuation of family enterprises is the result of strictness in successor selection, in which the previous generation put in a lot of deliberations. They are very strict with the screening process, e.g., the successor must be highly educated; and overseas working experience is preferred etc.

3. Corporation management — Three-level model

The management of German family enterprises deserves attention. Firstly, a three-level management model is adopted: at the highest level sits the owner of the enterprise, who is usually a family member; the second level is board of supervisors. Those with management experience tend to be included in board of supervisors, and they are not necessarily shareholders of the enterprise; the third level consists of the experts and consultants. The board of directors in German family enterprises is rather powerful. The board members are not appointed by shareholders. Rather, their nominations are subject to the confirmation of the board. As for the selection of CEO or president, the board of directors will decide on the nominations, then all the shareholders will vote for them, and the board of directors will then give their final confirmation. German family enterprises are very strict with the decision-making process. Approvals from both shareholders and board of supervisors are required. Shareholders or enterprise owners *per se* are not qualified to make policies. The board of supervisors serves as a consulting organization. Its existence makes the corporation more open, organized, and systematic. It not only helps to retain family advantages within the enterprise, such as loyalty and emotional bonding, but also makes full use of its professional background to provide up-to-date information. The communications among these three levels are very important, which is guaranteed by various communicative channels such as yearly report, monthly report, or daily report. In addition, German family enterprises attach great importance to strategy management. The long-term strategy should be formulated in written form. The enterprise owner does not have the authority to change it at his own will. A strict control is also exerted on the budget as well.

4.   Board of supervisors

Currently, a majority of German family enterprises have been passed on to the second generation, or even the third or fourth generation. Problems do exist during the transition. The first generation, or the pioneer, is not willing to hand the management over to professional managers. On the other hand, the third generation, since they are usually young at age, prefer appointing professional managers to take over management. They set up a board of supervisors to monitor the work of hired managers. However, they still hold the controlling rights. In some cases, the family will take back the management when the younger generation grows mature enough.

Inheritance is another problem bothering German family businesses as a whole. A survey shows that about 40% of the family enterprises will accomplish the power transfer during the period of 2003 to 2008. More than half of them prefer a family member taking over the management. The current generation, or the post-war generation, has grown up in a better-off environment. Unlike their fathers and mothers who had experienced the post-war reconstruction, the current generation enjoys the comfort of life, and endorses the value of freedom. They lack ambition and do not want to raise children. As a result, selecting successor is a challenge for family enterprises today.

Family Enterprises in Italy

Family enterprises in Italy are different from those in the US and Germany. Generally speaking, they are smaller in size, with both ownership and management in the hands of the family. Large listed family enterprises are rare in Italy. Italy is also known as "a nation of small- & medium-businesses", for such business forms are dominant. Statistics show that 99.7% of the Italian companies are small or medium in size with no more than 500 employees. These companies account for 70% of the country's GDP. The Italian businesses are famous for their expertise in leather-making, shoe-making, textile, furniture, jewelry, wine-brewing, machinery, marble exploitation, and electronic industry, etc. These industries feature high level of specialization, strong adaptation, and big export ratio. Many world-famous brands are rendered by Italian family enterprises. Strong competitiveness of Italian small & medium family businesses helps the country to rank top among the world's industrial nations.

1. Network of corporations group

For Italian family businesses, limitation in size determines the limitation in profit. Nevertheless, they adopt a unique method to strengthen themselves — that is, small corporations voluntarily gather together to form associations, or a sort of loose network, in which they keep close and frequent contact with each other. An individual enterprise is only a link in the product chain formed by the group. Obviously, such corporation groups has an edge over individual company, since limited resources can be put together to concentrate on specialized production or on a certain working procedure. In this way, family enterprises in Italy are able to adapt themselves to the constantly changing and highly classified market. Compared with large vertically integrated enterprises, Italy's family enterprises are still competitive. Consequently, Italian businesses, large or small, do not care too much about being comprehensive in production. For example, the Fiat Group owned by Agnelli family, one of the top automobile manufacturers in Italy, has a limited range of products. There are a number of small- & medium-sized corporations which carry out specialized production and provide certain auto parts not only to Fiat, but also to other auto manufacturers. Italian leather shoes are world-renowned. But there is not a single Italian shoe manufacturer that is capable of producing a complete pair of shoes. The production is also specialized. Some factories make shoe covers while others produce soles, and they coordinate with each other. A factory with more than 30 workers can be reckoned as a big one.

2.   Technology innovation capacity

Reputation is the life of family businesses. The quality of the products should be guaranteed to win more customers. That's why Italian family enterprises can enjoy both domestic and overseas fame despite their limitation in scale. To adapt themselves to the constantly changing market, these family enterprises pay special attention to technology innovation. They keep a close eye on the development trend of their competitors. The most advanced equipment and technology are applied in the production so that their products cater to the changing needs of the consumers. The competitiveness of Italian family businesses results from their technology innovation capacity. Many small- & medium-sized corporations in Italy have the tradition of establishing cooperation with scientific research institutes. For example, the second largest scientific research center in Italy — the Industrial

Application Research Institute which belongs to the country's Trade & Industry Department — has set up a research base whose primary job is to provide technology for practical application in small- and medium-sized corporations. The organization not only introduces solidification technology, such as advanced equipment, but it also helps the corporations to improve their production and management system. At the same time, the government pledges policy support, such as raising funds for technology innovation. Italy has set up "Rolling Fund on Technology Innovation" to back researches on significant scientific innovations. Free assistance takes up as much as 50%. The rest of the needed fund can be obtained through bank loan. Italian government also sets up various socialized service systems under different demands of small & medium family businesses, such as consultation organizations and finance organizations; scientific research centers based in universities or colleges; service organizations set up by trade or industry associations. These services organizations make great contributions to the development of family businesses by spreading technological knowledge and information, speeding up reform process in district economy, promoting technology cooperation, boosting the development of corporations group, providing various services including quality inspection, attestation, skill-training, etc., and creating a favorable development environment, and so on.

3.   Industry distribution — "One district, one industry"

The Italian government takes various measures to encourage specialized production and coordination among small- and medium-sized corporations, strengthening them in terms of technology. As for industry distribution, the country is featured with the pattern of "one district, one industry" — in other words, corporations in a certain area concentrate on one particular industry. Under such a plan, corporations of similar type tend to gather together, forming a close-knitted network. Massive cooperation and efficient coordination within the district boost scientific research and technology development. In addition, businesses organization and technical centers (including specialized schools) co-exist and rely on each other, establishing a unique industry structure featuring "3-in-1" collaboration. There are 20 districts, altogether 94 provinces, in Italy. Each province has its own industrial association, where the members of family enterprises can communicate freely with each other, and obtain information on economy analysis, market forecasting and technical consultation. Whenever a relevant policy comes out, the industrial associations will communicate with the government to ensure maximum interests for their member corporations.

Since their inception in last century, most Italian family enterprises have already celebrated their 100th anniversaries. They are currently in the hands of the third or fourth generation of the family. Similar to situations in France, Italy has a low degree of social trust. People tend to depend more on family members. Cooperation between family and non-family members are usually ineffective. Therefore, family inheritance is a common practice in Italian businesses. But in recent years, rapid technology innovation has brought about numerous new industries. Therefore, a large portion of family businesses have to face various problems in power transfer.

Case 5: Porsche Company — The Outstanding Second Generation

Introduction

On September 25, 2005, it was confirmed by Wendelin Wiedeking, the board chairman of Dr.-Ing. h.c. F. Porsche AG, that 20% stock shares of Volkswagen would be purchased by Porsche, whose high-class sports cars are renowned around the world. In light of the prevailing stock price of Volkswagen at that time, Porsche would have to pay about 3 billion euros for the purchase. This strategy would also make Porsche the biggest stockholder of Volkswagen. Porsche's expectation to become the biggest stockholder of such a big car manufacturer, ranking the first in Europe and fourth in the world, has caught the attention of the whole world.

The Porsche sports car is renowned around the world not only for its attractive and stylish appearance, but also for its superb engine performance. Porsche cars have been loved and pursued by car lovers and have been called "the king of the sports cars", owing to their advanced technology, attractive designs, credible safety, flexible details and the incomparable driving pleasure it offers.

Such a legend of sports cars has been created by the three generations of Porsche family. It is this family, filled with genius mechanists, vehicle designers, technical specialists and management experts, that built Porsche into a world-renowned and time-honored brand. In 1900, Ferdinand Porsche designed Lohner-Porsche, the first motorcar in the world to be named Porsche. It was a great success that laid a solid foundation for the future development of Porsche. In spite of the negative impact of the wars, Ferdinand, together with his sons and sons-in-law, ran the company successively with the innovative designs. This not only expanded a huge market for the company, but also established its own products and brand, and thus drove the development of the motor industry in Germany and even in Europe.

When Dr. Ferdinand Porsche died in 1951, his son Ferry Porsche took over the management of the company. Talented in design as his father was, Ferry achieved exceptional success in running the company. In addition, he insisted on applying the successful experience in racing cars to ordinary cars and successfully transformed Porsche Company into a joint stock company. At the same time, the daughter of Ferdinand worked very hard to manage the sales and trade of Porsche Company in Austria. She finally successfully developed the company into the largest trading company in Austria.

When Porsche was passed on to the third generation, however, the company found itself in trouble as a result of a power struggle between Butzi, Peter and Piech, the grandsons of Ferdinand, and irreconcilable conflict in the family. Finally, all the family members quit from the management of the company. They only retain the right of directorship and the right of choosing high-level managers for the company. Peter Schutz and Wendelin Wiedeking, two professional managerial talents from outside the family, revived the Porsche. In the past five years, the share price of Porsche increased by 500% and the wealth of the Porsche family reached 2.4 billion euros.

The pressure from the international motor market, competition, merger and brand, and the impact of exchange rates are getting increasingly intense. How can Porsche Company keep its competitive edge in the industry? Can the fourth and the fifth generation of the family control the company that is now run by outsiders? And how can they achieve it?

The Father of Porsche

The first vehicle bearing the name of Porsche — Lohner-Porsche — was manufactured in 1900. It was named after its designer

Ferdinand Porsche, who was the founder of Porsche AG and also a genius mechanist. Ferdinand Porsche was born in 1875 in Mattersdorf, a village close to Reichenberg, in what was then North Bohemia, later Czechoslovakia. The young Porsche worked as an apprentice in his father's blacksmith's store. Subsequently because of his fondness for electronics, Ferdinand left home and joined an electronics enterprise in Vienna. At first, he did only some sundries, such as sweeping floor and oiling the transports. Because of his hard work and sheer determination, Ferdinand was promoted within four years, to be the director of the testing department. When testing an engine for a carriage company, he was recruited by its director. Upon joining the carriage company, he started to design engines. His design won acclaims from around the world. This electronic carriage, which was 80 years ahead of Audi, helped Ferdinand became a famous automotive engineer in Europe.

Since then, Ferdinand found his interests in the field of sports cars, and set the direction for the Porsche development. By 1903, Ferdinand had already become a famous mechanical engineer. He spent several years studying and grappling the characteristics of the gasoline engine. In 1906, he took on the post of technical director in the Daimler firm, and brought his family to the new district of Vienna. After 17 years of peaceful life, Ferdinand hopped over to Mercedes-Benz based in Stuttgart. Ferdinand Piech, his eldest grandson and former chairman of Volkswagen, wrote in his biography that his grandfather, who was supposed to stay in Benz for quite a long time, went to build a villa in Stuttgart instead; which led to the split in the manufacturing of Porsche AG into two parts; one part in German and the other in Austria.

By the time World War II ended in 1945, Ferdinand was already a 70-year-old man. Nevertheless, he was still the most popular engineer. He was persuaded by many enterprises to take over the post-war reestablishment and rebuilding of motorcars. That year, he was invited to discuss the possibility of authorizing

Renault to produce the Volkswagen cars, but the French government had a different perception of what Ferdinand had done during the war. In the second round of discussion with the French government, Ferdinand, his son Ferry and his son-in-law Anton Piech were arrested by the French soldiers. Four months later, Ferry Porsche was released. In May 1946, Ferdinand and Anton Piech, who had a closer relationship with Volkswagen, were transferred to Paris. Meanwhile, he was also in charge of the later phase of manufacturing and testing for Renault's 4CS cars. In February 1947, they were sent to Dijon prison. Three months later in August 1947, Ferdinand and Anton Piech were released from prison without any charges. But the cumulated 20 months of prison life had taken a toll on Ferdinand's health which deteriorated to an incurable stage.

While his father was in prison, Ferry began to take charge of Porsche. He built on the reputation of his father, and began to design racing cars for others. Ferry had inherited his father's gift in the design of racing cars. He designed a car named Cisitalia for an Italian merchant. At the same time, together with chief engineer Rabe, Ferry also designed his first and very own sports car — named Porsche. In 1948, the first "Porsche" sports car was produced. Given that the car had undergone modifications over 356 times, it was named Porsche 356.

The time when Porsche 356 was put into production happened to be the time of the European economic recovery. German Volkswagen rose rapidly. Porsche had reached an agreement with Volkswagen for a patent fee of 5 marks per car payable to Porsche — the inventor of Beetle. In addition, it was stipulated in the agreement that Porsche 356 could also be sold in the sales network of Volkswagen, and its after-service would be provided by Volkswagen. In so doing, Porsche sports car could be promoted rather quickly in the markets. Since then, the highly qualified Porsche sports cars became a popular success in Germany, Europe and North America. When its production stopped in 1965, total output for Porsche cars had reached 75,000. In 1951, with support from Ferry, Porsche was moved back to Stuttgart Germany. In that very same year, Dr. Ferdinand Porsche passed away at the age of 76. However, the business created by him, including Porsche sports cars and Volkswagen cars, were still undergoing manufacturing at full speed.

The Torch was Passed and Carried Forward

After the death of his father, Ferry Porsche took the full control of the company's operation. Eagles do not breed doves. Under the leadership of Ferry, Porsche made a remarkable progress.

Ferry Porsche had always wanted to introduce his successful experience with racing cars into building the common cars. In 1972, Porsche had been transferred to a holding corporation, whose stocks were listed in 1984. The operation rights belong to the Board, with Ferry being assigned as its chairman.

Porsche sports cars are famous for their durability and longevity. Two-thirds of the Porsche sports cars produced since 1950 and three-fourths of the model 911 produced since 1964 are still in use today. By July 15, 1996, Porsche had already produced one million sports cars.

On March 9, 1990, Ferry Porsche left his post as Chairman of the Board at Porsche, and was conferred honorary chairman for life. On March 27, 1998, at 88, Ferry Porsche died in Austria.

Dr. Porsche also had a daughter named Louise, who was five years older than Ferry. Ferry and Louise were on very good terms. Even though they managed Porsche separately in Austria and Germany, they were reliable partners to each other. Despite their constant bickering eversince they were children, they always maintained a good relationship. Away from everybody else, they found comfort, confidence and solace in each other. It was Louise whom Ferry confided in when he was released from prison in 1947. Louise possessed the character of maturity, sobriety, persistence and resolution. Even Dr. Ferdinand himself had to acknowledge that his daughter was more outstanding than his son. At that time, Porsche was prepared to move their head-quarters from Gmund Austria back to Stuttgart. But the Austrian Porsche company needed to be kept as it focused on marketing and trading, and the sales of Volkswagen cars. In so doing, the stock shares of the Piech family had to be separated.

After the separation, Austrian Porsche, in addition to doing research on the Cisitalia formula cars, also carried on the busi-ness of cropper, handcart and cable car based on the conditions of raw materials, equipment and funds. One year later, due to the remote location of Austrian Porsche, it could not be used as the production center, thus the sports cars manufacturing plant was moved back to Stuttgart. With the success of Volkswagen and the industriousness and persistence of Louise, who had devoted herself to the family business, the Austrian Porsche grew to be the biggest private enterprise of Austria.

In this way, Porsche possesses two bases, one in Austria and the other in Germany. The Austrian company was in charge of trading and was managed by Louise. The company based in Stuttgart was in charge of motor business and was managed by Ferry. There was an unwritten rule in the family: members of Porsche family were in charge of motor company, while the Piechs (the daughter's branch) were to stay in Austria. Since the motor business seemed more attractive to the younger genera-tion, almost all the males in the third generation of the Porsche family wanted to work in Stuttgart. That planted the seed for hidden troubles which gradually led to family disputes.

According to tradition, all of the family property should be passed on to the eldest son. But in view of the contributions made by his daughter and son-in-law, Ferdinand ultimately decided to divide his estate into two halves. Furthermore, he did not appoint the person in charge. By the third generation, the division of the family estate had already taken the rule of equality. The estate had been divided into 10 parts, respectively owned by Louise, Ferry and their 8 sons and daughters (see Figure 3.2 — the structure of the Porsche family).

Another Brilliant Victory After the Turning Points

In the third generation of the Porsches, there were two young-sters named Ferdinand, both of whom had deep interests in the motor. One was Ferdinand Alexander Porsche (also called Butzi) — the son of Ferry Porsche. The other was Ferdinand Piech — the son of Louise Piech. The latter was to be the chairman of Volkswagen.

Butzi had a great passion for cars. He treated others in a friendly manner and took things in his stride. He had no interests in the company politics. In 1961, 28-year-old Butzi began to design the Porsche 356 — model 901, which later became the famous model 911. At the same time, he was also actively design-ing the Porsche model 904 racing car. Its body shell, shaped in a graceful curve, was made of fiberglass-reinforced resin. Model 904 was not only Butzi's maiden work, but also his masterpiece. He signed off on this car without any modification, revealing his talent in motor design. Later, the Porsche 911 which was also designed by him was admired worldwide. Porsche 911 broke 16 world records in the 1967 racing car rally and was voted the "best sports car" of the world. Many motor fans called it "the king of racing cars". Since then, the 9 series cars of Porsche have been granted great repute and credit.

Ferdinand Piech is several years younger than Butzi. He is the third child of Louise. Since his childhood, Piech idolized his grandfather. He liked to stay with him, asking him to tell stories about how he had resolved the technical problems and how he had won car races. Piech had witnessed the respect and adulation his grandfather had received. Ever since he was a boy, Piech had been eager for success, determined to model himself after his grandfather. Piech was fond of making all kinds of handicraft and doing various experiments. In his boyhood, Piech had helped Ferry — his uncle — to fabricate the first Porsche 356, which was also a contribution by Butzi. In April 1963, Piech graduated from the Swiss Federal Institute of Technology with a degree in mechanical engineering. After graduation, he worked in Porsche as a commissioner for racing car engines. Shortly after, his brilliant performance was marveled by even the senior engineers. Piech was in charge of modifying the engine of 911, which was to be used in the model 904. The modification involved doing research on a 6-cylinder engine, and increasing its power from original 130 horsepower to 180 horsepower. Piech had refitted the carburetor made by Ferry to downdraught carburetor, which could avoid flame out when the cars make their turns. Soon after, Piech became famous for his design of the engine 911. From the very beginning of his work, he did not blindly abide by the senior engineers. Unlike his easy-going cousin, Piech is irascible but energetic. He possesses a strong drive for accomplishment, which wins him the reverence from experienced senior engineers.

In 1965, Ferry realized that his nephew possessed outstanding nature on motor. Although Piech was crankish and irascible, Ferry offered him the management rights of the Porsche Inspecting and Developing Department. The first thing Piech chose to do, after taking charge of this department, was to assemble all the employees, appealing them to pull together to reach a prominent aim — design and produce the new generation of the sports cars to knock off the dominant positions held by Ferrari and Ford in the field of sports cars. Piech and Helmut Bott, another senior Porsche engineer, always stayed in the office the whole day to discuss all the details. Bott was a warm and accommodating old man. Piech unfeignedly admired his skills and talents. He treated Bott as his mentor and maintained good relations with him. Soon, 26-year-old Piech had established his own power foundation. He organized a deliberate and highly efficient team, completely constituted by young and dedicated engineers. There were no departmental boundaries in this team. It had absorbed many top talents. The employees quickly realized that if they could not adapt to the working intensity of Piech, then they would probably be fired.

The problem of nepotism had been existing in Porsche, ever since Piech entered the company in 1963. With the strength of Piech growing, especially after independently introducing Porsche 911, the conflicts among the Porsche's third generation also escalated. The conflicts had eventually escalated to the disputes on the heritors, because the one who inherited Porsche could justifiably kick the other out of the company. But by that time, Ferry was only in his early 60s. Thus the problem of inheritance had to be put on the table ahead of schedule.

As for the heirs in the branch of Porsche, Ferry had four sons. His second son had passion for nature, interested in farming and breeding, while his fourth son was still young and studying in college. His first son Butzi and second son Peter had already worked as senior managers in Porsche, both of whom had the capability of inheriting the company. Butzi had designed 911, obtaining preeminent accomplishment. He had been regarded as the most appropriate heir. But Butzi seemed to prefer design than management, and his abilities in execution and leadership were obviously inferior to that of Peter's. However, in the branch of Piech, Ferdinand Piech was young, energetic and anxious to inherit Porsche. But he is the son of Louise, not of Ferry. However, his mother Louise possessed an eminent position in the Porsche family. Originally, when she agreed to let Ferry manage Porsche, she had persisted that after Ferry retired, her son must be in an equal position to compete for the management rights of Porsche.

However, the emergence of heritage disputes did not wait for the retirement of Ferry. Under this circumstance, Louise and Ferry put forward the double leadership: Porsche family and Piech family could separately choose one person to undertake the duty of chairman in Germany and Austria. But Peter strongly opposed. He asked his lawyer to tell Ferry that he would like to cooperate with anybody in Piech family but Ferdinand Piech. He held firmly on driving Ferdinand Piech out of Porsche. On Piech's side, he thought that he was at the same age with cousin Butzi and they had been in good relations since childhood, so the two of them could form the best partnership to inherit Porsche. Due to the irascibility of Piech, the relationship between Piech and Peter came to the edge of a collapse. In the autumn of 1970, Ferry invited all the family members to his house, as well as enterprise development consultants from Vienna. But this time, the family conflicts broke out all around. At last, the eldest son of Louise — Ernst — proposed that all the family members should resign from the management positions, and retained experts to manage the company. As the eldest in the third generation, Ernst had some influence over the others. Therefore, his suggestion was taken as one solution. From the beginning, Ernst set himself as an example. He retired from the chairman position of Porsche at the age of 41. Then Peter left the position of production manager, coming to the Austrian Porsche. The position of production manager was temporarily taken by Ferdinand Piech. When it was time for Piech to leave, Ferry changed his mind. He wanted to remain the president of Porsche, but required all the youngsters to leave. This idea was opposed by Piech, who believed that everybody no matter old or young should leave the positions of management. In the summer of 1971, a final agreement was drawn within the family: that all of the family members should withdraw from the company. In March

1972, Ernst Fuhrmann assumed the position of general manager of Porsche, while Ferry was the board chairman. At the end of that year, Piech also left Porsche. And the Austria Porsche was entrusted to be managed by the professional managers. Since then, the Porsche family members only supervised their rights and interests in the board of supervisors, including the 100% original issue stock, and 13% preference stock of Porsche. Even in the board of supervisors, Ferdinand Alexander Porsche gave up the chairman's position to Helmut Sihler, former Henkal President.

Piech used to think that he would stay in Porshe for his lifetime. So, when his uncle made this decision, he was very grieved. Piech was very clear that he stood little chance to be the heir to his uncle, and he would always be the one considered after his cousins Butzi and Peter. Piech wanted to show his family that he was an excellent engineer and an outstanding leader. With this thinking, he was determined to continue fighting his way in the motor industry. At the beginning, Piech got a job in Benz. He left soon after, due to insufficient budget on research and development. He was then employed by Volkswagen, and worked in its separate design company located in Italy. In August 1971, he was transferred to Audi NSU to be in charge of the special programs management. Three years later, he assumed the director's position of the research and development department. Later on, in 1983, Audi 100, a milestone in the history of auto design, was promoted from the department led by Piech. In 1992, with a triumph over his main opponent — Daniel Goeudevert, Piech had eventually become the board chairman of Volkswagen.

When the family members were forbidden to get involve in the management of Porsche, the debate focus had shifted to how to choose a proper person to take charge of the company. Subsequently, Peter Schutz was assigned to be the CEO of Porsche, under whose leadership, during the decade of 1980s, the sales of Porsche achieved a record high. He had riled Ferry

Porsche and Piech by suggesting that if Porsche continued to undergo depression till the end of the 1980s, they should consider selling the company. Since then, the relationship between Schutz and Ferry cracked, for the proprietor of this family enterprise would always be reluctant to give up the control of Porsche. Consequently, Schutz was temporarily replaced by Heintz Braniski who had a strong financial background. In 1990, a young computer company director named Arnault Bern became the general manager of Porsche. But under his charge, the situation at Porsche worsened. According to the regulations at Porsche, in the face of crisis, Porsche family would suspend the rule of forbidding family members to be managers. Porsche family made the same promise to Piech: if he could rescue Porsche from the current plight, he would be assigned 5% stock shares of Porsche. After being driven out of Porshe by his cousins for 20 years, Piech was invited back to be the manager of the company. He refused this invitation. He was concerned that on the day when Porsche restored its prestige, the family conflicts would resurface. Moreover, Piech's career was very promising in Volkswagen, which made him more inclined to remain there. It was also Piech's expectations that he would show off his prominent capability in Volkswagen, a much bigger company than Porsche. In 1992, after defeating Daniel Goeudevert, his main opponent, Piech became the board chairman of Volkswagen. Another reason Piech chose to stay in Volkswagen was to protect the interests of his mother, whose company in Salzburg Austria had to rely on the relations with Volkswagen. Thus, his choice would ensure the steady operation of his mother's company.

Ultimately, the debate on who would be the right person to manage Porsche resurfaced. Piech recommended 39-year-old Wendelin Wiedeking to be the manager of Porsche, who had been in charge of production. His suggestion was opposed by other family members, for they thought he was too young to take that position. However, Piech had a different opinion. He really appreciated the accomplishments of Wiedeking, who had brought a dying German auto axletree company (another family enterprise) back to life. In fact, Wiedeking did bring Porsche a favorable turnaround. After he took charge, Porsche embarked on product transformation, from producing only sports cars to producing multi-purpose roadsters. In 1993, Porsche introduced a concept car named Boxster. As soon as Boxster was produced, there was a rush to purchase it around the world. Porsche's dream of introducing a public sports car with high quality and low price had eventually come true. At the turn of the 21st century, Porsche promoted another multi-purpose sports car. A brand new 911 open car was introduced at the Geneva motor exhibition. The two business transformations led by Wiedeking had successfully saved Porsche out of its plight. In the recent five years, the price of Porsche's stock has risen five-fold. The fortune of Porsche family had reached 2.4 billion euros (not including that of the Piech family).

However, the Porsche family was reluctant to completely entrust the management of the family enterprise to outsiders. After 30 years of being away from Porsche, Ferdinand Piech, who had already become the president of Volkswagen, still thought that if Porsche had been managed by him and his favorite cousin Butzi, the company would operate much better than now.

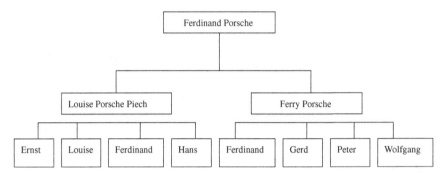

Figure 3.2:   Structure of the Porsche Family

Characteristics of Asian Family Enterprises

The differences in cultural backgrounds determine the positions and roles that the Eastern and Western families enjoy and play in their societies. Trained and edified by the church for more than 1,000 years, the Christians have the ability of organization and association that go beyond families. While in the Eastern Asia, families have always been the center for all kinds of relations and activities. In the society, there are only the roles that belong to families (monarch or subject, father or son, husband or wife, elder brother or younger brother, etc.), and the roles and rights of familism and pan-familism are played or enjoyed for the obligations of families. Naturally, the nature and essence of the family enterprises that are cultivated under such distinctively different soils will be different.

The combination of politics-oriented Confucianism and civilian-oriented Confucianism often takes different forms in different areas. Let us take Singapore, a Southeast Asian nation, as an example. The Chinese immigrants account for three-quarters of the local population. The country has been governed by the People's Action Party since its establishment, and its combination of tough governmental leadership and market economy is a successful example. Indeed, the leaders opposed the Western definition of freedom and they tried to advocate the Confucian ethics in the 1980s. Nevertheless, as a multiracial society, Singapore had never promoted the Confucian ideas to the position of state religion.

Unlike Singapore, South Korea has its own Confucian traditions. Many big enterprises, such as Hyundai, show obvious characteristics of family enterprise, which is closely related to the traditions. The nationalistic capitalism in Japan, based on the longevity system and life employment system, is apparently related to the Confucian ideas, which emphasizes loyalty for the country (or the monarch), filial piety for parents, and respect for the elders.

The East Asian society had long been under the influences of the Confucian "three cardinal guides and five constant virtues". Even after World War II, patriarchs had the sovereign authority in their families. There was no equality in the relations between father and son, husband and wife, and among brothers. The East Asian family enterprises are in accordance with the real family relations, attaching importance to the consanguinity, kinship and emotion factors. In these enterprises, the leaders possess the sovereign authority and therefore the conceptions of contract and equality are not so clear.

Family Enterprises of Japan

Japan is a developed capitalist country deeply rooted in Eastern culture. On the one hand, their management mode has referred to, transplanted and even recreated the advanced European and American operational measures. On the other hand, they have also maintained some of the unique features of their own culture. Japanese family enterprises had widely existed long before capitalism was established. After the Meiji Reformation in 1876, with the emergence of capitalist economy, family enterprises underwent great progress by combining the capitalist production mode with ardent support by the Meiji administration. Consequently, the plutocratic enterprises, influential both economically and politically, gradually came into being. These plutocratic enterprises had been deeply colored by families. They did not operate their administration according to capitalist economic theories, but fused their national culture into the concept of corporation. Up until the outbreak of World War II, about ten plutocratic enterprises, such as Mitsubishi, Sumitomo, Yasuda and Mitsui, had already emerged in Japan. On the basis of family administration, these plutocratic enterprises have directly or indirectly connected themselves to the government. Hence, the neoteric Japanese family enterprise configuration was formed, with features of separate operation, combinations between government and enterprise, between enterprises, and between enterprise and individuals.

Before World War II, Japanese enterprises adopted the system of cognation operation, following the mode of division of labor and cooperation around the key family members. They also adopted the "mode of family operation", advocating life-long employment, seniority and organized family enterprises in terms of kinship. When the joint-stock system was wildly used in family enterprises, a new type of enterprise configuration, the vertical administration co-existing with the joint-stock system, began to emerge. At the end of the 19th century, stock corporations had undergone great progress in Japan. But with the concern that their administration would be revealed to the public, some plutocratic families such as Mitsui, Mitsubishi, Sumitomo, Yasuda and Fukawa, had not adopted the joint-stock system after stalling for a long time. And the joint-stock system had not been used until the late Meiji era and early Taisho era. Compared with other stock corporations, plutocratic family enterprises had their own stock-holding form — the clan members circled around the key family member, who was the center of the whole family enterprise. Since the holding company was on top of the hierarchy, it could vertically administer other companies in the group. Furthermore, as this kind of enterprise group was constituted around the center of family enterprise, the family cartel of every production domains would naturally be established in the family plutocratic enterprises. Accordingly, the production and sales activities were tightly kept within the close administration networks.

After World War II, these Japanese family plutocrats were condemned as the most dangerous potential factors that would provoke another war. Therefore, after World War II, the US implemented three democratic reforms in Japan, including disbanding plutocratic enterprises. At that time, out of their own interests, the occupation authority headed by the US established the Regulation Committee of Holding Corporations to disband Japanese plutocratic enterprises. Its concrete measures included disbanding holding corporations, distracting stock shares and eliminating plutocrats' control over enterprises. In this campaign, many consortia had been divided into two and even hundreds of small companies. After the post-war democratic reform, the Japanese economy achieved rapid progress, during which enterprises underwent a series of purchases and amalgamations. New corporation groups, such as Mitsubishi, Fuji, Sumitomo, Dai-Ichi Kangyo emerged. However, as the traditional culture and corporation culture still had great impact, enterprises that were formed according to the new system still possessed the nature of family enterprise. Some of them, which were still at the command of the family members, were essentially family enterprises. The family members also have heritage rights of the enterprise.

Currently, the growth mode of Japanese family enterprises exhibits some unique characteristics:

1. The operation mode of loose association between Japanese family enterprises and Japanese government. Compared with those pre-war family enterprises, post-war enterprises have shaken off the close connection with the Japanese government. They still maintain indirect association with the government whose macro-control is greatly intervening in and guiding the activities of enterprises. Additionally, Japanese enterprises have always held the traditional idea and enterprise conception of "national interests first" and "invigorating industries for building countries", which have deeply influenced the operational behaviors and conduct of enterprises. Therefore, when necessary, they would integrate with the government to fulfill national interests.

2. Some of the family enterprises have evolved into Trinitarian big enterprise groups. Compared with pre-war plutocratic family enterprise groups, post-war enterprise groups have undertaken great changes either in the combination configuration or the compounding mode, becoming Trinitarian enterprise groups horizontally and organically combined by financial capital, production capital and commercial capital. They have shown the following features: firstly, in the aspect of association mode, they have established the cross stock-holding relations, rather than the vertical stock holding mode of pre-war plutocratic family enterprises; secondly, Japanese enterprise groups form an echelon economic circle centering financial capital; thirdly, within the

enterprise groups, individual corporations rely on each other, rather than adhere to each other, which means that although the combination is loose, it will not fall apart. There are two types of family enterprises in Japan: one is united enterprise groups, represented by Mitsui, Mitsubishi, Sumitomo and Yasuda; the other is large-scaled enterprise groups evolving from a single family enterprise, represented by Toyota and Panasonic.

3. Families control the enterprises through holding corporations or by way of directly holding the stocks. In Japan, two methods are often used by the families to control enterprises or enterprise groups: one is to hold stocks by family; and the other is to set up a holding company above all the corporations within the enterprise groups, and this organization has absolute authority over the rest of the corporations, but the most important positions are held by family members, which would simplify their control over a large number of corporations by only controlling the holding organization. Japanese enterprises, whose stocks are held by the families, are similar to those European and American ones. Before World War II, all the family enterprises were established by their founders and then accumulated on the original basis. As for proprietorship, in some of the family enterprises, the stock shares were completely divided. But most stocks were held by the proprietor, who together with his stockholder clan (paternal line, maternal line and relatives within three generations), could exert control over administration on the enterprise. But after World War II, the percentage of clan holding stocks had gradually decreased. However, due to the mutual stock-holding of different corporations or the high percentage of stocks held by operational groups, the clan could still maintain their control over the whole enterprise. The other family enterprise mode is a unique Japanese type, i.e., holding corporation, such as the monopolistic plutocratic enterprises Mitsui, Mitsubishi and Sumitomo. All of the plutocratic enterprises are developed on the basis of family relations. Take Mitsui as an example. By the Meiji Reformation, it had already lasted for more than 250 years. At its initial stage, Mitsui had been organized by 9 families (later 11)

of the same clan. Together, they dominated the property. Then, from the Meiji era to World War II, although it was reorganized many times, the system of clan management had never changed. Essentially, Mitsui is still a family enterprise. At the very beginning of its establishment, the founders had written in the regulations that "this chamber of commerce is called company, but it is essentially a business belonging to one family, completely different from other organizations set up by fund-raising."

In 1947, the "Anti-monopoly Law" was issued. According to Item 9, holding corporations were forbidden. In principle, the setup of holding corporations was illegal, and the enterprises were also not allowed to hold stock shares. Furthermore, the percentage of the stock shares held by the financial institutes was not allowed to exceed 5%. In this way, the stock shares originally in the hands of family and holding corporations had to be transferred to the hands of individuals. In 1949, the percentage of individual-held stocks had reached 69%. Setting up holding corporations also presented some advantages, such as rapid decision-making. In order to deal with the changing external environments, it became increasingly important to make proper and rapid decisions. Moreover, small-sized general company could be established through holding corporations. Therefore, only a small number of talented employees could effectively operate a big enterprise. Besides, the enterprise operation could also be strengthened, which would simplify the procedures of amalgamation and annexation. Consequently in 1997, the ban on pure holding corporations was released. Although there were some accessional conditions — holding corporations could not directly engage in the transactions and their incomes could only originate from the dividends distributed by the subsidiary companies they were holding — the setup of holding corporation is allowed.

With the changes of social environments and the development of enterprises, the family flavor of Japanese family enterprises had gradually faded. The original family enterprises had sequentially stepped away from going public, after a large amount of social capital went into the enterprises, greatly reducing the percentage of stock shares held by the family members. Contrarily, the big stockholders became banks or other corporations. But the families kept exerting influence on the enterprises. For example, Toyoda Sakichi established Toyota Automatic Loom Works Ltd (in 1933). Afterwards, his son Toyoda Kiichiro set up Toyota Motor Co. His nephew Toyoda Eiji, his grandson Toyoda Shoichiro and his great-grandson Tetsuro subsequently inherited the administration rights of the enterprise. Futhermore, in Toyota Motor and other related companies, the Toyota family has held a rather large part of their operations. The current Hiroshi Okuda is not a family member, but the enterprise is still strongly dominated by the Toyota family. Hiroshi Okuda, who has been assigned to the current position in 1995, is the first Toyota board chairman not belonging to the Toyota family. At that time, the business of Toyota Motor had begun to slide. Even worse, the 68-year-old Toyoda Tetsuro, who was Toyota's president at that time, suddenly suffered from palsy. Thus, Hiroshi Okuda was appointed by the elders of the family to be the president of Toyota. The percentage of stock shares held by Toyota family did not exceed 2%. But in Japanese enterprises, they often mutually hold stock shares. Therefore, although the percentage held by Toyota family was not that high, they still could indirectly control Toyota by holding the stocks of other enterprises. Consequently, they could determine the successor of their enterprise. Although the current president and board chairman do not belong to Toyota family, the family members are still assigned key positions in the enterprises.

4. The unique family culture of Japan is quite influential to Japanese family enterprises. Ito Masanori, the counselor of Japanese National Economic Management Research Center, has once written in his book *The Operation and Management of Japanese Enterprises*: ever since 2,000 years ago, Japanese had been planting rice. From seeding to ingathering, family members and even neighbors must cooperate with each other. Otherwise, based on their own efforts they could not complete the work. This habit of mutual cooperation had been formed during long hours of hard

work, which also evolve to the Japanese conception of recognizing hard work and cooperation. Therefore, "mutual cooperation in the group", which is equal to familism to some extent, becomes one of the Japanese values. As a result, the conception of "groupism" operation also becomes the instructive idea of the neoteric Japanese enterprise. Under the "family operation" concept, family enterprises focus on mobilizing the whole company, promoting integration of the enterprise, coordinating internal relations, inspiring individuals' wisdom, maintaining coordination and cooperation among members and simultaneously allowing the existence of personal actions and personal interests.

Furthermore, the Japanese family culture has its unique features. The first one is authority. Patriarchs possess irreplaceable authority within their families, which led to the emergence of some prominent Japanese families, and simultaneously helped to stabilize the Japanese society. As for family enterprises, this factor solidifies the authority of the family elders. Besides the Chinese traditional credos of "father guides son, male esteem, and proper formalities between the old and the young", the Japanese adherence to age order among brothers is much stricter than that in China. For example, Japanese families, including family enterprises, have adopted the system of inheritance by the eldest son, rather than equal division among sons. Some scholars believe that this system helps to protect the ownership of family enterprises. Unlike the complex connate organization of China, Japanese families establish a single and vertical family sequence, by way of sacrificing the "horizontal" brotherhood and sisterhood. This kind of family structure enables family enterprises to continue, and therefore Japanese family enterprises usually last much longer.

5. Small- and middle-sized family enterprises co-exist with large ones and face more risks in the market competition due to their comparatively small scale. As a result, family enterprises have to establish vertical and horizontal relations among themselves.

From the vertical perspective, many small-sized family enterprises have to rely on larger ones which would subcontract their businesses to smaller ones according to certain sequences, and therefore the market risks would be reduced. Take the automobile industry as an example. The field of auto assembly is constituted by various small- and middle-sized family enterprises, with every one of them in charge of a certain specialized production. For example, in Toyota, there are 40,000 small- and middle-sized enterprises working together, most of which are family enterprises. Only 30% of Toyota's auto parts are self-supported, and the other 70% are supplied by those subcontracted family enterprises. From the horizontal perspective, every enterprise constitutes one part of the coordination "pipeline" based on the industry association. Every working procedure is managed by one independent family enterprise. The order forms are sent together to one enterprise, which is in charge of general coordination. Then these order forms would be distributed to those relative enterprises. Moreover, those enterprises producing the same type of products would cooperate with each other to set the same price and adopt the same sales mode to maintain market order.

Family Enterprises of South Korea

Among Asian countries, South Korea is one of those which have reserved complete Confucian traditions. As early as the Wiman Korea era, Confucianism had already spread to South Korea, together with Chinese characters. Till the establishment of the Korean empire by Yi Seong-gye, Confucianism, as an official reigning thought, had dominated the fields of politics and culture for almost 500 years. Therefore, the teachings of Confucianism has penetrated into every corner of Korean society. At the end of the 19th century, with the invasion of Western capitalism, the political and economic systems of South Korea had undergone great changes. Since 1880, corporations and chambers of commerce emerged in the Korean society. With the Western capitalist culture flooding into Korean society, Confucianism still exerted dominant influence on Korean cultures. Up to the 1960s, this culture had been known as the "relations culture" to the Koreans. This means that both in social organizations and civilian groups, there was a thick color of relations, such as blood relations (relatives), geography relations (people from the same hometown), and school relations (schoolmates). This kind of culture has a deep impact on the formation of South Korean family enterprises.

The South Korean economy is led by the development of chaebol. Large-scale chaebol have been dominating positions in the national economy of South Korea. Most of these chaebol have been controlled by families. 43% of the top 30 South Korean chaebol's stock shares have been held by families. The percentage of family direct-hold stocks is 9.3%. Therefore, these large-scale chaebol are also called family chaebol. These families strengthen their control over the family enterprise group mainly by ways of dual-class share structure, cross-ownership ties, and stock pyramids. During the development of South Korean economy, family chaebol played a very important role. In 1981, during the era of heavy chemical industrialization, 24% of GDP was produced by the largest 46 family chaebol, while in 1973 it was only 9.8%. In 1995, the biggest 4 family chaebol of South Korea (Samsung, Hyundai, Daewoo and LG) provided 9% of GDP and 3% of the employment market. Moreover, the relative percentages of the top 30 enterprises were respectively 16% and 5%.

The development of South Korean family enterprises went through several stages with the following main features: firstly, all of the South Korean family chaebol are controlled by the founders and their family members. In the biggest family chaebol of South Korea — Samsung, Hyundai, Daewoo and LG — the positions of CEO are all assumed by their founders or family members. And most of the high positions are also taken by the family members. According to some researches, in these family chaebol, 76.9% of the presidents or board chairmen are family members and the number for vice-presidents or vice-chairmen is only 7.5%. Consequently, the rights of decision-making are in the hands of family members. Secondly, South Korean family enterprises are inclined to establish cross-ownership ties to strengthen their control over the enterprises. The so-called cross-ownership means that as the key stockholder, the stock-holding family could possess larger control rights by way of setting up enterprise group and making subsidiary companies to mutually hold stock shares. One of the main features of cross-ownership is to reserve the control rights over certain corporations of the group tightly in the hands of the family. Thirdly, South Korean family enterprises have many subsidiary companies. Many enterprises operate in the form of enterprise group. Generally speaking, the more the subsidiary companies, the tighter the control of family enterprises, and the more obvious the family features and influences. Until this day, many South Korean family enterprises have developed to a much larger scale. They take the form of enterprise group, with quite a lot of subsidiary companies. For example, Samsung, Daewoo, Hyundai and LG are all large enterprise groups, with multi-dimensional operations and a large amount of subsidiary companies. Taking advantage of their numerous subsidiary companies, these family enterprises have made many internal transactions. According to statistics, one-third of their annual incomes come from sales among their subsidiary companies. Furthermore, there are complex internal cross-subsidies. Once a certain subsidiary company undergoes losses, the family would transfer profits from other subsidiaries to top up. One research shows that 17 of the 21 subsidiaries, which have made profits from family enterprises, had ever undergone losses at least for one year in the past three years. And 4 of them could not even pay the debts. So, in order to reserve their control rights over these subsidiaries, family enterprises had to spend big sums of money for cross subsidies. Under this circumstance, it is very difficult for the South Korean government to supervise and regulate these enterprises. Therefore, the national economy would suffer potential risks. Most of South Korean family enterprises are large-scale establishments, with heavy debts and complex relations between parent and subsidiary companies. When the leadership is passed to the second or third generation, the enterprises would face the possibilities of breakup, disorganization and even bankruptcy.

After the Asian financial crisis of the late 1990s, the South Korean government implemented many new economic measures to reduce the control rights possessed by family enterprises. One measure limits each group to have only 3–6 subsidiaries. This measure limited the influence of family enterprises, transferring their unlimited interior expansion to centralization. In order to promote the rights and protect the interests of small- and middle-sized stockholders, the South Korean government loosened the requirements for minimum stock shares owned by stockholders who desire to participate in the management of the enterprise. To help strengthen the control over family enterprises, the South Korean government demanded these enterprises to clarify the property right; to separate management from proprietorship; and to attract outside talented professional managers to participate in the enterprise operations. It also requested that the percentage of non-family member directors must increase from 20% to 50%. A board nomination system must be introduced to improve the roles of outside directors and to heighten the voting rights of the institute investors. Furthermore, the existing legal audit function would be replaced by the Audit Committee formed by outside directors. The "Bankruptcy Law" has been modified to simplify the legal procedure of enterprise reorganization and bankruptcy. Meanwhile, the South Korean government also modified the "Law for Foreigner's Investment" to open the market of the enterprise's property rights, legalizing various activities of merger and acquisition, including hostile takeover and foreign takeover. Furthermore, the supervision of banks over family enterprises is also enhanced. In order to effectively prevent illegal transactions, including internal transactions, the South Korean government launched a legal proceeding for internal transactions to reinforce the management of the enterprise transactions litigation. The judiciary procedure has been introduced to assign the legal liabilities to leaders of family chaebol who have engaged in illegal transactions. For example, in 2003, the procurement agency of the South Korean government believed that stock transaction made by the president of SK group was not legal. Chey Tae-won — the president of SK — was put on trial. As a result, a series of external measures were introduced to rationalize the management structure of family enterprises, and brought South Korean family chaebols, especially those large-scale chaebols, in line with norms and operational modes of international enterprises.

Family Enterprises of Hong Kong

In 1841, Hong Kong became a colony under British rule. As a result, during the following one and a half centuries, Hong Kong had been in capitalist system and remained so for a long period of time after Hong Kong has become a special administrative region of China. The fact that capitalist system guarantees the continuation of individual wealth promotes the rise and sustainability of family enterprises in Hong Kong.

Family enterprises account for a significant part in the business field in Hong Kong, both in large-scale enterprises and small- and medium-sided ones, contributing a lot to Hong Kong's economy. The prevalence and flourishing of family enterprises in Hong Kong is related to the unique social and business environment in Hong Kong. On one hand, Hong Kong is greatly influenced by traditional Chinese culture and on the other hand, it is clearly marked with features of capitalist economic mode established and adopted by British colonist government. According to Professor Huang Shaolun, a sociologist from the Hong Kong University, familism is mutually caused by the two factors and probably, it is not a transient phenomenon but a long-term and essential characteristic of Chinese capitalism. Moreover, Hong Kong government has been adopting non-interference economic policies, which provides unique and favorable environment for the development of private enterprises.

Compared with Chinese family enterprises in other parts of the world, those in Hong Kong seem different in terms their large scale, long life span of more than three generations, and the many magnates they have produced.

Four Great Family Enterprises in Hong Kong

Some family enterprises in Hong Kong have grown strong, forming great families which are becoming even stronger by getting united through marriage, such as the four great families: Tung family, Tang family, Tien family and Rong family. Those four great families originated from South China before the liberation, gradually grew bigger and stronger and then move to Hong Kong, playing an important role in both business field and political circle. The Tung family has grown into a big family after Tung Chao Yung — the "Onassis of the Ocean" — accomplished a marvelous pioneering business adventure. His eldest son, Tung Chee Hwa, was the first elected Chief Executive of the Hong Kong Special Administrative Region. The Tang family was formerly based in Wuxi, Jiangsu province and the current Chief Secretary for Administration of Hong Kong, Henry Tang, belongs to this family. The Tien family came from Shanghai and Tien Yuanhao started from scratch to become a great manufacturer of trousers. His sons James Tien Pei Chun and Michael Tien Puk Sun were not only stars in the business field but also big names in the political arena. The Rong family also came from Wuxi, Jiangsu province and was developed by Rong Desheng and Rong Zongjing brothers. The Rong family was renowned as the first business family and its members were called red capitalists.

The rise of the four great families shares the following features: (1) they started in mainland China and enjoyed great fame in business field; (2) they went to Hong Kong around the Liberation period and made their enterprises bigger and stronger; (3) they entered the political field during the second and the third generation and developed into great families both in business and politics; (4) they went through the development process of rise, expansion, diversification and cooperation.

Apart from the four great families, there were other big families and rising magnates in Hong Kong.

Lasting Family Enterprises in Hong Kong

Many family enterprises in Hong Kong have lasted for several generations. Some of them have been operating ever since Hong Kong was opened as a free port and some of them have been growing for more than 100 years. Although there are many branches growing out from the family tree, the trunk is always kept intact, like Lee Kum Kee, The Bank of East Asia of Li Shek-Tang's family,

Li & Fung Group of Fung Pak-Liu's family, Lishi Group of Liniangyi Group, and Wing On Department Store of Kwok Lok and Kwok Chuen.

Lee Kum Kee was set up by Lee Kam Sheung in 1888 to produce oyster sauce. After Lee Kam Sheung, Lee Shiu Tang operated the company and then handed it over to Lee Man Tat who introduced Western production line to make the products well accepted. The Ho family was set up in 1889 and became the richest family in 1897. It has been more than 100 years since the family business has been handed over to the son Ho Tung and the grandson Stanley Ho. Stanley Ho is the "King of Gambling". Li Shek-Tang started his business at the end of the 18th century and Li Koon-Chun took over to develop it into the Bank of East Asia which is inherited by his sons and then handed down to the generation of David Li. In 1906, Fung Pak-Liu and his friend set up Li & Fung Group and later bought his friend's shares to control the company solely. When it was handed down to Fung Ho-Chu, the family business improved and became a listed company. Later, Fung Ho-Chu passed the company to the third generation — Victor Fung and William Fung — who introduced Western ideas into management. In 1897, Lee Yi-Liang set up Lichanglong and Jinxinghao by dealing in opium. The family business further developed in the hands of his son, Lee Hy-San, and later in the hands of his grandson, Lee Ming-Ze. Currently, Lee Hon-Chin from the fourth generation is in charge of the Group. In 1907, the Kwok brothers started their business by operating Wing On Department Store and handed the business over to Kwok Linmao, then Kwok Zhiquan and Kwok Zhiliang. Now, they are considering passing the business to the fourth generation.

Reasons for the long life of family enterprises in Hong Kong are as follows: (1) family business gets stronger during the process of transfer when the second generation expand the business set up by the first generation and the third generation innovate and reform to ensure the healthy development of the family business; (2) the introduction of new ideas on management, which usually happens during the third and the fourth generation and different enterprises show different features due to different ages; (3) industries that family businesses are involved in are always changing and occasionally there are separations but achievements have been accomplished in each industry; (4) emphasize individual development together with the development of family business, pay attention to the cultivation of offspring and successors who are, in recent years, well educated, making it easier for them to contribute to their family business.

Magnates From Family Enterprises

Besides great families and their lasting businesses, a lot of magnates have grasped the opportunities in Hong Kong to develop their enterprises, accumulating enormous family wealth.

Superman — Li Family

When it comes to the richest man in Hong Kong, Li Ka Shing, the president and general manager of Cheung Kong Holdings, will immediately jump into people's mind. Born in a common family, Li Ka Shing set up his own rubber factory through hard work, capability and thriftiness. In 1958, he began to invest in the real estate market and managed to develop Cheung Kong into one of the largest real estate companies. In 1979, it bought Hutchison Whampoa Limited — a British-funded company — and the controlling shares of Hong Kong Light Company in 1984. In December 1995, the market value of three listed companies of Cheung Kong exceeded US$42 billion. At present, Cheung Kong is mainly operated by Victor Li, the elder son of Li Ka Shing, and the younger son Richard Li is in charge of Hutchison Whampoa Ltd. Since Richard Li returned to Hong Kong from America in 1989, he had accomplished a lot in only ten years and thus earned him the name of a "superman". Consequently, the father and son — Li Ka Shing and Richard Li — are renowned as the "supermen".

Fok Family

The rise of the Fok family is the history of Henry Fok Ying Tung's drive for success. He was born in May 1923 in Hong Kong. Because of anti-Japanese war, he dropped out of school early and worked as a coal shoveler, helped his mother operate the grocery and later turned to shipping. In 1953 and 1954, he set up Ericson Ltd and Wing Ltd. Subsequently, he formed the Henry Fok Group to deal in real estate, architecture, shipping, hotel, lottery, restaurant, retailing and oil industries. He made his company bigger, earning great reputation and creating enormous family wealth.

The Richest Woman in Asia — Nina Wang

Sometimes, women can also start from scratch and the development path of female magnates seems more admirable. The president of Huamao Group — Nina Wang — is a good case in point. She moved to Hong Kong from Shanghai in 1955 and married Wang Teh Hwei. In the 1960s, they switched Huamao, established by the Wang family, from importing Western medicines to real estate and developed it into the largest private land agent after 10 years of effort. In 1990, Wang Teh Hwei disappeared after being kidnapped and Nina Wang had to operate the company by herself, managing to diversify its business into hotels, industrial trade and entertainment and thus emerging as the richest woman in Asia.

Rising magnates in Hong Kong have achieved their splendid careers, created a generation of great families. All of them have successors from their respective families, except Nina Wang, and their development will bring a new tide of flourish for family enterprises in Hong Kong. Given the significant role that family enterprises play in Hong Kong, family enterprises will remain a feature of Hong Kong's economy.

Family Enterprises of Taiwan

Taiwan is a region dominated by family enterprises, with two-thirds of the listed companies being family businesses. 80 of the 100 big

enterprise groups are owned and run by families. Due to its bur-
geoning market economy, the transformation of Taiwan's leading
economy from agricultural to industrial took place only in the past
30 years. Generally speaking, from the point of view of enterprise
development, Taiwan's companies belong to the middle-sized
enterprises, and the family management mode seems to work well.
Given that there is still a strong Chinese culture in Taiwan, family
enterprises are very common.

In Taiwan, there are four types of family enterprises. There are
enterprises that are respectively formed by blood relations, connate
relations, hometown fellow relations and partner relations, among
which the former three are dominant by quantity.

Taiwanese family enterprises are represented by the so-called "five
old big families" and "five new big families". The five old big families include: Yen family in Keelung, Lin family in Panchiao, Lin family in Wufeng, Koo family in Lukang and Chen family in Kaoshiung.
Most of these families had grown during the Qing dynasty and the
reign of the Japanese, based on land ownerships and relations with
the government. Keelung's Yen family got rich through mining. Its
later businesses had extended to shipbuilding, passenger transportation, shipping, metal industry, land investment and exploitation.
Panchiao's Lin family was the biggest landowner during the Japanese
occupation, becoming Taiwan's richest family through the business
of refining sugar. In Wufeng, the Lin family's wealth was dependent
on monopolistic business ventures in Taiwan from the time of the
Qing dynasty to the Japanese occupation. When Taiwan was ruled by
the Japanese, the Lin's turned to financial industry. In Lukang, the
Koo family's main business was salt production on saltern. The purchase of a large piece of land made them a wealthy landlord. In the
city of Kaoshiung, the Chen family had a dominant influence in
Tainan province by operating a large piece of land inherited from
their ancestors.

Taiwan's five new big families came into existence after World War II.
They were the Wang family of Formosa Plastics Group, the Tsai fam-
ily of Lin Yuan Group and Fubon Group, the Koo family of Koos
Group and China Trust Group, the Tsui family of Far Eastern Group,

and the Wu family of Shin Kong Group. The business growth of these families can be attributed to new industries, new capital and new talents; as well as their relations with government. Although there were only 200 corporations under the five families, their total takings had accounted for 10% of Taiwan's GNP; their total assets accounted for 5% of the total Taiwanese enterprise assets, and they had employed more than 220,000 employees.

Owned by the Wang family, Formosa Plastics Group is the king of the manufacturing industry. Its key corporation — Formosa Plastics Co Ltd — was founded in 1954 and very quickly occupied the dominant position in the industry. Formosa Plastics Group originally manufactured PVC products. It has three supporting corporations, i.e., Formosa Plastics, Nan Ya Plastics and Formosa Chemicals & Fibers. The three corporations produce PVC plastic powder, various plastic products and synthetic fiber respectively. In the 1990s, Formosa Plastics Group held the position of the biggest private enterprise group of Taiwan. Currently, the businesses under the Formosa Plastics Group include oil-refining, petrochemical materials, plastics manufacturing, fiber, textile, electronics, automobile, steam and electricity, mechanics, transportation, biotechnology, education and health care. It has as many as 70,000 employees. Wang Yung Ching — the founder of the group — has been the key person in the entire enterprise, and has been known as "the God of Management" in Taiwan.

The Lin Yuan Group and Fubon Group of the Tsai family had been Kings of the financial industry. In 1960, the four brothers of the Tsai family established Cathay Insurance Corporation. Two years later, Cathay Life Insurance Corporation was founded. Having made several investments, the powerful Cathay Group was eventually set up. In 1979, due to inner conflicts within the group, the Cathay Group was divided into four parts, namely the Lin Yuan Group, Fubon Group, Guo Xin Group and Guo Su Group. Once it was formed, the Lin Yuan Group rapidly expanded. In 1985, Cathay Life Insurance Corporation took the position as the biggest private enterprise in Taiwan. Besides finance and insurance, Lin Yuan Group also invested in medical treatment, time share, leasing, etc. Its employment once reached 40,000. The Fubon Group also invested in the financial and insurance industries. In 2001, Fubon Financial Holding Co Ltd was founded and expanded with employees numbering more than 20,000. Tsai Hongtu — son of Tsai Wanlin, who was the founder of Lin Yuan Group — was the key person of this group. Tsai Mingzhong and Tsai Mingxing, the two sons of Tsai Wan Tsai, the founder of Fubon Group, were the key persons of the Fubon Group.

The businesses of the Koo family's Koos Group and China Trust Group mainly focus on financial and cement industries. Its core enterprise used to be China Trust Commercial Bank, which was originally known as China Securities Investment Corporation. In 1970, this company was reorganized to become China Trust Investment Corporation. In 1989, the Group carried out an internal reorganization, establishing four systems of China Trust Investment, China Trust, Chailease Finance and China Life. In 1991, the group divided into two parts. China Trust, headed by Taiwan Cement Corporation, later changed its name to the Koos Group, focused mainly on the manufacturing industry with Koo Chengyun, the second son of Koo Chenfu, at the helm. China Trust Group, headed by China Trust Financial and Taiwan Cement, devoted themselves to the field of finance, with Koo Zhong, the son of Jeffrey Koo, at the helm. The Koos Group's business include paper-making, paper products, petrochemical products, pharmaceuticals, pesticide, electronics and electricity, informational product manufacturing, life insurance, construction, securities, time shares, banking and finance, etc. It has almost 20,000 employees.

The success of the Wu family began with the textile industry. Its founder Wu Huoshi was in the fabric business as early as the post-war era. Later, he turned to the textile industry. After the enterprise expanded, he extended upward by setting up a synthetic fiber company. He then expanded his business downward by setting up a dye factory. Eventually, a big "textile empire" was established. In the following years, the group extended its businesses to other fields, such as finance and insurance, hospital, hotel, import and export trading etc. It has about 40,000 employees. Wu Dongjin, the eldest son of Wu Huoshi, is a key figure in the group, assuming the position of board chairman of Shin Kong Financial Holding Corporation.

His second son, Wu Dongliang, another key person in the group, was appointed the board chairman of Taishin Financial Holding Corporation.

The Far Eastern Group of the Tsui family has textile as its original business. Its core company Far Eastern Textile Mill was first established in Shanghai in 1942. After moving to Taiwan in 1949, it continued its textile business. In 1953, Taiwan Far Eastern Textile Company was founded, producing cotton yarn and cotton fabric. In the following year, it united with Far Eastern Textile Mill as the current Far Eastern Textile Corporation. In 1957, Asian Cement Co Ltd was set up. The company underwent rapid progress and made great profits, becoming one of the main forces of the Far Eastern Group. Under the leadership of Xu Xudong, the son of the group founder Xu Youmo, the traditional image of industrial corporations was completely changed. Far Eastern Group formally entered the field of high-tech industry. The businesses of the group range from cement, textile, general merchandise and finance to transportation, construction, petrochemicals, and communications, and had gradually expanded to large-scale department stores and shopping centers. It had a total of 30,000 employees.

Today, some of the old Taiwanese family enterprises, with the aging of the first generation, are already under the commands of the second or even the third generations. When it is time to choose the successors, these family enterprises attach importance to the grooming of their heirs. They send their children to prestigious European and American universities to receive their tertiary education and professional training, where they could learn modern science and technology and even management skills needed by modern enterprises. As a result, current Taiwanese family enterprises have a combination of both modern and traditional family business. Also, in the 1980s, Taiwan's traditional conceptions went through many changes. Some important traditional values have been replaced by modern conceptions. Furthermore, under the influences of Western enterprise culture, some enterprises subsequently introduced the Western management ideas. Some family enterprise managers, with far-sightedness, realized the fatal weaknesses of family enterprises. They created some new mechanisms in the brutal market competition. As for employment practice, these enterprises have abandoned the traditional practice of nepotism, ranking talents much higher than material capital. As for the appointment of high-level managers, the enterprises gradually began to choose professional managers rather than family members. Consequently, in current Taiwanese family enterprises, there are many professional managers. For example, Taiwan Semiconductor Manufacturing Company Ltd owned by Zhang Zhongmou broke the traditional practice of Taiwanese family enterprises by establishing the model of professional managers. As for the reward mechanism, they placed emphasis on profit-sharing together with their employees.

Taiwanese family enterprises have made improvements in the aspect of enterprise system. They have introduced the regulation-contract mechanism, which seeks to distribute stock shares to family members based on their relative positions. By doing so, potential contests for family property could be effectively avoided by law. Furthermore, the nuclear control of the enterprises would also be strengthened, i.e., the integrated control of the stock shares would be kept in the hands of the family, and thus the centralization of property rights and the arbitration in property disposition rights would be prevented.

Family Enterprises of Southeast Asia

The life span of family enterprises usually lasts for about 20 years. Only 39% of all the family enterprises could continue to the second generation. Unfortunately, only as little as 15% would last to the third generation. The situation with Southeast Asian family enterprises is better. In the world of the overseas Chinese, most of the companies are family enterprises in industries or commerce. Most of these family enterprises are flourishing. How do they achieve that? The business climate and environment faced by the overseas Chinese family enterprises are quite unique. With internationalization and modernization, and for the sake of survival and development, these overseas enterprises have to explore a new approach combining the advantages of both the East and the West.

Most overseas Chinese entrepreneurs of the old generation were born during hard times and had grown up during national calamities. In their childhood, they were forced through hard work to make a living overseas. They built up their businesses from scratch to become self-made economic giants in local areas. Some of them even ranked among the world's wealthiest men. Their course of making a name for themselves represents the developmental history of overseas Chinese businesses.

Most of the overseas Chinese family enterprises are located in Southeast Asia. Since the 1970s, the rapid rise of Southeast Asia has broken the post-war dominance of the Japanese economy, influencing the whole Asia and creating a miracle marveled at by the whole world. As an important part of the Southeast Asian economy, the Chinese enterprises have contributed a lot to the rapid growth of the Southeast Asian economy. At the end of the last century, Chinese enterprises suffered severe losses during the financial crisis. However, these Chinese enterprises have not been destroyed.

Wang Gungwu, a well-known Chinese historian and former professor of the Hong Kong University, once made a prognosis of family enterprises: firstly, in the past 20 to 30 years, the business activities and industry development undertaken by overseas Chinese had achieved remarkable accomplishments. Secondly, with admiration for the Western, flexible and durable style of management, formed after the Industrial Revolution, the traditional Chinese family not only adapt to this big change but also strive for opportunities in competition with big enterprises in the West.

The Southeast Chinese family enterprise economy has been developed on the basis of family or connate operations. The overlapping of ownership, control rights and family is the main form of the early Chinese enterprises. In recent years, with their expansion and internationalization, these Chinese enterprises have gradually adopted the form of holding corporations. But at the same time, a family or connate operation approach has been reserved. These Chinese family enterprises possess some common characteristics with respect to management:

1. The overlapping of ownership and management rights — Most of the Southeast Chinese enterprises are monopolized and controlled by the Chinese families. The decision-making level has been dominated by Chinese family members and those related by marriage to the family. It is very difficult for outsiders to be involved in the enterprise's management. The decision-making level of the subsidiary companies is also almost dominated by the family or connate members. Even if the corporation stocks are listed, the listed companies are still under the control of the families.

2. The patriarch-leading system. Usually, the overseas Chinese enterprises or their core corporations are tightly controlled by families. The board chairman or the president of the enterprises is always the patriarch of the family. And the whole enterprise is regarded as a large family. The patriarch has to be concerned with all of the enterprise's routines. The Chinese families are not only the founders and owners of the enterprises, but also the key managers. Family and family interests are often the core and goals of the enterprise. The highest position is usually dominated by the founder or the patriarch of the family. The centralized management mode of "patriarch omnipotence" is often being adopted. And the management system is organized based on the kinship of the family.

3. The succession of father passing to sons. As the family heirs, the young generations of family members are assigned important positions in the family enterprises to train their leadership capabilities. Usually the young generations take their work seriously. Once the founders pass away, the heirs, who usually have already studied or achieved big accomplishments abroad, would be asked home to take over the family enterprises.

4. The business activities of the Chinese enterprises focus on Confucianism and mutual confidence. Being far away from home,

and due to cultural differences, they could not fuse themselves into the mainstream society. So the economic development of overseas Chinese largely depended on their special relationship networks of blood and geography. They hold trust and faith as their credo, promoting their connections to the external world based on the family, connate and provincial relations.

5. For the overseas Chinese, they take in traditional Chinese culture together with Western values. Therefore, the traditional culture they have inherited is unavoidably affected by assimilation. Under the "trans-national" and "trans-cultural" influences, the overseas Chinese became gradually unfamiliar with the traditional Chinese language and culture. In addition, the descendants of the immigrants are also eager to integrate into the local mainstream society, which leads to multi-dimensions of their current culture and the dilution of their traditional culture.

Suffice to say the overseas Chinese "love" for family enterprises is closely related to Confucianism, Chinese traditional family and connate concepts. After finding a foothold in foreign countries, the overseas Chinese would take their family members and even their relatives and friends there as long as the condition permitted, in order to banish the feelings of discrimination, loneliness and depression in a foreign land. As for the establishment of their own businesses, many began running their family stores only with the help of their spouses. When they have achieved some success, they would summon their relatives and friends to join them and worked together. When they should grow old, in order to maintain stability in the whole family, they would pass their businesses to their descendents. As the enterprises passed from one generation to the next, they eventually became family enterprises.

It may occur to some people that family enterprises are usually small-scale businesses, based on nepotism and conformism. Therefore, this kind of business operation should be abandoned. It is simply not true. There is a historical necessity for the emergence of family enterprises, which have their own merits. In most cases, ownership and management are combined. The combination tends to mobilize enthusiasm and commitment of the managers, and thus grants the enterprises more energy and passion.

Secondly, in most cases, there is a powerful core leadership in successful family enterprises, which would allow the enterprises to respond promptly to the changing demands of the markets. The patriarch, who is chosen based on seniority and talents and in accordance with the core leadership of the families, is the key decision-maker. Therefore, the decision layers in family enterprises are comparatively fewer, and its organizational structure tends to be flat and more flexible. From the viewpoint of management, the family enterprise mode helps to shorten the distance between the upper and lower levels, reduce the middle links between them, and speed up the information transfer, which would enable them to save costs and time in communication and decision-making. Consequently they are much responsive to the environmental and market changes.

Thirdly, if the secret of success lies in the ways of management, then the core management is to establish better interpersonal relationships within the enterprises. Not only are family members a community with the same interests, all the descendents share the same ancestors.

Overseas Chinese family enterprises have exerted both positive and negative influences. The family enterprises are passed sequentially from father to son and then from son to grandson. If they have many descendants, then naturally their family would flourish. But if they have no descendant, then it would be difficult for them to prevent the enterprises from being transferred to others. Furthermore, once the old family authority is over, all of the descendants would fight over the family property if the next authority is not selected in time. Therefore, under this circumstance, the family business empire would collapse. Generally speaking, the first generation leaders are very experienced and they are very capable in dealing with difficulties. To the second and third generations, for different reasons, the successor might be a mediocre or a black sheep, which would directly prevent the progress of the enterprises or even worse, destroy the whole business.

First, a good successor must be trained as early as possible. In the overseas Chinese society, either rich merchants or owners of small business are all concerned about whether they could pick a successor for their businesses. There is an old saying that "Wealth does not last for three generations" but no merchant would want the business created through their hard work to disappear just because there are no successors. In order to avoid the tragedy, many overseas Chinese businessmen began to explore other ways to sustain their family enterprises.

They attach great importance to the selection and cultivation of successors. According to the training experiences of Beijing Opera, they recognize the value of regular professional training, and advocated educating the children at the earliest time possible. Many Chinese businessmen introduce this method into their families. Many entrepreneurs sent their children to famous European and American Universities to receive higher education, learn modern science and technology and master modern enterprises management skills. Concerned about their character and leadership development, fathers are extremely strict with their children. Besides emphasis on academic pursuit, the entrepreneurs also pay attention to developing their practical experience. Upon graduation, some of the children will work in the family business, starting from the bottom, to be promoted along the way. Some have arrangements to work in other companies so as to gain experience in building business relationships, while others would go right into setting up their own companies.

When grooming their children, the entrepreneurs stick to some basic principles such as "sons and daughters rank first, and nephews rank second", and "making differences between male and female, and the eldest would be chosen first". But often these rules are not strictly adhered to. They pay more attention to morals and talents.

Second, they would introduce the "joint-stock" system. It helps to separate management rights from proprietorship and improve the operation efficiency. Today, many of the successful Chinese enterprises have already introduced the joint-stock system, with the outstanding ones becoming listed companies. As for individual stock holding, the stock shares are still being passed from one generation to the next.

Third, in order to flourish, overseas Chinese families have created a model of management that combines merits of both the East and the West, apart from introducing measures in succession planning and joint-stock system.

Starting from the traditional Chinese concept that "Harmony in the family is the basis for success in any undertaking", overseas Chinese family enterprises have been changing with the times, decidedly abandoning some demerits of traditional family enterprises; applying modern human resource management models; and eventually creating a new enterprise model that combines the merits of both the East and the West to respond flexibly to the market changes. By so doing, they not only protected the permanence of their enterprises but also created a unique Chinese family style of modern management.

Case 6: Case of Kikkoman: A Combination of Tradition and Modernity

Introduction

On a winter morning in 1997, the world's top-ranked entrepreneurs, scholars, and reporters assembled in World Economic Forum in Davos, Switzerland. A Japanese entrepreneur Yuzaburo Mogi, who is also known as the vice-chairman of an influential entrepreneur association, was addressing with fluent English at the Forum. Yuzaburo Mogi was raised in an old and traditional Japanese family, and he is currently handling a family business with a history of 370 years: Kikkoman Company — a company with long history and innovative spirit. Kikkoman Company aims at expanding international market for soy sauce, trying to make a traditional Japanese sauce an international flavoring. During the past 50 years, Kikkoman has been expanding market into more than 100 countries, becoming the largest soy sauce producer in the world.

"Sticking to the existing products and business hinders further development. Only under a strong leadership to carry out reforms can a company stand out with competitiveness in the 21st century's new global economy." Yuzaburo Mogi's evaluation of the present and his vision into the future exert great influence on the company.

As one of the oldest manufactures in Japan, Kikkoman has left deep imprints in the country's business history: earlier than other world-renowned Japanese companies such as Panasonic, Sony, Toyota, and Honda, Kikkoman was the first Japanese enterprise to set up a fully equipped plant in the US: in 1972, a plant was built in Wisconsin — ten years earlier than Toyota. Currently, Kikkoman's market share in Japan is 30% and the company supplies its products to 25% of restaurants and 99% of the supermarkets in America. Kikkoman has a history of 380 years. It was set up in 1630, and had gone through the Tokugawa period, the Meiji Reformation, the World War II, and modern Japan. Today, business is still in the hands of the founder's offspring. The evolution history of Kikkoman is like a splendid picture, revealing a legendary story of a traditional Japanese enterprise, by combining modern technology with traditional techniques, developing more than 2,000 related products, promoting them to over 100 countries around the world, and making itself an energetic multinational enterprise.

The three Chinese characters in the name of "Kikkoman" all have special meanings. "Kik" means longevity and luck. "ko" means first class or top rank. And "man" means forever. When put together, "Kikkoman" connotes that a top-rank company with a long history brings out first-class products. Kikkoman has achieved this! It is Kikkoman that provides soy sauce for the royal family in Japan. However, Kikkoman is far from satisfied. It continues to take innovative measures in management style and sales strategies. Besides soy sauce, Kikkoman has been extending into other areas such as sauces, wine, fruits and vegetables, and drinks. At present, ambitious as it is, Kikkoman intends to expand into fields like gene engineering, biology, and biochemistry. People have every reason to believe that this traditional family business will become more vigorous at the beginning of the 21st century.

A Brief History

The world-renowned Kikkoman soy sauce was first produced by Shige Maki, a female member of the Mogi family in the 17th century, the Tokugawa period. Her husband passed away in a power struggle, and Shige Maki, together with her only son, Bing Sanlang, fled from Osaka in 1930, and finally settled down in a small village called Tokasu, which was 50 kilometers north of Edo. There, Shige Maki changed her family name to Mogi, and changed her son's name to Qizuo Weimen, and that was how the Mogi family came into being. During the Tokugawa period, farmers led a hard life, and they were trying to seek other ways to earn a living. Many of them showed interest in producing soy sauce, for in the 17th century, soy sauce was considered as a luxury commodity, which only rich families could afford. Later, the urbanization process in Japan helped to make soy sauce popular among ordinary Japanese people and thus the demand for soy sauce increased sharply. Since soy sauce brewing became profitable, Shige Maki decided to take on the business. It was during that period that Shige Maki developed the secret receipe for brewing soy sauce. In 1662, when Shige Maki passed away, the Mogi family had secured its position as one of the outstanding soy sauce producers in Tokasu. Another famous soy sauce producer in Tokasu was the Takahashi family. In the following decades, the two families kept frequent and close business cooperation. In 1768, a marriage combined the two families together. Takahashi later became one of the eight branches in the Mogi family. On Mogi's side, five branches of members joined into the family during the period from 1764 to 1822. Another branch joined later. All eight branches made up Kikkoman Company in 1917.

In 1838, Zuopingzhi Mogi, the head of Mogi family, made a wise decision to ask for government approval to formally establish Kikkoman as the brand for their products. With strong brand-consciousness, Zuopingzhi Mogi knew better than anyone else the importance of brand promotion in arousing brand acceptance and loyalty among people. To achieve brand promotion, they offered funds to sumotori, printed the brand of "Kikkoman" on paper lantern and paper umbrella. The Mogi family was also considering international promotion. Therefore, when Japan shifted its political system from feudalism to constitutional monarchy, Kikkoman soy sauce was shipped to Hawaii and California in large quantities for local Japanese immigrants.

After a series of successful operations, Kikkoman had become one of the best soy sauce brands in Japan by the mid-19th century. Japanese government granted privilege to Kikkoman to exempt it from price control policies, which, undoubtedly, added fame to Kikkoman soy sauce in Japan.

In the early 1950s, in order to strengthen brand recognition among the Japanese, Kikkoman set up strategy planning and sales departments to conduct sales investigation, advertising, and consumer education. In sales strategy, the company stressed that soy sauce could be used to cook not only Japanese food, but also Western food. They funded cooking programs on TV, and sent cooking staff out to teach Japanese people how to cook non-Japanese food with soy sauce. They also offered soy sauce for free to brides to be who took cooking training courses before marriage. These sales strategies worked very well. Kikkoman's soy sauce enjoyed a high market share of 30%.

From 1950 to 1960, Kikkoman extended its interests to other areas. Besides soy sauce, the company developed a series of new products such as grape wine, fruit and vegetable juice, and traditional Japanese rack. In 1962, Kikkoman founded Katsunuma Wine Corporation to brew Western-style wine in Japan. They also researched and developed various food processing machines, medicines, and biochemical products, including ferment and essence which were for industrial and clinical use, and fruits and vegetables produced from genetic engineering.

The 1970s witnessed overseas expansion. Kikkoman set up plants in America and Europe, enabling their products to be processed and sold at the same place. In 1995, Yuzaburo Mogi assumed the position of CEO, further advancing the diversifying of products. He soon appointed seven product managers whose primary duty was to reinforce product research and development, and to strengthen the link between producers and consumers. In addition, a number of innovative strategies were implemented. In Japan's business history, Yuzaburo Mogi is regarded as a business giant with broad international vision, enjoying the same status as Morita Akio of Sony, and Kobayashi Yotaro of Fuji. Currently, Kikkoman has plants in many overseas areas, including America, Singapore, Taiwan China, and Holland. The overseas sales volume of Kikkoman soy sauce takes up 26% of the total income (US$2 billion). Kikkoman soy sauce has become one of the unique products in the world.

Management Concepts

As one of the oldest companies in Japan, Kikkoman has its unique style of management, which respects the traditions and emphasizes innovations. The unique style not only keeps the family enterprise integrated, but also maintains its energy.

As early as in 1917, 90 years ago, when the eight families jointly established Kikkoman, the six branches of the Mogi family, the Takanashi, and Jueqie made a regulation to abide by. The informal regulation includes 17 items (see the appendix), playing a critical role in the overall operational system of the company. The management tradition has long been adhered by Kikkoman for a long time. During his tenure, Qizaburo took the lead in putting forward the management concepts of the industrial spirit and corporation philosophy. In addition, from 1962 to 1974 when he was board chairman and president of the company, Mogi set up lifetime employment system, reconstructed manufacture process and treated the workers well. Responding to the innovative managerial steps taken by the company to adapt to the changes, the employees were all strongly attached and loyal to the enterprise. Emphasis on the employees and loyalty becomes a tradition of Kikkoman, which is also extended to its internationalized management.

Kikkoman has maintained the high quality of its products for more than several years. For that reason, Kikkoman has long been accepted and recognized by the Japanese. They have the strongest logistic system throughout Japan. One can find the products of Kikkoman even in a small grocery in the most remote area of Japan. Kikkoman sells soy sauce, one of the most traditional products in the world, but it adopts the most innovative steps in management, which is one of the reasons for its survival of more than 300 years.

Management Control

In terms of shareholding structure, Kikkoman is now an independent listed company, and is also listed in Tokyo and Osaka Securities Exchange. However, the family members own 3.41% of the company's shares by setting up Sensyusya, a financial association. Sensyusya is one of the ten top shareholders of the company, and the management right of the company has always been controlled by the Mogi family. After the development for more than 300 years, the family has many branches. In order to avoid the separation or disunity that may be resulted from the power struggle among them, Kikkoman made an unwritten regulation in 1917 when the eight family branches were set up. The regulation rules that only one male member of each family in each generation should be admitted into the company, which ensures that the power struggles among the branches be maintained at a healthy level. Generally speaking, each family branch would select and train a candidate (usually the eldest son), and try to rank him in the decision-making circle of the company. Non-candidates have to find jobs by themselves in other fields. Even when they enter the company for some special reasons, they can never be included in the power core. If one family fails to have a son, it can adopt male member of other family to represent itself in the company. The system guarantees that the power struggle among the branches of the Mogi family stay in a healthy and balanced condition, which can be reflected from the distribution of the ten presidents since the establishment of Kikkoman. Since 1917, there have not been two or more presidents from the same branch. Of the ten presidents, two come from the Bai family, two from the Yu family, two from the Zuo family, one from the original family, and three from other families. No matter which family the president came from, stability and selective risk have always been the style that Kikkoman sticks to.

Diversified Operation

Kikkoman began its process of diversified operation since the 1960s, and 90% of its activities was centered on soy sauce before that. Japan's soy sauce market was saturated by the 1960s. Aware that the development of new products and the exploration of new markets are crucial for the survival of the company, the Mogi family conducted a series of active diversified operations.

In 1962, Kikkoman set up Katsunuma Wine Corporation in an attempt to brew and sell port wine. At that time, the port wine from the Western countries was not familiar to and accepted by the Japanese consumers so its consumption was quite low. By propagating a favorable healthy effect for hardworking businessmen and anemic women, Kikkoman promoted its wine products and quickly opened up the Japanese market for family wine consumption. Together with other promotion programs, the consumption of port wine in Japan rose by 7 times during the 20 years from 1973 to 1993. The annual average output of Katsunuma Wine Corporation increased by 100 times compared to that of its preliminary stage, accounting for 10% of the total port wine production in Japan.

In 1963, one year after Katsunuma Wine Corporation was established, Kikkoman set up another food company, focusing on distribution and wholesale of foreign products in the Japanese market. Kikkoman established a set of unique selling channels for its soy sauce products, through which the Company can easily and effectively sell the foreign seasoning products. Kikkoman then signed an agreement with Del Monte, the top vegetable and fruit manufacturer and seller in the US, so that Kikkoman was authorized to produce and sell the tomato juice and tomato sauce under the Del Monte brand in the Japanese market. It turned out that the alliance of Kikkoman and Del Monte was a great success. When Kikkoman sells tomato sauce through its own selling channels, the market share of the tomato products under the brand of Del Monte reached as much as 30%, ranking second. The annual per-capita consumption of tomato products in Japan is three times as much as that in the US. Moreover, the alliance helps Kikkoman to establish its modern image in the Japanese consumers, minds as the Western companies did.

In 1990, Kikkoman extended its cooperative relationship with Del Monte. In addition to tomato products, Kikkoman was also awarded the permanent agent right of the Del Monte products in the Pacific area. Kikkoman made good use of the value of the Del Monte brand, and spared no effort in promoting innovations for its production process.

Internationalized Operation

When the demand for soy sauce in Japan decreased, it became necessary for Kikkoman to produce sauce products that satisfy the tastes of the Western consumers. The choice furthers Kikkoman's strategy of internationalization. Qisanlang Mogi and Yuzaburo Mogi, the father and son, planned and implemented Kikkoman's strategy of internationalization.

Yuzaburo Mogi was the firmest sponsor for the strategy of internationalization within the Mogi family. It was Yuzaburo who convinced the top level of the company, including his father, of the necessity of setting up factories in the US. His understanding of the market and people in the US contributes to his confidence, which stems from his experience as a student in Columbia University in pursuit of a master's degree of enterprise management. Aware of the necessity of conducting internationalized business, Qisanlang Mogi sent his son to the US as a pioneer. Located in the most diversified New York City, Columbia University, where Yuzaburo studied, is quite internationalized itself. To a great extent, his vision of internationalization was fostered in the period.

Yuzaburo traveled a lot while he was in the US. He tried to understand the natural conditions and social customs of North America, studied the distribution of Japanese food restaurants in the America, and thoroughly investigated the possibility of the soy sauce consumption by the American mainstream. In his spare time, Mogi was a product exhibitor for Kikkoman in the supermarkets in New York. He demonstrated how to make ported meat with Yakisauce (the sauce mixed from soy sauce, sugar and rice wine), and invited consumers to taste. Judging from the response of the American consumers to the food, Mogi was convinced that the American market was promising for Kikkoman's products. Moreover, Mogi associated and maintained close relationship with some outstanding figures that he acquainted in Columbia University, which laid a solid foundation for him to set up factories in the US. In 1961, Mogi graduated and returned to Kikkoman. He first worked as a worker in sauce factory and then moved to the accounting department, where he led the computerized reform. After that, Mogi was transferred to the planning department of the company, responsible for the overall operation and management of Kikkoman. It was in 1965 when he worked in the planning department that Mogi began his attempts to set up factories in the US.

Mogi's determination and willpower to prevail over all dissenting views led to the final success. In 1965 when Yuzaburo handed his study report for the establishment of factories in the US to the leaders of the company, they jumped to the conclusion that the sales volume cannot compensate for the cost needed for setting up a factory. While in 1970 when the sales volume of soy sauce in the US steadily increased, the top management of the company agreed to Mogi's plan to investigate, collect information in the US and formulate feasibility report. In December of the year, Yuzaburo and his team went to the US. They traveled around the country, trying to find a suitable location to set up the factory. They also sent mails to several state governments for information of foreign investment. To manufacture locally will save a lot of transportation costs. Moreover, soy sauce factory pays very low taxes to the US government. The raw materials needed for the brewing of soy sauce could be found everywhere in America.

However, it costs almost two-thirds of the annual capital gross of Kikkoman to set up a factory in the US. The inland transportation fee would also be increased. It was a risk for Yuzaburo to propose the establishment of a factory in the US. When proposing the plan, he was risking his own promising future — possibly the presidency of the company. If the plan ended up in failure, Mogi would lose the confidence and consequently the position of president. Nevertheless, he was willing to try. Fortunately, after Yuzaburo proposed for three times, it was finally accepted by the board. Since all the materials needed for the brewing of soy sauce could be found in the central and western area, a 200-acre land in Walworth Town, Wisconsin was chosen as the site of the factory.

On January 18, 1972, Kikkoman began to build the factory in Walworth. At the beginning of June 1973, the factory produced the first bottle of soy sauce. After five years of local operation, Kikkoman in America began to make profits. Ten years later, Kikkoman became the biggest soy sauce manufacturer in the America. In 1998, Kikkoman set up the second factory in Folsom in California. In 1996, Kikkoman built its first factory in the Netherlands. At present, the ordinary seasoning products made by Kikkoman can be found in 25% of all the restaurants and 99% of the supermarkets throughout America. Kikkoman has achieved great success in internationalizing its business.

Family Rules

The following rules are the guidelines and regulations to which the Mogi family has been adhering for several hundred years.

1. The family members must attach great importance to harmony, respect each other, work hard to keep the family prosperous, and maintain family wealth.
2. Religious worship is the basis for nourishing one's virtue; keeping faith equals enriching one's wisdom.
3. Loyalty and patriotism are the obligations of the family members. Respect and serve the country; understand and abide by national systems.
4. Courtesy is the basic quality of the family members. If the elder members lack courtesy, the young members cannot respond with loyalty; if the young members lack courtesy, negative influences will be invited. Courtesy is crucial for a self-disciplined and harmonious family.
5. Remember: virtue is the basis for making fortune. Never judge anyone by money.
6. Strict discipline is necessary. Treat every employee equally. Ask them to work as hard as possible. Class ethics of any organization should be kept.
7. Human resources are the most precious asset of the company. Every employee of the company should be equally treated without any personal prejudice. The employee should be respected and appointed to positions which commensurate with his capability and achievements. His self-worth should also be emphasized and promoted.
8. The education of the next generation is our undeniable responsibility for the nation and the society. The kids should be trained in morality, wisdom and physical exercise.
9. Treat everything in the world with kindness, which is the source of discipline and the mother of virtue. Words can

either bring luck or invite misfortune. A sharp tongue will hurt both yourself and others. Kind behaviors will make you feel easy even in a different situation.

10. Simplicity is a tradition that the family adheres to for generations. The doctrine of the mean is something that one must pursue in life.

11. Achievements come from diligence and effort. Gambling is not appreciated. Behaviors that violate social order or make advantage of others' vulnerability to accomplish one's own career should be strictly prohibited.

12. Competition is necessary for progress, but extreme and immoral measures should be avoided.

13. Any evaluation should be made publicly and equally. Rewards and punishment should be convincing. Rewards can stimulate the employees to accept new challenges, and punishments help to reduce unintended mistakes.

14. Decisions to enter new fields should be made after discussion with the family members. To reduce losses means to increase profits.

15. Never borrow in negligence; never provide guarantee for any debt; never borrow money for making profits.

16. Try your best to repay the society. Never ask for the return and never be self-satisfied.

17. Never make important decisions all by oneself. Discuss with people who are interested in the matter at any time. The exchange of ideas helps to foster correct working attitude.

(*Adapted from "The Kikkoman Chronicles: A Global Company with a Japanese Soul", authored by Ronald Yates, Mechanical Industry Press, 2003*)

Case 7: Samsung Group: From Family Enterprise to Global Brand

Introduction

Samsung Group, the largest South Korean trading group, is the umbrella organization for a 26-company conglomerate, with 300 juridical persons and offices in nearly 70 countries and areas worldwide. The group has an employment of 196,000 persons.

In 2003, the group's turnover was approximately US$96,500 million, equal to 10% of China's GDP. Samsung Group is the most powerful Korean conglomerate in the world's marketplace, with nearly 20 products ranking tops in terms of world market share.

The success of the Samsung Group should be attributed to two generations of the Lee family. Lee Byung-Chull, the founder of Samsung Group, built up the corporation from scratch. He was regarded as a mythical industrialist in the period of Korea's economic renewal. His pioneering work made Samsung a potential electronic magnate in the world.

In 1936, Lee Byung-Chull, founder of Samsung, founded a rice mill with the money inherited from his father. Lee Byung-Chull passed away in the year of 1987. After 50 years, Samsung Group had evolved into the largest trading group in Korea, with 37 subsidiary companies and 150,000 employees. Lee Byung-Chull established a number of world-renowned companies during his life. Considering the huge achievements he made to the country, the Koreans honor him as the "father of business".

In 1978 when his father was still alive, Lee Kun Hee was named vice-chairman of Samsung. In 1995, eight years after Lee Byung-Chull's death, Lee Kun Hee was in full control of the management right of Samsung after purchasing the shares held by New World and First Sugar. However, Lee Kun Hee's second "pioneering" began after he took over the leadership, and he accomplished self transcendence through the second phase of "Second Pioneering" and new "Change" management. And thus he built the largest enterprise in South Korea in the time of his father into a world-class trading group.

After the pioneering under the two generations for 70 years, Samsung realized its dream of becoming a state-of-the-art enterprise. However, it still faces challenges in the increasingly changing global market. How will Lee Kun Hee and the third generation of Samsung respond?

Lee Byung-Chull: The Founder of Samsung

Lee Byung-Chull was born in Jung-kyo-ri, Jeong-gok-myeon, Uiryong-gun, Kyongsangnam-do in 1910. In his grandfather's generation, the Lee family started out as a peasant family, became a landlord owning 1,000 shi's of land. His grandfather was an honest, diligent man who was willing to apply scientific methods to farming. His grandfather's way of doing things had great influence on the family as a whole.

He went to a private school, Munsan-jung, established by his grandfather, Munsan Lee Hong Seok. There, he studied the Chinese Classics from the age of five. As a teenager, he studied modern sciences in Jung-dong Middle School; then in April 1930, Lee Byung-Chull went to Japan to study economics at Waseda University. One year later in 1931, Lee Byung-Chull moved back to Korea. At the time, he was faced with three choices: politics, independence campaign, or business. Recognizing that the most urgent task was to establish national economy, Lee decided to join business. In the spring of 1936, Lee Byung-Chull founded a joint rice mill through a common investment with his acquaintances. He then expanded his business to automobile transportation with 20 trucks and a Japanese automobile company he purchased at that time. But the aftermath of the unexpected Sino-Japan War forced him to go into liquidation. He became penniless.

Then Lee Byung-Chull became engrossed in a new business plan, traveling all around Korea and to many cities in China, such as Changchun, Shenyang, Qingdao, Beijing, and Shanghai. After a careful consideration and planning, Lee Byung-Chull finally decided to start trading with China and Manchuria. On March 1, 1938, Lee Byung-Chull established Samsung Trading Company in Taegu. Apart from trading with China on fruits, vegetables, and fish, Samsung Trading Company also flourished in the noodle-making industry. Nine years later in 1947, Samsung Trading Company was moved to the capital city of Seoul and renamed as Samsung Corporation. Unknown to the public at that time, the company was ranked among the top seven trading companies in South Korea. Half a year later at the beginning of 1950, it was the first and biggest trading company in the nation. However, the Korean War devitalized Samsung. In January 1951, Lee Byung-Chull decided to move the company to the interim capital of Busan and formally changed the name of the company to Samsung Corporation, with 300 million won as the registered capital.

In the 1950s, Samsung traded in sugar and textile. In the 1960s and 1970s, the corporation adopted the strategy of multi-directional development and extended its business into areas of petrochemical, ship-building, finance, electronics, insurance, and communication, etc. During this period, 24 subsidiary companies and holding companies were established.

Lee Byung-Chull passed away in the year of 1987. After more than 50 years, Samsung Group has evolved into the largest trading group in Korea, with 37 subsidiary companies and 150,000 employees. Lee Byung-Chull had established a number of world-renowned companies during his lifetime. Considering his huge achievements and contribution made to the country, the people of Korea honored him as the "father of business".

Handover of Samsung within the Family

Contrary to common practice, Lee Byung-Chull did not select his eldest son to be the heir of his corporation. Instead he chose his third son, Lee Kun Hee, who was believed to be more talented in business and management. In 1987, Lee Kun Hee was named the vice-chairman of Samsung, and he stayed in this position for ten years, laying a solid foundation for his future development.

Apart from selecting a heir, Lee Byung-Chull did not make clear how his properties were to be divided among the family. After Lee Byung-Chull's death, the family spent eight years, after difficult negotiations and consultations, to finally settle the matter. The eldest son took over the management of First Sugar and Anguo Fire. First Textile and a media company were given to the second son and his wife. The eldest daughter inherited Jeonju Paper and the Korea Hospital while the second daughter got New World Departmental Store. The Lee family estate was settled peacefully, without causing any huge family rift among the siblings. The biggest controversy was about the stock right of Samsung Life Insurance Co Ltd, which was the most difficult dispute to solve.

The Lee family did not possess a large percentage of Samsung's stock. Lee Kun Hee was holding 0.45% while the rest of the family members held 1.54% in total. The management of Samsung was under the control of Lee Kun Hee, but the majority stock right was not.

The Second Pioneering Under Lee Kun Hee

Lee Byung-Chull founded Samsung and developed it into the largest enterprise in South Korea. Lee Byung-Chull's successor, Lee Kun Hee, made it a world-class trading group. Lee Kun Hee was born on January 9, 1942. Like his father, Lee Kun Hee had studied in Japan when he was young. He received a bachelor's degree in economics from Waseda University, and continued his MBA education at George Washington University. Lee Kun Hee had a keen interest in films. When he was in Japan, he watched 1,200–1,300 films. Lee Kun Hee developed a unique thinking method while enjoying films. He said a film can be felt differently if the audience were in the different positions of the supporting role, director, and photographer. Lee Kun Hee was also a sports fan. He was good at wrestling, judo, horsemanship, golf, and table tennis. Aside from his work in Samsung, he also assumed the position of chairman of an amateur wrestling association, and a position in the International Olympic Committee. Lee Kun Hee put some of the sports ideas into his management. In his 1993 reform, he required his employees to learn the self-discipline of golf, the cooperation in baseball, and the fighting spirit of football. Ever since his childhood, Lee Kun Hee was isolated, soft-spoken, and kept a low-profile. Little notable achievement was observed before he took the position of vice-chairman of Samsung. It was little wonder that people were suspicious when he pledged, in his inaugural address, to make Samsung a world-class corporation.

The Second Pioneering

Launching-out

Lee Kun Hee launched the "second pioneering" soon after his take-over of Samsung. At the beginning, he spent 14 months traveling around and visiting different enterprises both inside and outside South Korea. It was a preliminary period — a period of thinking and considering the future development of Samsung.

In March 1988, at the 50th anniversary of Samsung, Lee Kun Hee announced his plan for his "second pioneering." The main task of the second pioneering was to explore new business areas and to reform the current ones. Samsung's new interests included aerospace, genetics, and macromolecule. Electronics, semiconductor, and communication industries were combined to achieve operational efficiency. Lee Kun Hee set the goal for Samsung — to be a world-class family electronic appliances and communication products provider. To achieve this goal, Lee Kun Hee instituted some vigorous reform measures. As the world economies stepped onto the stage of globalization, Samsung should also grow to become a world-class corporation instead of being just the largest company in South Korea.

Reforms

1. Reform in organizational structure

The reform started with Samsung's think tank — the secretariat office. The secretariat office, whose job is planning and coordinating, was set up in 1959, imitating secretariat offices of large corporations and armies of that time. Initially, the secretariat office had a staff of only 20 people who dealt with routine affairs. In 1975, Lee Byung-Chull reshuffled the secretariat office, following the practices of Mitsubishi, Mitsui Chemical, and Sumitomo — the three giant corporations in Japan. At that time, Samsung was undertaking the project to expand commerce in the global market. Therefore, the group needed a specialized organization to take the job of managing an increasing number of subsidiary companies. In addition, this organization should shoulder a heavy responsibility of collecting and analyzing economic information. Obviously, the secretariat office gained power through the reform. In some cases, the head of the secretariat office can execute the power of the chairman: giving business orders to subsidiary organizations. The new secretariat office took on important duties, such as monitoring, advertising, planning, personnel, finance, technology, and management. Lee Byung-Chull relied heavily on the secretariat office for his decision-making. As such, the secretariat office was the place where the most outstanding individuals gathered. This secretariat office, like the brain of Samsung Group, has made great contribution during Lee Byung-Chull's time. Later, with Samsung's exponential growth in size, more and more subsidiary companies were set up. As the subsidiary companies were demanding autonomy in conducting business, disadvantages of the office began to emerge. For example, the secretariat office would do some preparatory work to ensure no one would say unpleasant things to Lee Kun Hee at the president's meeting. Subsidiary companies had limited power. Even a 1,000-won purchase was subjected to the approval from the secretariat office. Over-monitoring conducted by the secretariat office impaired internal efficiency of the group. Finally, conflicts erupted when Samsung Life openly protested against the secretariat office. Lee Kun Hee was aware of the problem and he admitted that the office had too much power. In 1991, Lee Kun Hee put forward the concept of self-discipline in management, restricting the power granted to the secretariat office. In 1999, the office was officially disbanded. Samsung's decision-making process regained efficiency as a result.

2. Reforms in personnel system

Samsung's personnel policy changed as the group was launching its globalization strategy. More employees were sent overseas to work. Usually, outstanding people were assigned to developed countries. In developing countries where the market potential was enormous, insufficient qualified people were sent there. Lee Kun Hee carried out the boldest personnel reform in Samsung's history. Altogether, 217 people got promoted and transferred. 38 and 17 technology and globalization talents were sent to production and overseas departments respectively.

3. Reforms in management

While Lee Byung-Chull adopted a traditional management style featuring power centralization, Lee Kun Hee favored power decentralization.

In the first five years, Lee Kun Hee's reform measures proved to be a success. At the time of Lee Byung-Chull's death, the sale of the group was 17,400 billion won, and the profit was 226.8 billion won. In 1988, one year after Lee Kun Hee's taking over of Samsung, sales were 20,100 billion won, with profit of 341.1 billion won. In the last year of Lee Kun Hee's reform, sales was 38,210 billion won, with a profit of 293.5 billion won.

Second Phase of the Second Pioneering — Samsung's "Change" Management

After five years of preparation and adjustment, Lee Kun Hee's Samsung was ready for a big stride forward to become a world-class trading group. In 1993, Samsung announced a "change" in management, signifying the beginning of the second phase in Lee Kun Hee's "second pioneering". But at that time, Samsung's products was still not recognized as "world-class" in terms of design and quality. Still, most Samsung staff were contented and proud of themselves. In order to achieve his strategy, in as early as 1993, Lee Kun Hee set his aims for the 21st century.

Change in notion: Four conferences

In February 1993, Lee Kun Hee went on a tour of his companies around the globe, addressing the overseas employees. After examining the markets in the US, Europe, and Japan, Lee Kun Hee held four conferences in these countries, with the intent to change the old mindset of the Samsung staff.

At first, Lee Kun Hee summoned a president's conference in Los Angeles. The US market, the largest market in the world, was vital to the Samsung Group. At that time, Samsung's products could not enter the big department stores, and were usually sold in discount stores at a low price. Lee Kun Hee said: "the old Samsung had already died in 1986. It is not a matter of how to improve management. It is a question of 'to be or not to be'. We should be courageous and determined to strive to be the first-class in the world. That is the only way out. Being the top within a country is not something to be proud of. I will be very angry if someone says that we are one of the best and are successful for beating other Korean corporations. The fact that we lag behind the world shows that we have wasted the past 10 years." Lee Kun Hee's speech aimed to arouse the crisis consciousness and sense of urgency within each president of subsidiary companies, to eliminate self-complacency, and frame a timetable for "change". Lee Kun Hee said: "As to the question that whether Samsung can become a world-class trading group, the following two or three years is very critical — it is the last chance for us!"

Then in Japan, Lee Kun Hee held a conference in which 46 subsidiary company presidents attended. The conference centered on how to improve Samsung's competitiveness. Similar to what he did at the Los Angeles conference, Lee Kun Hee led the presidents in visits to the sites of production and sales, such as Akihabala, the tsukiji-market, and Lalaport market. At the same time, they visited first-class electronics companies and machine companies such as Toshiba, NEC, FANUC, and Fujitsu. Lee Kun Hee made it clear at the Tokyo conference that his intention was for the presidents to learn and discuss the secret of Japanese corporations' success in business operations, ranging from product development, production, stocking, work coordination, to effective management, etc.

In the same year, Lee Kun Hee held another Tokyo conference in which more than 100 people attended. The main aim of the conference was to decide the details of "quality control". Lee Kun Hee spent nearly nine hours stressing the importance of quality, and he proposed to develop a new Samsung culture built on quality improvement. It was a fundamental change in Samsung, as Samsung staff had been used to the traditional business principle whose priority was given to quantity, not quality. For this conference, the 100 participants had to leave their managerial positions for more than a month. Despite the cost, Lee Kun Hee was determined to instill a crisis consciousness into managers, to change their mindset.

In a later conference in Frankfurt, Germany, Lee Kun Hee made an eight-hour keynote speech — the so-called "Frankfurt Manifesto". The speech was videoed and played to every employee of the Samsung Group. It was the turning point for the group.

From Los Angeles to Frankfurt, the four conferences lasted 68 days in total. Lee Kun Hee made 350 hours of speech. 1,800 employees attended the meeting and discussions lasted for 800 hours. After the conference marathon, Samsung put forward a guideline for "change" management — everything should be replaced except wife, daughters, and sons. In addition, Samsung decided that in electronics, the group should follow the example of Panasonic and Sony — the two world-class corporations in Japan, famous for their powerful innovation spirit and "early-bird-catches-the-worm" alertness. The textile company of Samsung set Toray Co as an example to follow and exceed. With an acute awareness of globalization, Toray Co turned itself into a world-class corporation in a sun-set industry. In stocks, Westinghouse Electric Company was a model for Samsung. As early as the 1980s, Westinghouse Electric Company spent US$7 million in purchasing an ERP system, standardizing the management in areas of finance, purchase, quality monitor and storage. The whole project was completed in 1994. In customer service, Nordstrom Department Store in Seattle, America served as a typical model. Eversince Nordstrom first entered the retail market business in 1975, it has evolved into a big umbrella of 77-departmental stores and 122-business site conglomerate. An important principle of the Nordstrom Departmental Store was to never say "no" to customers. The employee should provide the best service to customers. From Hewlett-Packard Development Company, Samsung would learn its production management. Hewlett-Packard Development Company applied production data management system, whose function is to trace and manage internal information on product development and improvement. The information included in the system covers a wide range — on components, products, files, computer-aided-files, and decision-making, etc. Even today, the system is still undergoing constant improvements.

Samsung's sales department modeled was after Microsoft, Helen Cosmetics, and the limited companies in the US. These companies wrote down the regulations in a small manual, which facilitated a standardized chain operation. In new products development, Motorola and 3M are the examples cited by Samsung. It is well known that Motorola stands out in the area of wireless communication. The company developed the first cell phone, the terminal of built-in microprocessor, vehicle hands-free phone, personal cell phone, and CDMA technology. Open communication and discussions are everywhere in Motorola, whether it is between superiors and subordinates or among colleagues. Freedom and openness in Motorola encourage various novel ideas. In addition, the company put huge investment into training and research. It was these merits that Samsung was trying to copy. The merit of 3M is its philosophy in management. The company encourages its employees to take challenges and never criticizes them if they make mistakes in their attempts. When it came to sales management, the brand manager system adopted by Procter & Gamble Company was of interest to Samsung. The brand manager is responsible for product-related work such as concept-forming, advertising, product promotion, price-setting, etc. Therefore, the sales personnel are rather powerful with their brand. In addition, Procter & Gamble Company spares no effort in training marketing personnel. Samsung's model in material flow is the American cosmetics company Mary Kay. The models in purchase and coordination are Honda and the Document Company. By learning from the achievements and best practices from world-class corporations, Samsung was more certain in its strategic direction and future development.

Change in organizational structure and strategy

The current framework of Samsung, whose main business areas are electronics, finance, chemicals, and heavy industry, was formed in the group's 1993 reshuffle. Samsung took drastic measures to cut down on non-essential business such as sugar production and textile to reshape the group's image. At the same time, the Group reformed departments with high additional value in accordance with national standards set for basic industries and most advanced industries. The 1993 reform paved the way for Samsung to become a world-class trading group in 10 years' time.

Change in management regulations

After the four conferences in Los Angeles, Tokyo and Frankfurt, Samsung turned its attention to quality control, and carried out a series of reforms.

1. Halting product line

To begin with, Samsung halted the production line of washing machines, color TVs, videos, video cameras, microwave ovens, and conducted a careful investigation. The results showed that if the disqualified products ratio can be reduced, the current profit would multiply. To seek optimal profit, Samsung decided to adopt Japan's production model and came up with a regulation that if the product quality went wrong, production and sales would halt until the problem was solved. Halts in the production line will result in reduced profit. Nevertheless, this regulation, which was totally different from past practices, went with the quality control advocated by Samsung. The managers of Samsung will have to be trained for about six months on the production line. If problems arise, they would have to go to the factory to solve them, instead of sitting in the office and dealing with numbers. Quality control scheme was also carried out in Samsung Heavy Industries Co. The scheme included five areas: a weekly announcement of failure cases; three-phase decision-making; regular education; embracing suggestions; and removing barriers among the different departments. Although Samsung had the tradition of demanding an explanation for mistakes, to publicize them was a big step forward. To make mistakes public is for everyone to draw a lesson. Previously, a policy proposal had to go through nine decision-making departments and 12 signatures were needed. But after the reform, a decision was made through three stages: proposal by individual or department; discussion or examination by directors and presidents; decision-making by a director representative. The 3-phase decision-making process greatly increased efficiency by reducing the time spent otherwise. As a result of these reform measures, disqualified product ratio decreased enormously. Take video, for example: the disqualified ratio decreased from 11% to 7%.

2. Concentration

Aside from quality control, Lee Kun Hee put forth the concept of concentration in pursuit of greater profit. Generally speaking, seven or eight departments will be involved in developing a new

product. For the sake of efficiency, these departments would
not be too far away from each other, and therefore, concentration is necessary. Samsung invested a large amount of money in
the construction of infrastructures, putting apartments, offices,
meeting rooms, hospitals, supermarket, schools, and kinder-
gartens into one area. Improved efficiency was achieved. The
"concentration" concept not only applied to construction, but
also to factories, sales, and business, etc. If an overseas factory
is to be built, the group needs to consider the following factors:
distance to the harbor, internal or international airport, convenience of highway, labor force, electricity and water price, etc.
Lee Kun Hee required that all the employees in Samsung
should develop coordination awareness. Every morning, a
10-minute video was played to promote these ideas. Improved
cooperation between internal and overseas departments or
among different divisions, led to increased efficiency.

3. Working hours system

Lee Kun Hee maintains that in order to become a world-class
trading group, self-improvement of the employees is of great
importance. In order to allow ample time for employees to
acquire knowledge, Lee Kun Hee adjusted the work schedule
from 9 a.m.–6 p.m. to 7 a.m.–4 p.m. In that way, employees had
a sufficient time after work to study and improve themselves. In
addition, the Group provided various training courses for its
employees, and even offered 50% tuition subsidy for foreign language education. These measures succeeded in creating a learning atmosphere within the group.

Personnel reform

In 1993, the Samsung Group carried out another large-scale personnel reform whereby 260 managing staff got promoted, and

34 were transferred. Technological talents and those with rich experience in overseas business stood a better chance of a promotion. For those whose only speciality was management, their prospect for a promotion was not so bright, which was different from the management practice of the Lee Byung-Chull's era. For the first time, the secretariat office suffered a reduction in size — its workforce shrunk from 200 to 100; two divisions were removed; the number of business teams reduced from 11 to 8 with the head of each team demoted.

At the same time, Lee Kun Hee attached great importance to outstanding talents. He once said: "A genius can support 100,000 to 200,000 people." In order to become a world-class trading group in the 21st century, Samsung had to develop world-class technology within two or three years. It could not be achieved without excellent technological talents. Lee Kun Hee set the rule that the ability to cultivate outstanding talents was an important criterion in evaluating the performance of managing staff. Failure in this respect could lead to serious consequences such as removal from office. This criterion took up 40% of the performance evaluation. Lee Kun Hee also believed that they should search the whole world for the most suitable people — the younger, the better. They could go to high schools in America, Japan, and China to look for promising youth, and give them scholarships if they promised to work for Samsung in the future. On the other hand, cultivating current core-employees was also an important reform measure. Samsung Electronics expanded the talent search team into a larger organization called the talents development institution. At present, among the 180,000 employees in Samsung Group, 12,000 hold a doctorate degree. Samsung Electronics has 1,200 PhD researchers, 300 MBA, 5,500 masters and doctorates. 25% of the management in Samsung Group have a master or doctorate degree. Even so, the group is not contented with the current situation, and targets outstanding students from both inside and outside of the country.

It is expected that the talent accumulation at Samsung could reach 11,000. Every year, the Group has 1,000 excellent talents entering the company.

Samsung picks capable people for important posts. Personal relations or blood relations are never a consideration for a promotion. Once, a cousin of Lee Kun Hee was turned down by the Samsung Group for his unsatisfactory performance in the recruitment examinations. Another cousin of Lee Kun Hee, who worked in a technology company of Samsung, retired as a technician. Yet, an ordinary but outstanding employee of Samsung, who came from the countryside, was successively promoted to positions of textile factory director, general affairs director, department store manager, and president.

Samsung adopts various measures to motivate its employees. As for core technicians and managing staff, Samsung offers high salary and stock options as well. The group puts emphasis on inspiring the employees. An important job is to arouse their sense of responsibility. Trust is another important factor in employee motivation. Samsung does not have the card-punching system or the last elimination system. Those who make errors at work will be given a second chance. Samsung set up a specialized organization whose function is to ensure livelihood for those who has left Samsung, and to help them find new employment. Such practice is unprecedented in South Korea. Samsung also makes efforts to arouse consciousness within employees. Lee Kun Hee put forth his "catfish theory". If a catfish is put into a loach pond, the loach will grow better. The same rule can also be applied to Samsung.

In personnel management, a drastic reform measure of Samsung was to enhance employee training. In terms of both quality and quantity, Samsung stands out in the world. Take Samsung Electronics, for example. The company's expenditure in personnel training reached US$82 million or $1,800 per person (3.35% of the salary). After years of evolvement, Samsung has developed a unique, systematic training system. The group offer opportunities for a paid education program at any employee's request. It was this policy that attracts people to Samsung. The new personnel training include the a 4-week education of corporation culture. The aim is to inculcate the right views on life, corporation, career, and to instill the spirit of cooperation. Overseas employees must be sent back to the Samsung headquarter for career training and education. The training course has a condensed schedule, starting from 5:50 a.m. to 9:00 p.m. every day, including weekends. The first week of training is about basic etiquette, work attire, and regulations of Samsung. Group training is also a required course, which enforces the spirit of cooperation. The second week of training is about Samsung's business concept, the group's influence on Korean economy, and the source of Samsung's competitiveness. The third week's training agenda is discussion on topics such as "service" and "challenge". The fourth week is a summary. After a four-week training, the Samsung culture and spirit were cultivated in each new hire. For the incumbent employees, the group provides plentiful educational opportunities. It is clearly prescribed that everyone in Samsung should receive a minimum of two weeks of training. Before developing a new product, the Group will also launch a training program. There are three education departments in Samsung: management capacity department, professional knowledge department, and corporate culture department. These three departments provide specific education to employees. At the same time, Samsung invites famous experts to lecture to its employees, and also sends employees to famous overseas universities and institutions for training on international law, patent, or finance. Samsung's training is diversified. The group provides different training content and adopts different training methods to different groups — new employees, core employees, and management. Samsung reserves special training courses for core-employees, such as courses for deans, presidents and managers. A "practical" training course is developed specially for sales staff. In addition, exchange-of-position method is often adopted. Samsung takes bold reforms in training methods. They put special emphasis on two-way education whose sole idea is to encourage independent thinking ability. The group requires that the employee should learn two foreign languages. An extra salary (10%–15%) will be given as an incentive for mastery of one foreign language. For the high-ranking management, Samsung set up a school intended for presidents. All the high-ranking employees are subject to six months' training in this school, and three months' training course overseas. It was these diversified and specific training courses that qualify and prepare Samsung's employees for globalization.

Change in corporation culture

1. Stress on change

Lee Kun Hee strongly believed that great changes would take place at the end of the 20th century, and the coming 21st century would be an era of creative technology and competition. Changes in the 20th century would be more than the changes in the past 5,000 years. As seen in the past 50 years, more changes had taken place than in the previous 100 years. In short, the world is changing fast. Lee Kun Hee required Samsung to change to combat external shocks, whether the changes are in management, business notion, or in corporate culture and product services. That "everything should be replaced except wife, daughters and sons" best represents Lee Kun Hee's notion of "change".

2. "Family" culture

Samsung tries to avoid faults in the family enterprise; such as over-trust in family members, mistrust in non-family members.

Instead, the group carries forward the advantages of family enterprises to their utmost, that is, to instill a "family" culture in the group. Samsung's concern for its employees is evident in every detail. Take Samsung SDI, in Shenzhen, China, for example. The company sets up a post office and a cash dispenser within the factory. This is a huge convenience for workers as they do not have to wait in long lines to remit money home. The company usually gives out salary in advance before a holiday or weekend. The workers dormitory building used to be 20-minutes' walk away from the factory. For safety consideration, the company built a new dormitory building for women workers, and transformed the storehouse into a dorm building for men workers. The construction cost 14 million yuan. To enrich the cultural life for workers, the company installed a television set on every floor of the dormitory building. Tuesdays and Fridays are movie days. Various sports or entertainment organizations are formed, such as football team, basketball team, and glee club. The company even opened an Internet café in the factory. Every year, the management of the company will mail a letter to each worker's family, to express gratitude for their work in the company. All these measures help to raise working enthusiasm. The workers can feel the warmth in the company and as a result, they can plunge wholeheartedly into their work.

3. Stress on etiquette and morality

Lee Kun Hee learned the importance of etiquette from golf. Samsung's culture was developed on the basis of morality and etiquette. Among South Korean corporations, Samsung's employees are noted for their politeness, which is reflected in their daily behaviors such as phone manners, receiving guests and visitors etc. *Constitution of Samsung* — a manual circulating around in Samsung — is mainly about behavioral regulations.

The content of this manual is based on Lee Kun Hee's explanation of corporate reform. To become a world-class enterprise, all the employees in Samsung should be people with morality and etiquette. Otherwise, Samsung can never achieve this objective. In Samsung, people are valued more than money. According to Lee Kun Hee, to stop and help a fallen child can be viewed as the beauty in human nature. As to morality, huge waste in Samsung reflects a lack of morality. Without morality, an enterprise is not capable of good products, and it cannot last long.

4. Encouraging innovation

Aiming to be a first-class trading group in the world, Samsung began its efforts to create an open and innovative atmosphere in the group. Its employees are inspired to break the old work and thinking modes and to put forward their plans, ideas and suggestions. They are also encouraged to form various interest groups, to set up related reward measures and to compete with their colleagues. The group made it clear that failures made in their process of work exploration are acceptable. At the same time, Samsung ensured the efficiency in information system so that information can be gained and shared easily. At the time when there were no e-mails, the faxes of the presidents and the chairmen were accessible 24 hours a day. With these measures, creativity and devotion of the employees are greatly stimulated.

Lee Kun Hee's failure

Although he was chosen as the most respected entrepreneur by the media, Lee Kun Hee did make mistakes when he was the chairman of Samsung. At the end of the 1990s, influenced by the concept of "big enterprise, big production", he made a wrong decision. He invested billions of dollars in the auto industry when there was an obvious surplus in domestic motor manufacturing. Finally, Samsung Motors was forced to be sold to Renault SA at a very low price. Because of that, Lee Kun Hee was once regarded as a failure. To the Korean media, to establish Samsung Motors was not only a blind decision but also a failure of the bureaucratic management system. Some media even thought Lee Kun Hee had succeeded in nothing since 1987 when he took over the helm at Samsung. But Lee Kun Hee faced up to the failure and shouldered the responsibility. He donated 2 billion won from his personal savings and was praised as a responsible CEO who held himself accountable for mistakes in the investment policy.

New Challenges for Samsung

Lee Kun Hee's first objective for Samsung — a first-class corporation in the world — has been achieved. Lee Kun Hee is holding a bigger dream for the future — a super-class enterprise with emphasis on electronics, finance, and services. The current problems with Samsung are: immature nano-composite and biotechnology, incomplete reforms in the financial industry, and an absence of a development focus for the next 5 to 10 years. Samsung is facing great challenges in the constantly changing global market. In its 70 years of history, Samsung went through the hands of two generations of the Lee family. When it comes to the future development of Samsung, it remains to be revealed by time.

Case 8: Lee Kum Kee: A Family Enterprise Whose Wealth Lasts over Five Generations

Introduction

In 2005, Nanfang Lee Kum Kee Health Products Co Ltd, affiliated to Lee Kum Kee, received two awards for human resources achievements, including the awards of "Best Employer in Asia" and "Best Employer in China" by Hewitt Associates LLC. In addition, the Health Food Group was chosen by Fortune China as one of the "Great Workplaces".

Lee Kum Kee is a famous brand in Asia. Its oyster sauce products cover a market share of 88% in America and held the second position in Japan. Its products of more than 200 varieties can be found in more than 80 countries and regions throughout the world. At the end of 2004, it had more than 30 branch companies and nearly 2,000 authorized stores. The company boasts not only of its production of 200 kinds of sauces, but also its product line of health food. The sales volume of health food from 2002 to 2005 increased by 100%.

Unbelievably, the thriving family enterprise went through nearly 120 years of history and the Lee family's control of the company has been passed on to its fifth generation. The curse that "wealth does not last for three generations" seems inefficacious in this case.

Nevertheless, Lee Kum Kee is still confronted with the succession problem. In July 2006, Lee Huimin, the president of Lee Kum Kee and also one of the successors of the fourth generation, told the press with worry, "We have to consider the problem of 'wealth does not last for three generations', and it seems that the members of the fifth generation have little interest in managing the family enterprise." Lee Kum Kee had to make a significant decision, i.e., to find a non-family member to shoulder the responsibility of being the president of the company before the end of 2006.

History and Development of the Enterprise

In 1888, Lee Kam Sheung established Lee Kum Kee, a company focusing on the production of oyster sauce in Nanshui Town, Zhuhai, Guangdong province. During the day, Lee would purchase oysters from villagers and decocted oyster sauce in the night. His oyster sauce was decocted in optimal fire and produced in modest concentration. Moreover, his sincere and enthusiastic service also attracted clients from not only nearby, but also from Jiangmen, Shiqi, Guangzhou and even Macau. In 1902, the oyster sauce factory of Lee Kum Kee was destroyed in a fire. It then moved to Macau to be re-established. Lee Kam Sheung, the founding father of Lee Kum Kee, died in Macau in 1922. Thereafter, his three sons inherited the cause of the father and further developed Lee Kum Kee by constantly exploring food variety and improving manufacturing craftsmanship. In 1932, Lee Shiu Tang, the eldest son of Lee Kam Sheung, expanded the base of oyster sauce production from Macau to Hong Kong. Since the 1950s, Lee Kum Kee grew to become a powerful enterprise, with its oyster sauce business flourishing and markets expanding in Hong Kong, Macau and Southeast Asian nations. In 1972, Lee Man Tat, the third generation of the Lee family, took control of the enterprise. With a pioneering spirit, Lee Man Tat further expanded the business by strengthening management and improving craftsmanship. Besides the production of traditional oyster sauce products, the Lee Kum Kee Group also manufactures a series of ten products, including sesame oil, sauce and beverage. Its products sell well in more than 80 countries and regions, including Southeast Asian nations, Japan, Britain, Germany, France, Canada, the US and Australia, literally realizing that "where there are Chinese, there are the products of Lee Kum Kee". In 1992, the Lee Kum Kee Group entered the mainland China market. During the first 10 years in China, the group's business grew by leaps and bounds. In 2004, its soy

products were awarded the famous brand in China, and its product line of dark soy sauce and light soy sauce were chosen as
national quality-inspection-free products. In Hong Kong, Lee
Kum Kee was awarded "Top Ten Enterprises in Hong Kong in
the Millennium" and "The Most Unfailing Enterprise for Brand
and Reputation".

Culture: Win-Win Relationships and Others' Interests Come First

Lee Kum Kee attributes its prosperity to the loyalty for the core
values: practicality, reputation and constant exploration. The
core values are expressed as "shared dreams, shared policies and
shared efforts" in the company. Lee Kum Kee has been emphasizing that the development of the enterprise should do good to
both the enterprise and employees. The mutual beneficial relationship, embodied as "others' interests come first when we are
making profits", has long been a target of Lee Kum Kee. The
essence of the enterprise culture was distilled by Mr. Lee Man Tat
from a traditional Chinese verse "Practicing ethics not for making oneself known, and working hard only for the interests of
others". As the essence of the corporate values, the principle
should be implemented in every field of business of the company. Lee Kum Kee made it a task to develop sauce products, a
task to spread the traditional food of the Chinese culture to the
rest of the world. As such, the task of developing health food is
to spread the health food, made from Chinese traditional herbs,
to the rest of the world. Each year, Lee Kum Kee would evaluate its employees to measure the conditions they are in. Two
measuring indices are: feeling and pressure level. According to
Lee Kum Kee, only the good condition of the employees can
guarantee the good condition of the enterprise. Therefore, it is
of great significance to shape an equal and harmonious cultural
atmosphere within the enterprise. For example, when a member

of the Lee family enters the enterprise, he should be treated like any other employee and start from the bottom. He may be rewarded for good deeds and punished for bad ones. There is a dragon boat team in the group, whose captain is an ordinary employee. Although members from the higher echelon of the Lee family also join the team, they are treated as ordinary team players and have to obey the captain of the team. So the employees will not regard themselves as outsiders. The essence of the enterprise culture of Lee Kum Kee is making the interests of all the employees, instead of the interest of the family, its basic foundation. Within the enterprise, a concept of equality, fairness and righteousness is advocated. All the family members are educated to sincerely communicate with the ordinary employees, to share with them the happiness and woes. This allows the employees to regard themselves as "owners" of the enterprise. Staff will consciously recognize the values and long-term goals of the enterprise, and pledge their utmost loyalty to the company.

The principle of "others' interests come first" is also embodied in its corporate social responsibilities. Nanfang Lee Kum Kee made donations to the construction of the Infinitus Hope Project primary schools and social welfare institutes. In addition, it made donations to improve the educational facilities, set up scholarships and help needy students to receive medical services. It invested more than 10 million yuan in the hometown of the Lees to set up middle schools, donated HK$10 million for the library of the School of Medicine, Tsinghua University. Its donations during these years added up to more than 50 million yuan. In return, these acts undertaken for the public good won public praise for Lee Kum Kee.

The Lee family and the enterprise emphasize pioneering and innovative spirit. It was with this spirit that Lee Kum Kee realized its breakthroughs. For example, at the beginning of the 1990s, the expansion of soy sauce products around the globe was quite successful, literally realizing the target of "where there are Chinese, there are products of Lee Kum Kee". For all the good reasons, it was a good choice to continue to focus on the sauce products. However, Lee Kum Kee Group did not stop there. Instead, they continued to expand their sauce products and sought other market opportunities. At that time, the international trading volume for herbs reached $10 billion, with products from China constituting less than 5% of the total. Apparently, this was disproportionate to China's status as a great country with centuries-old excellent tradition and culture in herbal medicine. With this view in mind, Lee Kum Kee decided to enter the field of health food even though the domestic market for health food was not very promising at that time. To this day, Nanfang Lee Kum Kee has made great achievements in this field. With more than 10 branches and 800 authorized stores throughout the nation, the company became a large-scale enterprise in the production of health food. Herbal health food with the brand "Infinitus" was developed into three product lines with over 20 varieties. With the opening of Hong Kong Disneyland in 2005, Lee Kum Kee began to redefine its sauce product types and clientele base. As an "Official Sponsor for Asian Sauce", the company cooperated with the chefs at Disneyland Hong Kong to develop sauces and spices in independent packaging.

The Family

For most family enterprises, it is a great challenge to deal with conflicts and disputes within the family without exerting negative impact on the routine operation of the enterprise. Invariably, there were conflicts and disputes in the history of Lee Kum Kee. When Lee Kam Sheung, the founding father of Lee Kum Kee, divided the enterprise into three even parts, significant differences in opinions arose among his three sons concerning the future strategic direction of Lee Kum Kee. Lee Shiu Tang believed that they should expand the enterprise with all kinds of projects and he personally set some ambitious targets for the company. The other family members, however, were more conservative, thinking that it would be a huge risk to make any amendment to current formula. Lee Shiu Tang and his eldest son, Lee Man Tat, firmly believed that their assessment of the future development of the company was good and correct. As a result of the significant differences in opinions among the family members, Lee Shiu Tang had no choice but to purchase the stock held by the other members. Since Lee Kum Kee was a private enterprise then and the channels for financing were limited, Lee Shiu Tang shouldered the heavy financial burden. Because of the buy-over he was ostracized from the other angry brothers for the rest of his life.

It came down to the generation of Lee Man Tat, who had seven younger siblings: one brother and six sisters. The sisters did not participate in the management of the family enterprise, and the only youngest brother entered the financial service industry. Thus, Lee Man Tat inherited all the shares of the company from his father. However, soon after the father retired, Lee Man Tat transferred a large portion of the stocks to his brother and invited him to run the company. Growing up in the family enterprise, Lee Man Tat had his own great vision for the future development of the company, whereas the brother was content with the status quo. Thus, significant differences occurred over the developmental direction of the company. The young brother filed a suit against Lee Man Tat in an attempt to take control of the company, which ended with the elder brother regaining all the stocks of Lee Kum Kee. By then, Lee Man Tat had already paid huge costs economically and emotionally.

Family Committee

Drawing lessons from the experience, Lee Man Tat firmly believed that the key issue lay in the harmony of family members.

Any discord would pose challenge to the family's survival and exert negative influence on the development of the enterprise. Only when the family relations are properly dealt with can the enterprise be better managed and operated. Therefore, Lee Man Tat set up a family committee and established a family constitution, trying to manage the family coherence. In 2003, the family committee was established to coordinate the family, enterprise and investors. The committee consists of almost all the 26 family members. Many family members without holding any company stock were also in the committee. The seven members holding the stock of the company were core members. The family committee comprised the family office and the family foundation. It was responsible for making major decisions, leading the Lee Kum Kee Group. The committee organized all kinds of activities to maintain family unity. The committee convened 4–5 day meetings every quarter and the meetings were hosted in rotation by the core members. Topics in the meetings were determined by the hosts. Problems with business operations were generally excluded from the meetings. In the first day of the meetings, wives were included to discuss the situations in the family. They strolled about together and enjoyed the happiness of the family union. On the second day, the participants would discuss five key problems: office of the Lee family, family foundation, family investment, family constitution and training center of the family. Before the meetings, the hosts would ask the participants to read a predetermined book related to the topics of the meetings, so that they could be prepared; and through this communication, they could reach a shared understanding. The Lee family tried to make the meetings interesting so as to engage the family members. When one meeting had ended, they could hardly wait for the next meeting. These family meetings became a favorite platform for communications among the members. These meetings were an opportune time for family members to settle any conflict and dispute that exist within the family, reach a consensus that would strengthen the ties, deepen the understanding and sentiment of the family members, especially the younger generation, all for the sake of the enterprise. These family values were passed from one generation to the next, forming a shared core value within the family. The outcomes of family meetings were recorded in the family constitution and serve as key issues aiming at maintaining the long-term interests of the family. The operational rules of the family committee were determined by the family constitution.

Although members of the family committee were also members of the board, their functions were separated. Decisions on major issues about the development of the enterprise, including organizational and strategic planning, employment, stock transfer, and dividend distribution, were made in board meetings. The affairs of the family, however, would be discussed at the family meetings instead of at the board meetings. Thus, the enterprise affairs and the family affairs were effectively separated. Moreover, the same person was divided in his different roles as a family member, a shareholder, a director and a manager, thus avoiding abuses.

The Lee family wrote issues of family management into the family constitution. Thus, with the reference to the constitituion, the family members were ruled and family conflicts were properly dealt with. In addition, the constitution reduced the negative impact of family conflicts on the enterprise operations.

In order to solve the family conflicts, Lee Man Tat, at an early stage, stipulated in the family constitution that children of the family may work in the family enterprise upon completion of their college education. They must also obey the following two provisions: firstly, everyone can only have one family and one wife. If he has another family after marriage, he will have to quit from the board; secondly, anyone who divorces will have to quit from the board and will never be allowed to join the company. Nevertheless, he may keep his stock, but cannot participate in any decision-making. The mandate was settled and widely recognized by the offspring. Lee Man Tat had been asking his children never to forget their ancestors. As a tradition, each year, the family would hold a "Memorial Ceremony for the Ancestors" before the Qingming festival in Hong Kong to commemorate the first- and second-generation founding fathers of the Lee family enterprise. The participants, who were mainly from the company's many dealerships, outstanding employees from around the globe and all the family members, get together to pay their respect and offer thanksgiving to the pioneers. They cherished the values and traditions of the century-old cause, and highlight the contributions made by the pioneers to the society as a whole.

As far as power transfer to the fifth generation is concerned, the Lee family stipulated that firstly, all members of the fifth generation must graduate from college and have worked in other companies for at least three years before they can join the family enterprise. Secondly, family members of the fifth generation can be admitted into the company only when they pass an examination, just like others, and they must start from the bottom. Thirdly, any member who is found to be incompetent for the job may be given another chance in a different position. However, if his performance is not improved, he will be fired as well. These stipulations are settled with the consent and signing of all the family members and written into the pages of the family constitution.

Challenges

The family members of the third and fourth generation enjoy a harmonious relationship. When the father Lee Man Tat called for his sons to join and help the enterprise, Lee Huimin, Lee Huixiong, Lee Huizhong and Lee Huisen readily responded without hesitation. Having graduated from famous universities in the US, all his four sons were well educated. They took on various positions in the enterprise and cooperated with each other harmoniously. Lee Huimin took the office of chairman of the Sauce Group; Lee Huixiong took the post of chairman of the American, Latin American and European branches; Lee Huizhong was chairman of the booming China business; and Lee Huisen was the executor of diversification of the group and chairman of the health food group (see Figure 4.1).

The harmonious relationship among the brothers came from their shared experiences in childhood. However, their children did not share the same experience. Moreover, many are not interested in working in the family business. Succession is an issue in the fifth generation.

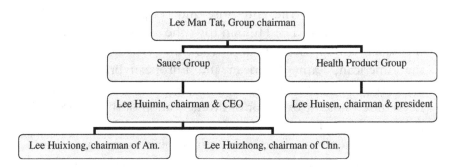

Figure 4.1:   Organizational Structure of Lee Kum Kee Co Ltd

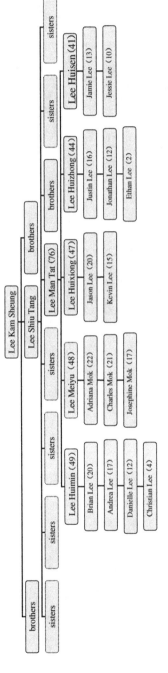

Figure 4.2: Family and Ownership Tree of the Lee Family (Partial)

Source: Documents of the company.

Section III

DEVELOPMENT OF FAMILY
ENTERPRISES IN CHINA

5

Merchants from Huizhou and Shanxi during the Ming and Qing Dynasties

Not only could history tell us about legends of the past, it could also predict our prospects for the future. Family enterprises around the world, accompanied by the ups and downs of the world economy, have presented a variety of winding stories. There were fortune's favorites going with the historical trend; there were tragic heroes suffering defeat on the verge of victory; and there were also enterprise giants lasting as long as a century. No matter what the destiny and outcome were, there is always one persisting truth — the stories are seemingly deeper than what is presented on the surface.

When Chinese feudalism was developed in the Ming and Qing dynasties, the Chinese private economy and private enterprises had undergone rapid progress, accompanied by the emergence of some wealthy and influential merchant groups, such as the Hui merchants and Jin merchants. All these merchant groups exhibited a strong flavor of clan and family. And they could be regarded as the embryo of the neoteric Chinese family enterprises.

Merchants from Huizhou, Anhui Province

Hui merchants were a powerful force in the commercial community of the Qing dynasty. Its influence lasted for hundreds of years in the Chinese neoteric commercial arena. The Hui merchants group possesses distinctive features of the family and clan, and it is an enterprise group of the extensive family type. Therefore, how could they keep developing and flourishing in the Chinese economic arena for hundreds of years?

213

Geographically, Huizhou, the place of origin of Hui merchants, was an old town including Jixi, Xixian, Xiuning, Yixian, Qimen and Wuyuan, which is presently under the administration of the Jiangxi province. According to geological studies, the aboriginal land to the south of Changjiang River heaved upwards to form a mountain range with an altitude higher than 1,000 meters. This mountain range, known as Huangshan (Yellow Mountain), is located to the north of Huizhou. To the south of Huizhou, there lie the cone-shaped hills of Baiyue and Qiyun. This unique geographic location gave Huizhou the features of "being separated by mountains, and its inhabitants sheltered from the influence of customs from other places". This unique geographical position has made Huizhou a relatively closed society, with its unique local folklore, special customs and public sentiments. Most of the inhabitants in these villages, surrounded by the mountain ranges, belong to the same clan. In Huizhou, connate fellows living together is a universal custom. According to the custom, the first chapter in *Huizhou Fuzhi* was compiled during Kangxi's reign, "the local inhabitants are respectively living together with their connate fellows without intrusion by people from other family names". Therefore, Huizhou is a region prevailed by familism, and as a result it is deeply colored by the family culture. Family custom and culture have played an important role in the commercial activities of the Hui merchants, and have been regarded as one of the originations of the family enterprises. The Huizhou region has its own special geographical landscape — "70% of this region is mountainous area, 10% is water, 10% is farmland and the remaining 10% are roads and gardens". Under this circumstance, Huizhou's limited fields are heavily populated, which contributed to the crisis mindset of the people in Huizhou. Therefore, in order to survive, local inhabitants ventured out of their hometown to make a living. According to the local proverb, "if one was not ever a kindhearted person in his pre-existence, then he would be born in Huizhou, and by the age of 13 or 14, he would be abandoned in the outside world". As a result, merchandising became an important means to make a living. Inhabitants of Huizhou have acquired outstanding business skills and acumen. Moreover, the inhabitants of Huizhou attach great importance to blood and family relationships, and possess a strong conception of clan. The locals "paid attention to establishing long-time connate relations; families in the same village had constructed the same ancestral temple; and when the New Year approached, they would make sacrifices to their ancestors together". In so doing, a great commercial power, known as Chinese Hui merchants, had been breeding in this region; and they exerted great influence on Chinese commerce for close to 400 years.

The Hui merchants' influence over human and financial resources, derived from the regional monopoly and association of the same clan, was prominent in the pawn-broking industry. Their competitive strategy was in uniting their connate and hometown residents to work in the same industry. Relying on the abundant funds and their coordination, they could reduce the pawn profits and thereby supplant those non-local merchants who were out to make much higher profits. Hui merchants led their connate fellows to expand their monopoly of pawn-broking in Shanghai and other places. In the 1880s, there were 69 major pawn brokers in Shanghai, half of whom were Hui merchants. And this could be regarded as one of the models that Hui merchants monopolized the markets, by virtue of their connate influence. Moreover, the superior position in the field of pawn-broking also greatly promoted their development in other commercial fields. Let the industries of salt and tea, the most profitable businesses at that time, be an example. The sales and operation cost of one batch of salt required at least 20 million taels of silver. Most of this money came from loans. Additionally, substantial funds were needed to ensure the operation of tea business, because in order to make timely purchases of large quantities of cheap but high-quality tea, the tea merchants had to pay enough money before the tea-picking season. After the tea-picking, they also had to make the remaining payment. With the addition of the costs of processing and packaging, long-distance transportation, and road taxes paid, the tea merchants had to invest a large amount of capital. The Huizhou salt and tea merchants usually borrowed money from their hometown or connate fellows who, taking into consideration the close relationships, asked for much lower interest rates than the average market loans.

Consequently, when it came to costing, the Hui merchants could utilize their advantage to occupy a better position in the competitive market against the others.

In the Ming and Qing dynasties, Hui merchants adopted different forms of capital combination, and shaped a huge network that literally included everybody in the town. This personal relationship network greatly helped the commercial activities of Hui merchants. As a result, Hui merchants relied much on their connate fellows, and this enabled them to effectively combine and consolidate capital in their commercial activities. By the consolidation of capital, they could strengthen the geographical and blood ties among them to enhance cohesion within the Hui merchant group.

More interestingly, Hui merchants adopted many concrete methods to solidify their connate culture. For example, they established merchant guild halls all over the nation to reinforce the unity of Hui merchant groups. This kind of merchant guild halls, based on geographical and blood relations, had provided much convenience for merchants of the same clan or family. Some large-scale merchant guild halls had their own shops, storehouses, piers, and free schools, which were used to help Hui merchants to convey goods or provide education for their children. At the same time, merchant guild halls were used to help merchants prop up their power in the local society. When Hui merchants were bullied by local forces from non-local merchants, merchant guild halls would assemble all of the Hui merchants to provide assistance. In addition, the merchant guild halls provided public welfare to unite the Hui merchants and saw them through thick and thin. Furthermore, merchant guild halls could represent the merchants in negotiating with the local government. Besides, the system of monthly subsidy had played an important role for the long-time prosperity of Hui merchants. It assured the provision of monthly subsidies to those merchants and their children who were in need of financial assistance. In the early era of the Qing dynasty, the phenomenon of helping and succoring those in poor, originally existing only within family, had become extensively systemized. At that time, appropriate funds provided by the salt administration of the Hui River supported the relief house, the elders' house, lifesaving house and

Yizheng Study in Yangzhou. By so doing, the self-identity of the Hui merchants had been greatly enhanced, and the inner cohesion had also been reinforced.

Moreover, Hui merchants placed great emphasis on their reputation within the family and the respect from their connate fellows. Many merchants donated money to buy public property for their clans. They paid large sums of money to buy fields for their clans, donate religious sacrificial properties, construct ancestral temples and build public burial grounds. Till this day, we could still find some of these buildings intact. These grand and luxurious buildings played an important role in strengthening the connate cohesion.

Merchants from Shanxi Province

Merchants from Shanxi are well-known throughout the country for their business in money transfers and currency exchanges. As the cradle of the banking industry in China, this business catapulted the Chinese banking industry to an unprecedented height. As it is commonly known to all, the magnates of Shanxi in the Ming and Qing dynasties were all from family enterprises. The Fu banking firm of the Qiao family in Qi county, the Wei banking firm of the Hou family in Jiexiu county and the Rishengchang banking firm of the Lee family in Pingyao were all started by a family and passed on from one generation to another over several hundred years.

Located to the west of Taihang Mountains, Shanxi is a place known to the rest of the country for its dangerous terrain and untainted folk traditions. The special geographic position of the province provides a uniquely favorable advantage for Jin merchants. Shanxi is closely adjacent to the Great Wall in the north, which is a natural division between the farming community and the grazing nomadic tribes. Seizing the complementarity of the two civilizations, the Jin merchants made good profits in the business of communications and exchanges of goods between the two communities. With the accumulated capital in their long-term business ventures, the Jin merchants started to establish branches throughout the country. Since the Qing dynasty had not set up its own national banks yet, the banking firms rapidly covered the entire country with its business network infrastructure.

The famous Fu banking firm owned by the Qiao family was set up by his ancestor Qiao Guifa when he was trading in beancurd north of the Great Wall. Three generations later, the business was passed on to the sons of Qiao Quanmei, and Qiao Zhiyong, with his remarkable business acumen, took over the firm. The firm named "Zaizhongtang" was well run and prosperous. Apart from others, Qiao Zhiyong handed the firm to his grandson Qiao Yingxia when the former could hardly find a competent candidate among his six sons. Qiao Yingxia was so talented and competent that he achieved unprecedented success for the company. It was estimated that the capital of the Fu banking firm at that time was worth four to five million taels of silver. Adding the land and the house, its actual assets could amount to several million taels. The Fu banking firm was initially established in Baotou city, and there was a popular saying circulating in the city that "we have Duke of Fu before we have the city".

The firm owned by the Fan family in Jiexiu County was a typical family enterprise. Carrying on with the trade in Zhangjiakou, the ancestor Fan Yongdou was ranked among the eight royal merchants towards the end of the Ming dynasty. It was passed on to Fan Sanbo, the son of Fan Yongdou, and then to the generation with the name of Yu, and finally to the generation with the name of Qing. As rewards for their contribution to transporting food for military use, the firm was protected by the imperial government and hence gained rapid growth and development. Through the painstaking efforts of the Fan family merchants over several generations, its position as a royal firm was established. The firm had transported food supplies of more than 1 million dans for the army of the Qing dynasty and saved more than 6 million taels for the government, thus gaining its distinction. At the same time, the family made huge profits from dealing with salt and the transportation of foodstuff for military use and copper products. The assets of the family totaled several million taels. Other merchants could hardly rival its eminent political position. According to statistics, in the single generation with the names of Yu and Qing, we could find more than 20 members who were granted with official positions and titles. Fan Yubing was bestowed with "the Title of Taipu Temple Dean Togged Akin the Second Rank Officials". The Fan's were so rich and powerful a family, with backing of the imperial government, that nobody dared to challenge them.

Strict Managerial System

The main reason that the Jin merchants could develop their business from workshop family enterprises to large-sized firms lay in the fact that they overcame the common fault of nepotism in such kind of enterprises and adopted a strict business managerial system, including "shareholder-employee-partnership", managers' responsibility system, apprentice system, joint operation system and accounting system. The systems and regulations were quite specific and detailed, and were instilled in each member of the firms as habits. Nothing can be accomplished without norms or standards. The strict managerial systems not only helped the merchants from Shanxi to achieve great successes, but also marked a step towards modern commercial development.

Shareholder-Employee-Partnership System

By adopting the original "shareholder-employee-partnership" system, the Jin merchants avoided the abuses in family-oriented management caused by the identity of the right of ownership and the right of operation. Through effectively separating the two rights, independence and specialization of management were guaranteed and the enterprises were run in accordance with the market discipline. The "shareholder-employee-partnership" system was a kind of improved stock-holding system. It was improved and perfected from the individual ownership system, which featured individual investment and management; the loan capital system, which featured borrowing of money from others to run business, and the friend-partnership system, which featured the capital from one person and the collective management by friends. In the "shareholder-employee-partnership" system, the boss was supposed to provide capital and the employees were supposed to work for them. It clearly defined the separation of the right of ownership and management. Those who invested should be the owners of the firms, and those who worked for them should be the managers of the firms and responsible for the management of the firms. Both the owners and the managers held shares of the firms. The investments of the bosses were called the primary shares, which were subject to dividend distribution and unlimited liability. The secondary investments deposited in the firms by the bosses were subjected to interests instead of dividends. There might be several or more investors in the system, but there was only one general manager. Therefore, the core of the system was the full authorization of power to the general manager. Once a general manager was employed, the investors must never intervene with the affairs within the firm. General managers had the rights of fund distribution and personnel management. The investors must never preset rules and regulations for them, nor randomly employ people by his own favoritism. It was impossible for the investors to take out or borrow even one tael of silver. It was clearly prescribed by some firms that the investors must not carry out public activities in the name of the firms and should even pay for his own accommodations in the firms. The investors should only take charge of the auditing of the annual reports. Such strict and standardized managerial systems in China's commercial enterprises several hundred years ago surely deserve some praise and admiration. Owners of family enterprises in modern China should ponder over this.

System of General Manager Responsibility

As for daily management, the Jin merchants adopted the system of general manager responsibility. Full authorization guaranteed the independence of management and operation. The restrictions imposed on the investors protected independence of management from being hampered. In doing so, the management of general managers who focused on market demand could be guaranteed and the abuses of overlapping management could be prevented from the source.

The investors were responsible for the results and supervision, whereas general managers took charge of the process of management. With each concentrating on and emphasizing different things, there was no interference amongst them. The immediate and vital interests of the employees, represented by the general manager (storekeepers), were closely connected with the performances of the firms by being shareholders through their labor. Their interests accorded with those of the investors, so everyone spared no effort when working for the firms. The smartly designed systems used by the Jin merchants are quite similar to the ideas in modern enterprises of power separation, shareholding by managers and by employees, thus effectively reducing the costs of management.

Employment of General Managers

A lot of family enterprises founded by the Jin merchants had the same names and the major investors were from the same family. This guaranteed the control of the enterprise by the family. However, the system of employing a general manager was implemented in the enterprises, whereby general managers should be employed in accordance with the principle of "preferably hiring fellow villagers but never relatives". This meant that fellow villagers are more likely to be employed as general managers than relatives such as sons, son-in-laws or uncles. The Lee family owned Rishengchang, known as the first firm in the nation, and they hired Lei Lutai as the general manager to run the firm. Fully trusted by the Lee family, Lei Lutai spared no effort in running the banking firm. Their successful combination had created the splendid achievements of the "Nation's Top Banking Firm". Similarly, the six associated firms with the name of "Wei", including Weitaihou and Weifenghou set up by the Hou's family in Jiexiu did not hire members of the family to be the general manager. Instead, they spent a lot of money hiring Mao Hongyu, the former vice general manager of Rishengchang. Mao's talents in management were put into full use in the firm. In the short span of 30 years, Mao managed to set up branches in many major cities, making the Wei banking firm famous around the country. Mao himself got rich too and earned millions for the Hou family. They had successfully established a win-win relationship.

Dividing Family Property But Not Business

Another reason for the development and unity of the powerful enterprises for several hundred years lay in the adherence to the principle of "dividing family property but not business". It has always been a challenge for family enterprises to divide the property. Once the formerly abundant family assets are divided up into several parts, management on a large scale could not be achieved any longer. In addition, when family enterprises were passed on for several generations, with more and more branches of families emerging, family members could hardly be as united as the founders were. The ownership will also gradually be dispersed. Thus, one of the most important challenges for family enterprises was to maintain cohesion in power. It was only a matter of time when the Jin merchants would deal with the problems associated with this. Eventually, they only divided up the ownership into several parts, but business management remained united. Thus, they actually restructured the former sole proprietorship or joint venture into several stock enterprises with equal shares. This set a higher benchmark in the market. The Hou family became quite rich ever since Hou Wanzhan transported silk products from Suzhou and Hangzhou for sale during the years of rule under Kangxi. The family was known as "Hou the Millionaire". When Hou Xingyu was old, he divided the family property into six equal parts for his six sons. Thus, the family entered the generation that carried the name "Lai". The six brothers did not choose to run it separately, but entrusted the business to Hou Qinglai. With the efforts of Hou Qinglai and his son Hou Yingchang, the properties of the six sons of the Hou family were combined to form an associated banking firm under the Wei group of companies which were well known throughout the country. The family enterprise owned by the Cao family in Taigu was established by Cao Zhengxi. He divided his property equally for his seven sons. Similar to the Hou family, each of the seven sons provided 100 thousand taels to form the "Caoqihe", an organization to carry out unified management for companies of the seven sons. Later it was changed to "Liudehe". In spite of a different name, the companies of the seven sons were run collectively. Its branches could be found throughout the country and even abroad, with businesses in tea, silk products, leather products, banking firms and pawn-broking. Economically, each family was an independent accounting unit. Thus, the dispersion and outflow of capital were effectively avoided, which facilitated the large-scale development of the enterprises.

Loyalty and Integrity

The well-developed business culture and inner quality of the Jin merchants made it possible for them to stand out among all the merchants from around the country and made their enterprises bigger and stronger. Riehthofen, a German scholar, once said that "among all the Chinese, those who are the most developed in the special meters, numbers and measuring concepts of China and the tendency of banking based on the concepts are undoubtedly people from Shanxi and Shaanxi. As the keepers of the oldest culture, they have acquired a sense of superiority over their neighbors and residents of other countries. The tribes with such kind of sense may still manifest the achievements of spiritual superiority through the developed numerical concepts and banking talents, even though the offspring have lost political powers...the people of Shanxi are endowed with outstanding business competence and the spirit of large-scale enterprises." "The oldest culture keeper" and "spiritual sense of superiority" in his speech refer to the concepts of honesty, integrity and loyalty that the merchants from Shanxi have long been adhering to. Upholding benevolence and righteousness, the Jin merchants insisted on making profits only from legitimate operations. Jin merchants were aware that everyone needed a return of investment. Business can only be carried out when both sides could make a profit. Righteousness and honesty guaranteed the long-time prosperity of the firms of the Jin merchants. The basis of the "investor-employee-partnership" system was honesty. The solid relationship based on trust between investors and employees was the root to guarantee the interests of both sides and the fate of the business. Since the unlimited liability system was implemented, the investors, instead of the managers, should bear all the losses. If the managers were not fully trusted by the investors, the former could hardly carry out his managerial concepts and strategies. As such, if the managers were not honest to the investors, corruption could hardly be avoided and the so-called agent cost would be very high. Even if there was no definite provision for prohibiting interference, it was also impossible for the investors to intervene with the business of the firms personally, because the branches were located far away from the headquarters and the investors were unable to interfere with the detailed matters of the branches due to the inconvenient communications. As a result, the relationship between the investors and the managers could only be maintained by honesty and righteousness. It was by virtue of honesty and righteousness that Qiao Guifa, the founder of the "Top Merchant in the Country", together with his sworn brother Qin, had accomplished his original accumulation of capital. They had experienced hardships and difficulties in setting up a business firm "Guangshenggong". However, the manager once failed in the business, making Guangshenggong suffer losses of more than 100,000 taels of silver. It was undoubtedly a disaster for Qiao Guifa and Qin. However, Qiao never complained; neither did he punish the manager. On the contrary, he contributed all his wealth and had the manager run the firm again. But Qin lost confidence in the manager and quit his shares. With the full support from Qiao, the manager learned from the lesson of his failure and devoted all his attention to the operation of the firm. Soon it overcame the crisis and picked up momentum. So as the investor, the Qiao family took the opportunity to change the name of the firm from Guangshenggong to Fushenggong. With the name "Fu", they established a long-lasting prosperity for the companies.

Similarly, the famous company by the name of Dashengkui was jointly set up, by virtue of honesty, by Wang Xiangqin, a poor farmer from Taigu, Zhang Jie and Shi Daxue from Qi county. Initially, the three people were peddlers in the army. They took care of each other like brothers. Meanwhile, Zhang Jie and Shi Daxue quit and went into agriculture because the business was not doing well. Later, under a more favorable business condition, Wang Xiangqin personally invited the two to return to the company. It clearly demonstrated that they attached more importance to friendship and honesty than business.

A much-told story of the Cao family in Taigu about "Losses for Three Times, Invest for Three Times" clearly explained how the Jin merchants trusted their employees. In those years, Cao set up the Fushengjun banking firm in Shenyang in northeastern China with an initial investment of 70,000 taels of silver. However, several years later, the firm suffered huge losses, but Cao did not blame the manager. On the contrary, he consoled him and invested once again. However, good luck failed them again. Too ashamed to face the investor, the manager decided to resign. But, Cao invested again. The manager was deeply touched by the sincerity and trust that Cao had in him. So he seriously learned lessons from the failures and changed the approach to management. The manager quickly turned losses into profits. Not satisfied with just that, he set up several taverns and made a considerable profit from the operations of the banking firm and the taverns. The trust of the investor was repaid with profits. From the example we could see that the relationship of trust was a mutual one. The investor trusted the manager and the manager repaid the investor. There was another example. Rishengchang, the so-called "Top Banking Firm", set up a small branch somewhere in Sichuan. Because it was a small banking outfit, plus the inconvenient transportation and unstable economic condition at that time, the boss at the headquarters thought business in Sichuan might have been closed down. Thirty years later, the general manager of the headquarters was replaced and the old investor had passed away. No one in the headquarters knew anything about the manager in that small branch in Sichuan. Then one day, the manager from that small branch came to the headquarters to hand in the capital and dividends. Both the new boss and general manager could hardly remember the branch and were unwilling to accept it. Finally at the insistence of the Sichuan branch manager, the headquarters accepted the return of that investment. In more than 30 years, the manager had run the branch with painstaking efforts and loyalty. If he had been slightly influenced by the notion of selfishness, the story would have turned out differently.

These true stories offer enlightenment in the solving of problems like the incentive system for managers and the problem of how to better deal with the relationship between distributors and agencies, which are frequently discussed in modern enterprises.

Restrict Pursuit of Individual Interests through Honesty and Integrity

If the relationship of trust was the root of prosperity of the Jin merchants, honesty in operations was the key to profits. "To restrict interest through honesty and righteousness" was the credo adhered to by Jin merchants. The reason why the Fu banking firm owned by the Qiao family prospered for several hundred years lay in the trust that they *had won* from their customers. The quality of the products under the brand of Fu was guaranteed. It would never short-change the customers or cheat customers with inferior products, so Fu was the guarantee of quality. Before silver was used as currency, the brick-shaped tea produced by Dashengkui could even be used as currency for exchange. Tea, silk products and cigarettes sold by Dashengkui and horses, cows, sheep, camels and medical materials sold by the Mongolians and Russian merchants could all be traded using the brick-shaped tea products. This is a case in point to explain the credit of Dashengkui. Fan, the famous royal merchant had obtained the contracts for transporting foodstuff for the army and copper products due to his integrity and honesty. The Jin merchants had encountered challenges that tested their integrity and honesty, but they managed to carry through such beliefs even in turbulence. During the Turmoil of Gengzi in 1900, major companies set up by the Jin merchants were all destroyed and robbed, among which the banking firms suffered the greatest loss. The manager of the Beijing branch of Weishengchang banking firm had absconded with the bank's account book and escaped to the west. However, he was robbed by bandits in Baoding and the account book was gone. No sooner had the manager got to the headquarters in Pingyao than the senior officials who escaped the turmoil in Beijing arrived. The officials came to withdraw the money they had saved in Beijing branch with the deposit receipts. Weishengchang specially designated employees to handle the business and paid them in accordance with the memory of the accounts of Beijing branch. The firm was widely praised for its deeds. When the officials returned to Beijing, they helped the branch a lot in their business. Moreover, the forgiving attitude of Fushenggong towards debtors who were unable to repay the debts also won it good fame. For example, when a firm was shut down, it owed Fushenggong 50,000 taels of silver. The manager called at the Qiao's and apologized to Lord Qiao, who just consoled him and never asked the manager to repay the debt. Another example was that when a store owed 1,000 taels to Fushenggong, and the manager of Fushenggong just took an axe from the store as a symbol that the store had repaid the money.

The operations, managerial system, human resources system, governance structure and inheritance in the banking firms set up by the Jin merchants were quite unique and advanced. The systems, work ethics and corporate culture, which were close to those of modern business, are the significant reasons for their splendid success in the modern economic history of China.

6

Family Enterprises in Modern China

The *Forbes* magazine provides the most reliable richest people list each year. Since the founding of the People's Republic of China, no one from mainland China had been included in *Forbes* list until the year of 1995 when *Forbes* publicized 21 billionaires from China. In 2002, *Forbes* listed the top 100 richest people in mainland China. The total assets of these 100 entrepreneurs reached US$19 billion, while in 2001 this number was US$18 billion. It was observed that many families were included in the 2005 *Forbes* list on the richest people of China. More and more wealthy families have gradually been springing up around us. The names of their enterprises are sounding more familiar to our ears. Strong as they are, no one could ignore the power of these family enterprises. When we marvel at the fortune of these families, which amounts to hundreds of millions, we also become aware of the great power of their enterprises in earning wealth.

Compared to their overseas counterparts, family enterprises in mainland China have a much shorter span of development. Research on family enterprises, especially on the sustainable development of China's family enterprises, do not receive due attention among the academia in China. This chapter aims at analyzing the background, current conditions and challenges faced by family enterprises based on Three-Dimensional Development model. This chapter also tries to point out the dilemma that China's family enterprises might face and offer tips for the sustainable development of family enterprises in China.

Proliferation of Family Enterprises in China

Since the 1980s — a period of economic system reform and social structure transformation — a non-public-owned economy began to emerge and develop, later becoming an indispensable part of China's market economy. Currently, the majority of private enterprises in China are owned and operated by families. Familial management mode is adopted in both family enterprises and companies of other types, such as township enterprises, collective enterprises, partnership enterprises and joint stock enterprises.

China's private enterprises took the first step with the country's reform and open-door policy. "Deng Xiaoping's address in the south" heralded the golden period for private enterprises. According to statistics from a sample survey conducted by Chinese Academy of Social Sciences in 1999, private equity took up at least 90% in private enterprises in Zhejiang Province. The biggest stock holder possessed as much as 66% of the stock right, being in absolute holding position. The siblings also took up a large percentage, about 14%. The owner and his siblings held about 80% of the stock right of the enterprise.

Since China's reform and opening-up, China's family enterprises have increased in number and expanded in scale. At the same time, the industry structure has been upgraded, and management improved.

Since 1990, China's family enterprises have been witnessing drastic increases in quantity, employment population, registered capital, and scale.

The number of private enterprises increased by 23.8 times — from 98,000 in 1990 to 2,435,000 in 2002 (Table 6.1). In terms of scale, there were only 662 private enterprises with registered capital of 1 million yuan in 1991. In 2002, this number increased to 415,400. The output value gained by China's private enterprises increased from 12.2 billion yuan in 1990 to 1.5338 trillion yuan in 2002 — an increase by 125 times (retail price rise excluded). In more than one decade, the main organizational format has shifted from sole investment enterprise and partnership enterprise to limited company and

Table 6.1: 1990–2000 Number Increase and Scale Expansion of Private Enterprises[a]

Year	Enterprises	Increase Rate (%)	Average Registered Capital/ Enterprise (10,000 yuan)	Increase Rate (%)	Output Value (100 million yuan)	Increase Rate (%)
1990	98,141	8.35	9.86	4.38	122	23.17
1991	107,843	9.89	11.41	17.83	147	17.11
1992	139,633	29.48	15.83	38.77	205	32.33
1993	237,919	70.39	28.62	80.83	422	81.87
1994	432,240	81.68	33.5	17.04	1,140	121.98
1995	654,531	51.43	40.06	19.58	2,295	75.37
1996	819,252	25.17	45.8	14.33	3,227	32.53
1997	960,726	17.27	53.5	16.82	3,923	20.61
1998	1,200,978	25.01	59.93	12.02	5,853	53.18
1999	1,508,857	25.64	68.18	13.75	7,686	35.37
2000	1,761,769	16.76	75.54	10.7	10,740	39.73
2001	2,028,548	15.1	89.78	18.9	12,317	14.68
2002	2,435,282	20.1	101.66	13.3	15,338	24.53

[a] Statistics on Commerce & Trade Management (1991–2002) State Administration for Industry and Commerce.

company limited by shares. According to the survey of "Research Project on China's Private Enterprises", which was co-sponsored by the sociology department of Chinese Academy of Social Sciences and China Federation of Industry & Commerce, the average profits of private enterprises in year 2000 were 439,000 yuan, the annual sales volume was 6,075,000 yuan. As for those top-level industries, such as agriculture, fishing, real estate, architecture, research, the average taxation paid was 302,000 yuan.

In the 21st century, which is marked by speedy development of information technology and global economy integration, China faces fierce competition after entering WTO. Therefore, family enterprises are confronted with unprecedented challenges, as well as opportunities. Some older family enterprises have stepped into the

phase of second pioneering. They have already accomplished original capital accumulation and are heading for capital market. At present, several family enterprises have gone on public listing in
mainland China.

Types of China's Family Enterprises

China's family enterprises began to take shape when the reform and
opening-up policy was adopted in 1979. China's economic reforms
have gone through ups and downs. Inevitably, the pioneering private
enterprises had to shoulder both market risk and policy risk. Only the
most outstanding ones survived. In order to start their business, some
entrepreneurs quit their jobs in state-owned enterprises, governments,
and research institutes. They sought help within their families, and
took effective measures to gather resources, overcome difficulties in
land, workshop, capital and technology, and become individual entrepreneurs. Some people who come from different families co-invest and
work together as partnership business. Most partnership enterprises
appeared after 1990. Both the partners and their families were involved
in the business operation.

Affected by different policies at different reform stages, China's
family enterprises can be classified into the following forms:

Individual/Family Entrepreneurs

After China's reform and opening up, a group of entrepreneurs
were actively engaged in setting up corporations. Family enterprises
began to develop. In the early stage of their development, family
enterprises had some unique characteristics due to their backgrounds and locations.

a. Some entrepreneurs came from state-owned enterprises, govern-
    ments, and research institutes. They mainly focused on trade and
    small-scale industries. Small size and flexibility enabled their
    enterprises to gain benefits on border trade and transnational
    trade.

b. Due to the household contract responsibility system in the 1980s, agricultural productivity in countryside improved greatly. At the same time, economic reforms were taking place in cities. Therefore, a great number of entrepreneurs emerged in villages and towns. They combined manufacture and trade by setting up factories and shops. They possessed obvious advantages in small commodity production and circulation channel. Wenzhou area was a typical example. It was called "Wenzhou Model".

c. In Guangdong, Fujian, Jiangsu and Zhejiang, many family enterprises focused on processing and supplementary trade. Such industries set a high demand on technology. Usually, the countryside was not densely populated and most people were related. The entrepreneurs took effective measures to gather resources, overcome difficulties in land, workshop, capital and technololgy. Relying on relatives and family members was effective at that time.

Partnership Enterprise

Partnership enterprises refer to two or more individuals (not from the same family) investing in the same business. Such enterprises first appeared after 1990. Instead of working alone, they cooperated with other investors. The partners combined their resources to achieve integration advantage. Both business partners and family members were involved in the business operation.

"Red Hat" Enterprise

"Red Hat" enterprises referred to public ownership in name, but the family was actually both the investor and management of the business. Enterprises of this type appeared in the period from early 1980s to early 1990s. Due to the policy constraints and ownership requirement, such enterprises were registered by relevant local administration department in the name of public ownership economy. But in nature, they are family enterprises. The purpose of such practice was to facilitate business operation in certain areas which were forbidden to non-public ownership entity. After initial business success, "red hat" enterprises would inevitably be confronted with the problem of ownership. Presently, many "red hat" enterprises had removed their "hat" and restored the name of "family enterprises".

System-Transformed Enterprises

Some family enterprises fall into the realm of system-transformed enterprises. These enterprises had previously been owned by government, belonging to public ownership economy. Due to ineffective management, the management of these enterprises was transferred through individual contracting and lease. Even the ownership can be partly or wholly transferred to individual through currency exchange and debt-sharing. Family enterprises of this type were mostly local small or medium-sized enterprises.

The suitability of various forms depended on the specific circumstances at the time the enterprise was set up. Sichuan Hope Group Co Ltd was an example. This company belonged to the individual/family entrepreneurial form. In the early 1980s, when mainland China began the reform, the four brothers — Liu Yongyan, Liu Yongxing, Liu Yongmei, and Liu Yonghao — were in a lifelong secured job. The eldest brother Liu Yongyan worked in Chengdu 906 Computer Science Institute. The second brother Liu Yongxing was engaged in designing and maintenance of electronics equipment. The third brother Liu Yongmei was a public servant at the Agriculture Bureau in the town. The fourth brother Liu Yonghao was a teacher in Sichuan Mechanism Management Cadre School. Learning from others' success stories in doing business, the four brothers decided to quit their jobs and began to engage in aquaculture.

Starting from family aquaculture, they developed their business into a cross-industry and cross-regional group of companies with 1 billion yuan of assets. They are presently holding 2 billion group assets. The annual turnover of the group is above 5 billion yuan. Currently, the group has more than 100 subsidiary companies with 15,000 employees, becoming the largest family holding enterprise in

China. For many times, Liu brothers were ranked by *Forbes* to be the richest persons in mainland China. In 2002, they even appeared on the cover page of *Forbes* magazine.

China's first listed company holding by natural persons — Tiantong Holding Co Ltd — was developed from a "red hat" enterprise. Originally, this family company was registered as a township enterprise. Later, it restored its identity as a family enterprise. In 1984, the father and son — Pan Guangtong and Pan Jianqing — pooled 800,000 yuan and set up an electronic component factory in Haining. This factory was registered as a township enterprise in Guodian. After 17 years, the factory removed the "hat" of township enterprise. Later, it developed into a private limited company, and gradually into an integrated company with 40 million public shares. On January 18, 2001, the company was listed — the first listed company directly held by natural persons, with Pan Guangtong and Pan Jianqing holding 21.48% of the stock right.

Another example was Panpan Group Co Ltd, which was originally a collective enterprise. Through system transformation, contractor Han Zhaoshan gradually developed the company into a private one. Formerly, Panpan Group Co Ltd was a metal products factory in Yingkou. In 1982, this factory was on the verge of bankruptcy, with 12 grass houses, 2 machines, 12 workers, and 86,000 yuan in debt. The vice director of the factory, Han Zhaoshan, took over the management based on a contract. According to the contract, he must pay 30,000 yuan in the first year and an additional 10,000 yuan each year after. Han Zhaohan, together with a dozen people under him, stepped on a hard pioneering journey. In 1991, his company actualized 28 million yuan of output value, and 2.4 million yuan of pre-tax profit. In 1993, Han Zhaoshan continued his contract. During the second contract period, the company gradually expanded its scale, and the economic interest rises at the same time. In 1998, Han Zhaoshan signed the transfer agreement with the company. He purchased both the tangible and intangible assets of the factory. After system transformation, Han Zhaoshan took absolute control of Panpan Group. At present, Panpan Group is still under expansion through share purchase and is seeking overseas listing.

System-transformed enterprises were the results of China's state-owned enterprise reform after the 15th National Congress of the Chinese Communist Party (CCP). The contract system was similar to the farmland contract system in the countryside. Except taxation and contract fees, the contractor could keep all the remaining assets. Management contract imposed restrictions on production expansion. Therefore, the contract system evolved into lease system. The contractor could take advantage of the fixed assets, supply channels, sales network and enterprise credit of the state-owned enterprise, and combine them with his own experience, skills, innovation, capital, and employment to launch independent production and management. With the development of the enterprise, public-owned assets shrank while private assets increased. By purchasing and transferring the remaining public property right, new family enterprises evolved.

Management Practice of China's Family Enterprises

A majority of China's family enterprises are founded on family wealth, relying on family members and their social connections. Family members work for the enterprises with low pay. In decision-making, centralization is adopted. Usually, one or several persons are responsible for policy-making. Since the fate of the enterprise is closely connected with that of the family, the decision-makers are highly centralized. In addition, the flexibility in management enables the enterprises to be more adaptive to the changing economic environment.

Firstly, family enterprises emerged when China's economic system was undergoing drastic reforms. In order to gain an edge in a constantly changing market, private enterprises have to sometimes test beyond the policy limits and adopt various effective measures to overcome restrictions. Therefore, the owners must keep an eye on the loyalty of the top management; otherwise internal betrayal may lead to interference of government. The uncertainty in the social and policy environment has led to the preference of familial management and rely largely on the loyalty of family members. It is perceived to be a safer mode of business operation.

Secondly, unavailability of professional managers and a lack of social trust lead to low confidence in recruiting non-family-member managers. At present, for private enterprises, the fundamental principle in employing managers is reliability. First of all, the manager employed must be reliable. Without reliability, his managerial ability will be in an inverse proportion to the damage he might incur to the business. A stable and clear legal system and a transparent evaluation system are absent, hence contributing to the low confidence between the owner and professional managers. As a result, the owner of the enterprise has to choose someone he can trust from the family as the manager.

Thirdly, family enterprises rely on the family for initial finance support. At present, China's finance system mainly serves the state-owned enterprises. For family enterprises, they have to obtain financial support from the family network. During the initial period, business operation is at great risk. Such investment risk is akin to that in high-tech development. According to statistics, the founding capital of China's private enterprises mainly comes from the owner's previous savings, which takes up 56.3%. Loans from relatives and friends take up 16.3%. The capital composition mode is particularly evident in family enterprises in Jiangsu and Zhejiang provinces.

Fourthly, the operation cost of family enterprise is relatively low in a constantly changing environment. At the earlier stage, familial management mode helps to lower production cost and communication cost. Moreover, familialism guarantees trust within the enterprise, and therefore monitoring cost can be saved. Since the decision-makers and managers are from the same family, a speedy information exchange can be achieved, and problems can be solved immediately. A family enterprise is also viewed as an interest unity. As a result, efficiency can be greatly improved. Even when the enterprise is trapped in a financial dilemma, family members can help to cushion the blow by working without pay.

Three-Dimensional Development of Family Enterprises

According to Kelin E. Gersick, family enterprise can be represented by three independent and intersected subsystems: enterprise, ownership,

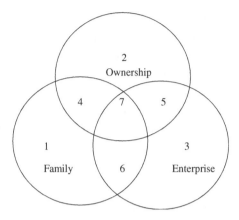

Figure 6.1:　Three Subsystems of Family Enterprises

Source: Kelin E. Gersick, Generation to Generation: Life Cycles of Family Business, p. 14.

and family. Each component in the family enterprise can be placed somewhere in the seven intersected areas (shown in Figure 6.1).

The three circles reflect the profile of the family at a certain period, which is of great significance to the understanding of the company. Nevertheless, with the time lapse, a family company also faces difficulties concerning changes in organization, family, and ownership distribution, etc. When time as a factor is added into these three circles, "three-axes" development will vary from enterprise to enterprise (as shown in Figure 6.2). In the three subsystems of ownership, family, and enterprise, each one has its own stages of development. Being interactive as well as independent, each circle develops at its own pace.

Ownership Axis

Kelin E. Gersick, an American scholar, believes ownership is an important criterion for identifying a family enterprise. He found that the family enterprise will go through three stages along the ownership axis. These three stages are one-person holding company, sibling-partnership company, and cousin-partnership company. Ownership development indicates the development trend for the enterprise.

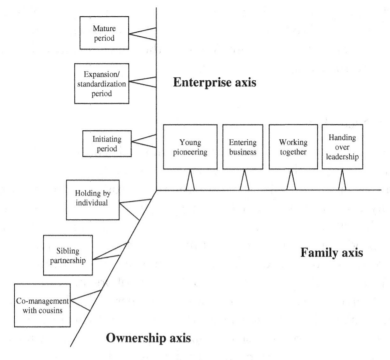

Figure 6.2:   "Three-Axes" Development

A majority of family enterprises start with sole ownership. After a long period of development, it will reach sibling partnership stage, and then cousin partnership stage. Thereafter, the ownership will decentralize and professional managers will take over the management. Part of the ownership will be transferred to non-family members, and therefore directorate will be formed with non-family members in the majority.

Family Axis

Family is a powerful and inevitable social organization. Based on development of family which includes individual development and family life circle, Kelin E. Gersick divided family axis into four successive stages: young pioneering family, entering business, family members working together and leadership handover. Family axis is different from the other two axes, for the division of axis is based on the common task faced by the family. Aging of the family members is a key factor for the advancement of family axis.

Enterprise Axis

Kelin E. Gersick maintained that although family enterprises do share some similarities, the differences between a street shop and a transnational company are substantial. In enterprise axis, growth and complexity are the two criteria for determining different phases in the growth process. The three developmental phases in this axis are: initial period, expansion period, and mature period. In each phase, the enterprise will take on different features in scale and structure.

At the initial stage, there may not be a formal organizational structure. Seated at the central position is the owner who takes charge of management. After the initial period, the company will enter the second phase — expansion/standardization period. The characteristics of this phase are expansions in many aspects, such as turnover, products, and employment, and standardization in organizational structure and procedure. During the expansion period, an enterprise will shift from a founder-centered structure to a more formal hierarchical organization. The companies are pressured to recruit professional managers for key positions. The owner will gradually transfer some of the power to non-family talents. Sooner or later, the enterprise will enter the mature phase featuring stable organizational structure, customer base and operation.

The Characteristics of China's Family Enterprises

Ownership Axis — Absolute Ratio Share

The ownership of China's family enterprises is affected by policies and social circumstances. Currently, there are the following various types of ownership.

Private Shareholder Holding Absolute Ratio Share

Prof. Zhang Houyi from Chinese Academy of Social Sciences conducted a research project "Study on Management Structure of China's Private Enterprises" in which board chairmen, general managers, and vice general managers from 179 private enterprises were involved. The survey showed that a majority of shares were privately held. The average holding ratio was as high as 85.1% (shown in Table 6.1). Among private shareholders, the owner holds the largest ratio of share, followed by the siblings, cousins with different family name, technicians, and non-family top management personnel. Usually technicians and non-family top management staff obtain enterprise shares through stock option, which is an incentive measure for attracting professional talents.

Table 6.3 shows that collective-owned shares amount to 6.8%. Some of the enterprises were previously collective-owned. After the transformation, the government keeps a small ratio of shares. According to statistics, on the average, each private enterprise has 14 private shareholders (Table 6.2). The mode of private shareholders is 1. Individual share-holder is the largest ratio. On the average, private shareholders hold 64% shares of stock. The medium is 60%.

Private Share-Holding Structure

A small part of the ownership of private shareholding companies belongs to public-owned organization, and top management staff. There are four explanations for the emergence of enterprises of this type:

a. At a certain stage, due to limitations in business scale and operation qualifications, family enterprises will be confronted with difficulties in market competition and project bidding. Therefore, they are willing to collaborate with public-owned economy for improvement.

b. During expansion period, in order to maintain rapid development, the owner of family enterprises will take some of the stock

Table 6.2:   Share Holding Rate

Stock	Average Ratio (%)
Private stock-holder	85.1
Collectively-owned	5.9
Legal person (other companies)	4.1
Government in village, town or city	0.9
Overseas investment	0.3
Others	2.2

Table 6.3:   Shareholder and Stock Ratio

	Number of Private Shareholders (person)	Shares of Stock (%)
Mean value	14.36	63.67
Medium	2.00	60.00
Mode	1	100
Standard deviation	69.95	32.04
Standard number (person)	151	141

out and grant to professional talents as a motivation and long-term incentive.

c. When the "red hat" is removed, the public organization takes part of the stock right.

d. Government departments sell some of the state-owned owner-ship to individuals, or co-invest with private capital in setting up limited liability companies. Therefore, state-owned enterprises will be transformed into privately-owned ones. Nevertheless, the state still holds a small percentage of ownership.

From the analysis above, we can see that China's family enterprises are obviously featured with one person holding majority stock right. With expansion in production and business scope, the ownership tends to be diversified but still in the control of the founder. Even some listed companies are still in the "absolute ratio share" with a major shareholder. These characteristics will remain in the Chinese family business for some time.

Technicians and managing staff holding shares is a positive phenomenon. On the one hand, it helps to narrow or remove the distance between the "boss" and "employees". Traditional labor-capital relationship has been improved. On the other hand, stock-holding makes the employee feel connected to the enterprise. Business risks decreased as a result. Nevertheless, since these non-family members obtain shares through stock option, they can obtain the share dividends, but have no voice in decision-making.

Family Axis — Autarchy

According to the *Study on Governance Structure of China's Private Enterprises* (Table 6.4), in one out of five family enterprises, relatives and close friends of the chairman are involved in business management. Usually, they assume the position of general manager, vice general manager or finance director. Besides professional skills, trust is a primary consideration for appointments in these positions.

Study on Governance Structure of China's Private Enterprises also investigated some family enterprises in Huizhou, Guangdong province. Among the 76 enterprises being investigated, 84% had family members in top management. Companies with both husbands and wives taking part in management took up 95%, and they usually assume important positions in finance, and human resources. 89% of the enterprise owners were male. 19 of them were under 35, taking up 25%. Fifty owners were from 35 to 49, taking up 65.8%. 7 were above 50, taking up 9.2%. 90% of the owners were married with one or two offspring. 52 owners (68.4%) reported that they would uphold the "enterprise first" principle in solving problems concerning the conflict between the enterprise and the family. From the owner's perspective, family business was obviously a major reason to bind the family together.

With a short history, a majority of China's family enterprises are still at the initial stage of development. For most entrepreneurs, they

Table 6.4:   Management Personnel Analysis

	Public Recruitment	Internal Promotion	Relatives of Board Chairman or General Manager	Close Friends of Board Chairman or General Manager	Appointments from Government	Other Sources	Total %
Number of managing staff	43.8	29.42	11.66	8.59	0.58	6.11	100
General manager	16	25	42	3	1	12	100
Vice general manager	29.33	23.55	24.33	11.05	1.5	10.34	100
Chief engineer, chief accountant, chief economist	50.11	28.19	9.86	5.63	0.69	5.52	100
Finance supervisor	40.58	24.57	16.37	12.9	1.01	4.57	100
Stock supervisor	36.15	36.45	15.85	6.79	0.75	4.01	100
Sales manager	41.87	35.6	15.39	3.89	0.46	4.6	100
Warehouse supervisor	34.5	42.1	13.76	4.5	1.5	3.63	100
Other managing staff	37.5	41.44	9.01	3.11	0.17	8.76	100

Source: Development Report on China's Private Enterprises No.3, 2001, p. 181.

engage themselves in every business activity, from pioneering work to market competition. They have little time to deal with family affairs. Since family members spend most of their time on business, their enterprise is also a "family" for them.

The founders usually occupy the central place in business, and sometimes they are reluctant to retire. From their perspective, they build their career from scratch, and they know better than anyone else how hard it was to set up the business. They also believe that only they themselves are capable of strong leadership. As a result, they tend to be extremely authoritative and confident. The founder's aspiration for power will pose a big threat to power transfer to the next generation or to non-family professional managers.

Due to the short development history, most family enterprises in China have not reached the power handover stage. Nevertheless, power transfer is a big challenge for family businesses in time to come. Currently, this issue has not been put in agenda in most family enterprises, not to mention planning for a smooth transfer. The family should make a long-term plan to solve this problem.

Enterprise Axis — A State of Disunity

According to statistics from China's Industrial & Commercial Administration Bureau, by 2002, there had been 2,435,000 private enterprises in China, with total registered capital of 2,475,622 million yuan — 112 times as much as that in 1992. The yearly increase rate is 60.3%. 415,400 enterprises have a registered capital of more than one million yuan. 327,400 of them are with a registered capital between 1–5 million. 53,700 are with a registered capital of 5–10 million. 34,300 are with a registered capital of 10–100 million, and 658 with more than 100 million.

In 2004, the Private Enterprises Research Center in the Chinese Academy of Social Sciences made a sample survey. In 2002,

China's private enterprises took on the following development characteristics:

1.   Industry distribution

Wholesale and retail trade, together with food and beverage, took up the biggest ratio of 39.56%; manufacturing, 32.27%, ranked second; social service, 12.44% was third; architecture, 3.41%; agriculture, forestry, animal and fishing industries, 1.76%; transportation and storage, 1.47%; mining and quarrying, 0.76%; and other industries, 8.33%.

2.   Types of enterprise

There were 1,740,000 limited liability companies, 71.45%, ranked number one; proprietorship enterprises, 23.41%, ranked the second; partnership enterprises, 5.12%; joint stock limited company (512), 0.02%.

3.   Registered capital

Above 10 million yuan, 8.26%; 5–10 million yuan, 12.92%; 1–5 million yuan, 78.82%.

4.   Regional distribution

Eastern part of China, 68.91%; Central region, 17.25%; Western region, 13.84%; Jiangsu, Guangdong, Zhejiang, Shanghai, Beijing, and Shandong, 55% in total.

Based on its spot check of 178 large-scale enterprises, the *Study on Management Structure of China's Private Enterprises* showed that (Table 6.5):

1.   Founding date

Among the 172 enterprises being investigated, 49 of them (28%) were set up before 1991. The remaining 123 were founded after Deng Xiaoping made his famous address in southern China, and the 14th National Congress of the CCP which erected the principle of "Insisting on the Public-Ownership as the main body and Develop the Non-Public Economy".

Table 6.5: Registered Capital of China's Enterprises in 1998

	Unit: 10,000 yuan
Average value	364.927
Medium	60
Mode	50
Total	178

Source: Development Report on China's Private Enterprise No. 3, 2001, p. 171.

Table 6.6: Total Assets

	Total Assets	Fluid Assets	Fixed Assets	Receivable Funds	Outward Investment (10,000 yuan)
Average value	2211.743	633.3257	1262.509	303.2164	169.4815
Medium	180	50	100	30	2
Mode	50	10	20	3	0
Valid sample	175	175	75	134	54

Source: Development Report on China's Private Enterprise), No. 3, 2001, p. 172.

2.   Registered capital

The average registered capital of the 178 enterprises was 3,690,000 yuan. Different industries have different requirements on capital needed. Enterprises with 500,000 yuan registered capital were in the largest number.

3.   Total asset scale

According to the 175 valid questionnaires (Table 6.6), the average total asset scale was 21,220,000 yuan. Average fluid assets was 6,330,000 yuan. Average fixed assets was 12,630,000 yuan. If we rank the 174 enterprises according to asset scale, the medium would be 1,800,000 yuan. Those with 500,000 yuan of total assets were in the largest number. Big variation is present.

4.   Employment

According to the 176 valid questionnaires, 104 enterprises with less than 50 employees took up the largest percentage — nearly 60%; 24 enterprises with 51–100 employees (13.6%); 37 medium-sized enterprises with 101–500 employees (21%); eight big enterprises with 501–1,000 employees (4.5%); three enterprises with more than 1,000 employees (1.7%).

5.   Organization

95.4% of the surveyed enterprises set up general manager or factory director office. 54% set up directorate board. 43% had stockholder meeting and 33.3% set up board of supervisors.[1]

From the statistics and analysis above, we can see that a majority of China's family enterprises have a short history of no more than 15 years. In terms of registered capital, total assets, and employment, they are small and medium in size.

---

[1] Development Report on China's Private Enterprise, No. 3, 2001, p. 178.

Case 9: Hope Group: Making Family Enterprises Bigger and Stronger

Introduction

In October 2006, the list of "Top 100 Richest of Hurun" first issued "Female Rich List of China 2006". Liu Chang, a 26-year-old girl, ranked top with 2,500 million yuan, becoming the youngest and richest female in mainland China. People would not be surprised if they know that this girl who frequents the "*Forbes* Rich List" is the daughter of Liu Yonghao — the chairman of Hope Group. However, this event can be viewed in another perspective — the media exposure of the second generation of the Liu Family. People cannot help wondering if the second generation occupies the power center, will they be able to maintain family harmony as well as prosperity? Or will they uphold the spirit of independence and continue their own way?

On November 4, 1997, Hope Group published an announcement in *Economic Daily* and *China Securities Journal*: "according to the resolution made by the board of directors of Hope Group, the Group would set up only four second-grade industrial companies: Continental, East China, West China and South China." Liu Yongyan, Liu Yongxing, Chen Yuxin and Liu Yonghao would respectively be responsible for the management of the four companies. It was also decided that from June 3, 1997, chairman Liu Yongxing would work as the legal representative of the group and would carry out all the activities on behalf of Hope Group; general manager Chen Yuxin would take charge of the daily management of the group; Liu Yonghao would no longer be the legal representative of the group. The announcement invited various social discussion. In fact, it was only a small adjustment in Hope Group. The former legal representative Liu Yonghao was replaced by the second brother Liu Yongxing. However, it was the rumor about the split-up in the Liu family that attracted public attention. As early as 1995, when

Liu Yongxing set up the East Company and Liu Yonghao set up the South Company, the "split-up" rumor began to spread. However, the Liu brothers had been silent, providing no explanation.

Another concern was that the New Hope Group, which was owned by Liu Yonghao, was still attracting much media attention. In recent years, through extensive media exposure, New Hope had surpassed Hope Group in fame.

People are wondering what is going on within Hope Group. Can the enormous family enterprise, which has developed for more than 10 years at an astonishing speed, maintain its splendid development?

Pioneering Process

The Liu brothers and their family are now well known in mainland China. Actually, even when they were not rich, the brothers and the family were some sort of celebrities in their hometown — Xinjin county, Sichuan province. Their father was an intellectual who took part in the revolutionary activities promoted by CCP and served as the director of Agriculture Bureau in Xinjin County after the founding of PRC. Their mother was a student of the famous Whampoa Military Academy and devoted herself to education thereafter. She gave birth successively to the four brothers: Liu Yongyan, Liu Yongxing, Liu Yongmei and Liu Yonghao (the names combined indicate well-disciplined speech and behaviors). Liu Yongmei, the third brother, was brought up by a peasant Chen, so he was also named Chen Yuxin. The four brothers have a little sister Liu Yonghong. Nurtured by the sound family environment, the brothers were admitted by colleges or technical secondary schools. College students were rare in mainland China, especially in small counties like Xinjin. The story of the brothers was much told in the county.

At the beginning of the 1980s when mainland China implemented the policy of reforms and opening-up, the four brothers graduated and got lifelong secure jobs or positions. Liu Yongyan worked in Chengdu 906 Computer Science Institute, Liu Yongxing was engaged in the designing and maintenance of electrical appliances, Liu Yongmei (Chen Yuxin) was a cadre in Xinjin Agriculture Bureau and Liu Yonghao served as a teacher in Sichuan Mechanism Management Cadre School.

1982 was a new era for the rural areas in China. Peasants were unprecedentedly positive. While the pessants threw themselves into the traditional planting agriculture, they also sought other ways to get rich. Encouraged by some successful stories, the Liu brothers decided to start aquaculture. With 1,000 yuan which was earned by selling watches and bicycles, the Liu brothers went to Liu Yongmei (Chen Yuxin)'s home in countryside and began to breed quails. Their business turned out to be a huge success. In 1983, Chen Yuxin left his position in Xinjin Agriculture Bureau — actually, his position was retained with salary suspended — and threw himself into business. And then Liu Yongxing quit his job to join his brothers in the establishment of Yuxin Breeding Factory in the name of Chen Yuxin. Chen worked as the manager and the legal representative, while Liu Yongxing was the vice manager. Liu Yongyan and Liu Yonghao quit their jobs successively in 1986 and 1987 to engage in the business.

In the initial stage, the market for quails breeding was so weak that many farmers withdrew from this industry. The brothers found out that the high price of quails, which resulted from high cost of breeding, was to be blamed. After a thorough analysis, they concluded that "there might be weak market, but there is no weak product", and that the key to success is technical innovation (this expression was not popular in the mainland China then). As long as they could reduce the cost of quail eggs to three or four cents, they could definitely occupy the market, make profit, and revive this industry. In order to decrease the cost, they consulted lots of materials, used computers to distribute feed and chose a fine breed, thus created the leading pattern of all-dimensional breeding. They fed pigs with dung of quails, fed fish with dung of pigs, fed quails with fish meal. Finally, the costs of the quail eggs were reduced and Liu brothers regained the market.

At that time, the brothers lived on very little and pooled all the money together into reproduction, thus forming a "communist family". In 1983, the brothers divided the profit equally and each received 180 yuan. Yongyan bought a batch of quails with the money to expand the size of the farm. Following the eldest brother's example, the Liu brothers never kept profit for themselves, but put money into reproduction whenever they made profits. Liu Yongxing had sighed with emotion: "without the batch of quails bought by the eldest brother, we could never set up Hope Group."

The brothers made no distinction on ownership rights. Even till now, they can hardly tell the investment ratio of the initial 1,000 yuan which they first put into their business. The brothers admitted that they had never thought of getting the money back when they put money together. Since the second brother and the third brother had invested more and made greater efforts in the initial stages, the four brothers verbally agreed that "the second brother and the third brother should hold the majority of ownership rights". In 1988 when they made huge profits, these two brothers initiatively put forward the principle of "equal distribution of profits". Nevertheless, the ownership rights were still in an ambiguous status. For the four brothers, their wealth did not belong to any individual, but to "the four of them as a whole".

At that time, the only thing Liu brothers cared about was how to make more money and expand their business. Nobody cared about personal fame or gain. Due to more public exposure, the third brother Chen Yuxin was the most well-known one. Once, some reporters visited the breeding factory and were received by the second brother Liu Yongxing. Liu Yongxing introduced himself as "Chen Yuxin", trying to avoid self-promotion.

Their father was dead when the brothers started quail-breeding in Xinjin County. It was their mother who did all she could to help the brothers with their business until she passed away in 1993. She played an important role in the initial stage of the pioneering process. As the brothers recalled, the opinions of their mother were influential, if not decisive. Especially in the judgment of the merits of the four brothers and in balancing their interests, she played a pivotal role.

In business operation, the four brothers cooperated with each other and went all out to run the business. Somebody once said that the cooperation of the brothers was a perfect combination. The eldest brother Liu Yongyan was the power center and it was him who brought up the idea of quails breeding. When the brothers were confronted with a major setback in the second year, it was the determination of the eldest brother that encouraged the other three. The second brother Liu Yongxing is an expert in techniques and management. Diligent and dependable, the third brother Chen Yuxin played a primary role in the pioneering period. Good at communications, the youngest brother Liu Yonghao is responsible for purchase and sales. With the joint efforts of the four brothers, the business of the breeding factory flourished. In 1986, the annual production of quail eggs was 150,000. They had established a sales network covering 16 provinces and municipalities, and even foreign countries and regions such as the former USSR. In 1988, their family assets stood at over 100 million yuan.

China's Feed King

In the 1980s, with the reform and opening up being carried out in rural areas of China, the livestock and poultry breeding industry was growing rapidly. At the same time, the demand for feed was also increasing sharply. China's feed market became an enticing big cake. However, those who shared this big cake were the feed enterprises from foreign countries. They dominate major shares of China's feed market. By the end of the 1980s, there had been over 30 Sino-foreign joint feed enterprises in Mainland China. Only Chia Tai Group earns hundreds of millions yuan of profits from the China market each year.

Early in 1985, seeing the huge opportunity in China's feed market, Liu Yongxing proposed to invest 2 million yuan to establish Hope Science and Technology Research Institute, focusing on researching and developing live pig feed, named Hope Feed. Meanwhile, they also invested 4 million yuan as scientific research fund, employing over 30 experts and professors as full-time or part-time scientific researchers. To conduct information exchange, they sent their employees to foreign countries and regions, including the Soviet Russia, the US, Poland, Australia, France, Hong Kong, etc. and often invited the well-known experts home. Huge resources were put into developing high quality and cost-effective live pig feed. For example, nearly 50 million yuan was invested to improve porket feed transformation rate and daily growth. Nearly a hundred prescriptions were trial-produced, and 33 prescriptions were selected for testing. Also in the same year, they invested 3 million yuan to establish the first feed plant as an experimental field.

In addition to giving full support in all aspects, the Liu brothers participated in the research themselves. The four brothers were so talented that they figured out many solutions in testing. They often used some cheap resources that were available in the local area to replace the high-cost raw materials that were hard to obtain, while ensuring that the quality of the feed matched foreign feeds. Fishmeal is a necessary ingredient in porket nutritious feeds. When the quality of the domestic-made fishmeal is poor, importing needs a lot of foreign exchange. Liu Yonghao thought of a substitute that was available everywhere in the local area — silkworm chrysalis, which are also rich in protein. Liu Yonghao and the researchers tried to mix some silkworm chrysalis and the fishmeal. After repeated tests, the result indicated the effect of this mixed feed was almost the same with that of fishmeal, while the purchase price of silkworm chrysalis was much lower. From the idea of silkworm chrysalis, they decided to use the milk liquid of the dairy companies as residual material, and apply scientific prescription to industrial milk powder to improve the porket feed transformation rate. The idea proved feasible and effective. The feed made this way not only fully complied with the nutritious standard and greatly improved transformation rate, but also reduced the cost significantly. On March 15, 1989, the Hope No. 1 Porket Feed was successfully developed. The experimental results indicated that all the parameters were very satisfactory. Having killed the remaining 100,000 quails in breeding, the Liu brothers started to fully embark on the feed industry.

Soon after being launched in market in the beginning of 1990, the porket feed was welcomed by farmers, with demand surpassing supply. Immediately, the Liu brothers invested 10 million yuan to conduct the second phase project — mature pig feed research and feed plant construction. The research went smoothly and was an immediate success. Fed on mature pig feed, the piglets, after weaning, would grow up within 3 or 4 months, which was 5 or 6 months shorter than the normal growth cycle. The expansion project of the feed plant was completed within three months, producing an annual output exceeding 100,000 tons. One year later, Hope brand No. 2, No. 3, No. 4, concentrated feed Hope extract, additive Hope Ling were developed successively and put into production. Among them, three scientific research items of Hope brand feed were listed on the National Spark Program for promotion and application.

Surviving fierce market competition, the Hope Feed quickly secured its position in feed market, and gradually expanded its market share. By January 1990, the monthly sales volume of the

Hope feed exceeded 40 million tons, surpassing Chengdu Chia Tai Co Ltd by a large margin. With the increasing sales volume, Hope Group quickly expanded its production capability to meet the market demand. In 1990, the sales volume of the Hope feed reached 60,000 tons, making Hope Group the largest feed manufacturer in terms of production and sales volumes in the Sichuan market. Just one year later, the Hope Group, with annual sales volume increasing to 100,000 tons, exceeded 100 million yuan in sales volume. Its profit and tax payment reached 10 million yuan, undoubtedly sat on top in feed market of the whole southwestern area of China.

In the spring of 1992, the Liu brothers decided to leave the South-West area and venture into the national market. For the first war, they chose to fight in the central part of China — Henan province. After hard negotiation and coordination with the local officials of Jun County, Henan province, they signed an agreement on joint operation of Jun County Hope Feed Plant. In April 1993, Jun County Hope Feed Plant was set up and put into production, whose products were well-received by farmers of Henan Province. One year later, the Hope feed produced in Jun County occupied the broad market in dozens of counties around. The sales income of the plant reached 100 million yuan, and the profit and tax payment exceeded 17 million yuan.

They then went eastward to Shanghai, southward to Guangdong and Guangxi, northward to Heilongjiang, Liaoning, and westward to Xinjiang. They successively established over 100 Hope Feed plants by means of sole proprietorship and joint venture in 29 provinces, autonomous regions, directly administered cities. The annual output reached billions of yuan, and there were over 30,000 sales outlets across the whole country. From the original Yuxin Fine Seed Plant to a giant feed producer who enjoys nationwide fame, the Hope Group is called China's Feed King.

New Noble of Forbes

The first separation

After Deng Xiaoping made his famous address during his inspection tour of south China in early 1992, China's economy stepped into the track of rapid development. The macro-economic environment provided opportunities for the private enterprises. In addition to the feed industry, many other areas have also taken on great investment potential. With the rapid expansion of the Hope Group's business, the Liu brothers had some divergences on operation concepts, investment directions and interest preference.

In that year, the eldest brother Liu Yongyan who graduated from the Chengdu Electronic Science and Technology University advised that they should expand business not only to other regions, but also to other industries, preferably high-tech industries. His proposal was approved in the board meeting. Thereafter, the Liu brothers divided their business into three parts, and the four of them chose to be in charge of a certain area according to their own interest and speciality: the eldest brother Liu Yongyan selected the high-tech area; the third brother Liu Yongmei was responsible for the existing industry and real estate; the second brother Liu Yongxing, together with the youngest one, Liu Yonghao, was in charge of setting up new feed plants and branch companies in other parts of the country. Thus, the four brothers started to run business separately under the single brand of Hope. At this moment, Liu Yongmei and Liu Yongxing decided to abandon the original agreement which gave them a larger part of shares, and divided the assets into four equal parts, with each brother holding 25% shares. For the first time, the four brothers clarified the boundary of property rights. They did not consider too much about their initial investment ratio. What matters was their brotherhood. Due to the generosity of the second and third brothers, the asset-dividing process went quite smoothly, without any disputes.

Immediately after, the Liu family was faced with another event — the third brother Chen Yuxin retreated from public sight. Before the opening of China People's Political Consultative Conference (CPPCC) of 1993, there were rumors that some private entrepreneurs would be elected as CPPCC commissioner, and the Sichuan government nominated Chen Yuxin to be the candidate. Chen Yuxin, preferred to be a doer rather than a symbolic figure, thus he suggested someone else from the family. Since the eldest brother Liu Yongyan was involved in scientific research, the second brother Liu Yongxing, a technical and managerial expert, was preoccupied with setting up branches companies all over the country, the fourth brother Liu Yonghao, with good public communication skills, became the most suitable choice. In late 1993, the third brother Chen Yuxin decided to give up his legal representative status. After the approval by the board of the directors, Liu Yonghao assumed this position. Since then, Liu Yonghao had been acting as the representative of the family to be interviewed by reporters. His three elder brothers fully supported him to in the building of his public image, and credited all the achievements to him, just as they did to Chen Yuxin in the past. By doing so, the three brothers all got on their own way, contented with their own work.

In 1993, Liu Yonghao became the CPPCC commissioner in the 8th CPPCC meeting, and at the end of the year was selected as the vice chairman of All-China Federation of Industry and Commerce. He became one of the representatives from private entrepreneurs to join the politics. Talented in public relations, Liu Yonghao was active in various social occasions, and as a result, the fame of the Hope Group has been greatly enhanced. Meanwhile, the second brother Liu Yongxing concentrated in expanding the business and his talent in production manage-ment and market expansion was utilized fully. The third brother Chen Yuxin managed the industry base of the family Liu in perfect order and the eldest brother Liu Yongyan made great progress in the high-tech research and development. The family Liu entered another golden period.

During the period of separate operation, since the four brothers had great commitments to their own positions, the Hope Group made significant progress in all areas. Closely coordinating with each other, the four brothers were able to exert their own special capabilities. Especially the second and the fourth brothers, they learned from each other and brought out the best in each other. Liu Yongxing was good at operational management, while Liu Yonghao was good in public communication, sales, and negotiation. The two brothers had clear divisions of work, with Liu Yongxing responsible for the internal affairs, and Liu Yonghao for external affairs. In the company, they shared one office, worked face to face, and made decisions together. When conducting negotiations, they spoke like one person. In April 1993, in just seven days, the two brothers signed four feed plant agreements in Hunan, Jiangxi and Hubei provinces. They built 10 profitable feed plants in the year of 1993. By the end of 1994, the Hope Group had set up 27 branches companies around the country. Liu Yongxing admitted afterwards that, he learned a lot from the youngest brother to improve his public communication skills during this period. At the same time, Liu Yonghao also gradually became familiar with the internal operation and management. This mutual improvement enabled the two brothers to run the enterprises independently.

In 1994, the second brother Liu Yongxing aired the opinion that the Hope Group had reached a mature stage in business expansion. The problem was how to carry out rapid replications. Binding two brothers in one project would be a huge human resource waste. Each of them should fully utilize their own special talent. Meanwhile, the overlapping operation also caused some interest disputes, and overlapping decision-making led to bewilderment of their employees. The original division of responsibilities should be replaced by the separate development model, which was more beneficial to the rapid development of the group.

The rapid expansion of the Hope Group around the whole country aroused concern from foreign feed magnates, who regarded the Hope Group as an emerging strong competitor in China market, and started taking containing measures. Meanwhile, tempted by Hope's success, some domestic enterprises also entered the feed industry. Therefore, the Hope Group had to face not only the pressures from the powerful foreign enterprises, but also the challenges from the new domestic competitors. Staying between Scylla and Charybdis, the Hope Group took quick actions to secure its position in fierce market competition. Therefore, in the board meeting in March 1995, the issue about separate operation of the second and the fourth brothers was put forward for discussion.

The second separation

In April 1995, it was decided through the negotiation of the Hope Group's board of directors that all the assets and funds of all the branches of the group were frozen, cash flow and appropriation were forbidden from April 13 that year. Meanwhile, they divided the assets of the group equally. Liu Yongyan and Liu Yongmei stayed where they had been. As for the new divisions, the second brother Liu Yongxing got the northeastern region and established the Hope East Company, while the fourth brother took the southwestern region, and set up the Hope South Company. At the same time, it was strictly stipulated that all the expenditure of the board members should not be reimbursed by the group's headquarters; that the inter-region expansion between the two regions was forbidden; the flow of the cadres between the two regions should be approved by both parties. Though the assets were divided, the Hope Group remained an integral group. In order to balance the power among them, the four brothers took four senior positions of the group respectively: the eldest brother Liu Yongyan assumed the office of chairman of the board of directors, the second brother Liu Yongxing took the position of the group's board chairman, the third brother Liu Yongmei served as general manager, and the fourth brother Liu Yonghao acted as president. To show their endorsement and sincerity about the above arrangement, the four brothers held a signing ceremony.

After the separation, the cooperation among the Liu brothers started to take on a different form. Business cooperation was based on clear boundary of property right. The four brothers determine the shares of the assets strictly according to their proportions of investment. Though they still ran their businesses under the same banner of the Hope Group, the four brothers began to develop their own business independently according to their own preferences.

Independent development

Today, the four brothers are respectively leading and developing four sub-group companies under the same brand of the Hope Group: the Continental Hope Group (Liu Yongyan), East Hope Group (Liu Yongxing), Huaxi Hope Group (Liu Yongmei) and New Hope Group (Liu Yonghao). With independent business operation, the four companies all maintain good development status.

Eldest Brother: Liu Yongyan

The eldest brother Liu Yongyan has committed himself to scientific and technological invention. In order to change the public image of Hope Group as a feed enterprise, which is deeply rooted in people's mind, he made a huge investment into his Continental Hope Group to embark on the high-tech industry, especially high-tech manufacture, in hope that his efforts would contribute to prosperity of the enterprise and the country. The group's two subsidiary manufacturing enterprises, namely Chengdu Hope Shenlan Transducer Manufacturing Company and Sichuan Hope Shenlan Air-condition Manufacturing Company were listed into the National Spark Program, the National High-Tech Enterprises, Sichuan Province Key High-Tech Projects and the West Region Key Development Strategy Projects, and have rapidly become the leading enterprises in the industry. Shenlan Transducer Company, especially had emerged as the top brand of transducer in China in the past three years, and had passed the CE certification of German Rhine TUV, getting the access license to the EU market. Shenlan Hope had become the largest central air-condition production base in the west of China. Its product, Shenlan Central Air-condition, was selected as one of the national key new products. Meanwhile, he had expanded his business into many other industrial areas including energy, chemicals, construction, tourism and financial investment, establishing over 30 subsidiary companies all around the country. The group had developed into a compre-hensive, strong, stable, and promising enterprise group.

Second Brother: Liu Yongxing

After separating with Liu Yonghao, the second brother Liu Yongxing established the headquarters of the East Hope Group in the Chengdu High-Tech Development Zone, which was moved to Shanghai Pudong in April 1999. The East Hope still focuses on feed production, mainly on expanding to the upstream and the downstream along the feed industry chain. By then, the Sichuan Hope Group would be able to rank top in the global feed industry. Apart from two feed companies in Vietnam, the East Hope Group led by him had 68 subsidiary companies in 16 provinces, cities and autonomous regions of China, whose main business area was feed production, together with some other related industries such as flour, food, bioengineering, fertilizer, electrolytic aluminum and investment. During the 20-year development in feed and investment areas, the group had been made rolling development by relying on its own capitals. Its investors include Mingsheng Bank, Mingsheng Insurance, Guangda Bank, Guangming Diary Industry, Sino-Korea BBQ Western Fastfood, Beijing Nanshan Skiing Field, etc. In order to build a world-competitive industry chain incorporating aluminum and electricity, the group had been engaging in a series of projects: electrolytic aluminum plant with an annual yield of 160,000 tons and a power generator set with an annual yield of 310,000 kilowatts in Liaocheng; two phases of construction of 500,000-ton electrolytic aluminum plant and auxiliary generator set and bio-engineering project in Baotou of Inner Mongolia; alumina project in Sanmenxia, Henan Province. East Hope Group had over 70 subsidiary companies across 16 provinces, cities and autonomous regions in China, with a total asset of billions of yuan, and nearly 10,000 employees. The Board Chairman Liu Yongxing had thus won a variety of social honors. In 1999 and 2000, Liu Yongxing, Board Chairman of East Hope Group, together with his brothers, was ranked by *Forbes* as the second most successful businessman in mainland China for two consecutive years. In 2000, Liu Yongxing was selected as one of the most influential 20 persons in future China by *Asia News Weekly*. In 2001, Liu Yongxing ranked first on the *Forbes* list, thus becoming the focus of the media and the society. In 2001, he was selected as one of the ten entrepreneurs attracting most attention by China's Entrepreneurs Association. In April 2002, East Hope was selected as an Advanced Enterprise in Terms of Economic Work in Pudong Urban Area by Pudong New District Urban Area

Work Commission. In December 2002, East Hope was selected as an outstanding enterprise in implementing Shanghai's first "Going Outside" strategy by Shanghai Municipal Foreign Economy and Trade Committee. In that same month, East Hope was selected as one of the Top Hundred Feed Enterprises of China by China's Feed Processing Association. In 2002, Liu Yongxing was selected as one of the 2002 CCTV Top Ten Persons in China's Economy and the Sohu 2001 Top Ten Finance and Economy Persons. In May 2003, East Hope was appraised as A Category of Tax-Paying Honest Organization in 2002 by Shanghai Municipal National Taxation Administration and Shanghai Municipal Local Taxation Administration. In September 2003, Liu Yongxing won the Medal for China's Glorious Cause because of his long-term support of the economic construction of the old, minority, border and poor regions and the Middle and West China. In September 2003, East Hope was appraised as the 39th largest enterprise in the year 2002 by All-China Federation of Industry and Commerce.

Third Brother: Liu Yongmei

The Huaxi Hope Group of the third eldest brother Liu Yongmei (Chen Yuxin) took over the feed industry in Sichuan which was left by the former Hope Group before the first separation in the early 1992 — mainly Xinjin Hope Feed Factory and the Feed Research Institute. At the same time, he also extended his business to real estate industry. By the end of 2004, Huaxi Hope Group had over 30 fully-funded, holding and joint stock enterprises, with 2 billion yuan in total assets, about 200 million yuan in the annual profits and tax, over 3 billion yuan in annual sales amount, and nearly 5,000 employees. In addition to its leading industry — the feed industry — it has made exploring investment in the modern agriculture, animal medicines and retailing areas. Currently, it has made an investment of 35 million yuan in building Guangan Wanqian Feed Company in Deng Xiaoping's hometown, which was regarded as the most excellent enterprise in the national feed industry, and had become the sample project of the glorious cause that allocate equal stress on both justice and profit, morality and practice. Moreover, the feed companies in Neijiang Wanqian, Guigang Wanqian, Baoding Wanqian and Luohe Wanqian had become the local star enterprises and good example projects. The Huaxi Hope Agriculture Science and Technology Research Institute built with an investment of 20 million yuan had been recognized as a feed enterprise research organization with the largest investment, the best environment, and the best equipment in the whole China. The Animal Pharmaceutics Enterprise established by cooperation with Chuqing Pig Breeding Scientific Research Institute that was the largest pig breeding research institute in China is going forward to the first phalanx of the same industry in China. Besides, as the sponsor shareholder of China Minsheng Banking Corporation (CMBC) and the second largest shareholder of New Hope Agriculture Joint Stock Corporation, Huaxi Hope Group also participated in industries including finance, chemical industry, diary, etc. with noticeable business performance. The Meihao Garden and Homestead International Hotel, which were co-invested with Continental Hope Group, was also engaging in tourism and restaurant industry. Having organized many large events since its opening in September 2003, the operation of the hotel was quite satisfactory. According to the enterprise medium and long term development strategy, Huaxi Hope Group would still focus on the feed industry, and would continue to explore in the new areas of modern agriculture, animal medicine and retailing industries.

Fourth Brother: Liu Yonghao

After taking over the South Company, the fourth brother Liu Yonghao changed its name into New Hope Company. After

separation from the Hope Group, the New Hope had made a
leap-forward development, for which Liu Yonghao made significant contribution. Liu Yonghao had always been showing a special interest in capital operation. He maintained that operating
an enterprise was comprised three steps: in product operation,
wealth is earned by cents; in brand operation wealth is earned by
ten cents; and in capital operation wealth is earned by dollars. So
after the separation, Liu Yonghao's main strategy was to carry
out capital operation, in order to achieve speedy expansion
through rapid capital collection. In early 1997, Liu Yonghao
used South Company's subsidiary enterprises as the base and
four enterprises as the main body to establish New Hope Group.
He was actively preparing to issue shares to be listed in
Shenzhen, to speed up the transition from a traditional family
enterprise to a modern enterprise, and a social-oriented joint
stock company as well. In 1998, the New Hope Group succeeded in issuing A shares in Shenzhen Securities Exchange, and
Liu Yonghao's 22-year-old daughter Liu Chang assumed the
office of board chairman. Three years later, the net assets of the
New Hope's listed company reached 1.2 billion yuan, 10 times
of the original one. The number of subsidiary companies had
increased from 4 to over 20. Meanwhile, the New Hope was also
the main sponsor and the largest shareholder of China
Mingsheng Banking Corporation, and also one of the main
sponsor shareholders of the Mingsheng Insurance Corporation.
The New Hope invested in establishing New Hope Investment
Company in which the World Bank Group International Finance
Company holds an investment of US$45 million, accounting
19.9% shares. Additionally, the New Hope Group was also a
major shareholder of Fujian Lianhua Trust and Investment Co
Ltd. Solid facts have proved the power of New Hope Group in
the finance industry. As for other business areas, New Hope
Diary was the largest diary industry consortium in West China
with 1.5 billion yuan in total assets, and 500,000 tons/year of

liquid milk processing capability. The New Hope Real Estate had developed over 1 million square meters of top- and middle-class urban residence. In the second half of 2000, the New Hope purchased Chengdu Qianjiang Chemical Industry Factory that was worth 73 million yuan, and aligned with World Bank Group International Finance Company and Chengdu Chemical Industry Group Company in building Chengdu Huarong Chemical Industry Co Ltd — the largest high-quality potassium hydroxide chemical enterprise in China. New Hope was the second largest phosphor and calcium producer in China. Currently, the New Hope Group has 35,000 employees, and its business covers many areas including feed, dairy and meat food processing, real estate, finance and investment, basic chemical industry, commercial logistics, international trade etc.

Conflicts and Flourish

When New Hope was listed, many confused New Hope Group with Hope Group, for they were similar in name. Even now, many Chinese are not clear about the differences of the two groups. Even the media carried reports that confused the assets and profits of the two groups, thinking that New Hope was the further development and surpassing of Hope Group. In this regard, New Hope Group might have the intention to publicize itself with the well-established fame of Hope Group. And the three senior brothers did not think it is proper. They held different opinion as for the issue of being listed, thinking that it was not a good time to be listed. They urged the fourth brother to be prudent and calculated the negative effect of being listed. However, the fourth brother Liu Yonghao insisted on having his New Hope listed and thus the other three felt it was hard to stop him. Nevertheless, the three elder brothers asked Liu Yonghao to strictly distinguish New Hope from Hope Group in public promotions, for the one being listed was not Hope

Group. Even till today, among the second-grade companies affiliated to Hope Group, New Hope Group is the only one who has more than ten listed subsidiaries.

Although the group was divided twice especially after the announcement on the replacement of legal representative that invited public conjecture was published in 1997, Hope Group still kept its momentum to develop. The names of the brothers became well known throughout China. Till 2004, the group became a national enterprise and one of the largest private enterprises in China, focusing on the industry of feed and covering more than 20 industries such as electricity, central air-conditioning system, construction, power, salt chemical industry, hotel, food, finance, real estate, biological industry, milk industry and aluminum industry. It has more than 200 factories and 50,000 employees. The annual sales income of the group stands at 30 billion yuan. The brand of Hope has become a well-known one in the country. The products of the group were successively awarded more than 20 medals such as No. 1 of the Top 500 Private-owned Enterprises in China, No. 1 of the Top 100 Private-owned Enterprises in Technological, Industrial and Trading Income, No.1 of the Top 100 Private-owned Manufacturing Enterprises in China and National Spark Model Enterprise etc. The four brothers are continuing Liu's brilliant legend in business in their respective fields.

Epilogue

The brothers were quite calm when they were listed in the *Forbes* global millionaires and ranked first in China.

Liu Yonghao smiled and said that he regarded fortune as "symbol". As he recalled, when somebody had 100,000 yuan, his desire for wealth is the strongest. When he has 10 million in his pocket, he feels he has everything. At this stage, people are most likely to lose momentum and fortunately Liu does not stop there. When his wealth increases to 1 billion, he would feel that he has only 0.1 billion in his pocket and the rest 0.9 billion seems to have nothing to do with him, which is exactly what happened to New Hope agriculture stock during its rapid development period when its capital increased from 0.1 billion to 1 billion. Today, Liu Yonghao, together with his brothers, possesses the wealth of more than 8 billion yuan. The stock assets exceed 1 billion. He confessed that money is nothing but a "symbol" for him. "Wealth is nothing for me and the accumulation of wealth means making contributions to the society", Liu Yonghao explains his endless pursuit of wealth, "many people lose momentum after getting rich and forget his responsibility for social development. I am not this type."

Liu Yongxing said that he does not feel excited of being listed in *Forbes*. He preferred a peaceful life. Wealth is not important, and what matters to him is how to change the environment around and improve the living status of the people. As an old Chinese saying goes, wealth did not last for more than three generations. So if the children get too much from the parents, they will forever remain where they are.

Although wealth is only a "symbol", the Liu brothers never stopped their pursuit for wealth. They constantly expanded the business scope, invested in new fields, pursued new points of profit growth, increased their wealth. However, can the snow-ball of wealth be rolled forward all along? Especially when the brothers are separated and focused on their own fields and regions, will the snow-ball disintegrate and eventually be vaporized? Wang Shi, president of Shenzhen Vanke Group, pointed out the key problems in business expansion during his meeting with the second brother Liu Yongxing: "It is comparatively easy for newly-emerged enterprises to complete a rapid initial accumulation. However, two billion yuan is a challenge, and five billion will be another one." According to Wang Shi, when Hope Group earns 2 billion, the Liu brothers should abandon the traditional family-oriented management pattern to overcome the challenge. Today, Hope Group is faced with the next challenge of 5 billion yuan. Wang Shi said, "In the face of this challenge, an enterprise will be seized by a sudden impulse to expand its business across regions and industries. Owing to the dispersion of fund and assets, many enterprises decline at the time." Wang Shi had made his point. What he said was precisely the present case with Hope Group. However, Wang Shi forgot a more important issue: the joint unity amongst people. Can the Liu brothers overcome the challenge?

In addition, there seems to be another less urgent problem for the brothers to ponder over. At present, except Liu Chang who is acting as board chairman of New Hope, the second generation of the Liu family are all studying in the US. As the Liu brothers are in their 50s and the eldest brother is nearly 60, the day of power transfer to the next generation is not too far away. Since divisions are inevitable even among the four Liu brothers, can the second generation stay united after taking over the Hope Group? The answers are to be revealed in time.

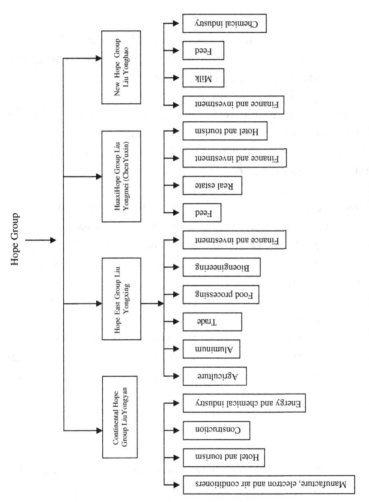

Figure 6.3:   Hope Group and Its Industrial Distribution

Case 10: Wanxiang Group — Three Axes of Family Enterprise: Family, Enterprise and Ownership

Introduction

On December 29, 2001, CCTV's Top Economic People of China, regarded as China's Oscars in the economic world, held a grand awards ceremony in Beijing Hotel.

"Carrying a legend of more than 20 years, he is an ever-green among Chinese private entrepreneurs. From a shabby workshop to partner of General Motor and Ford, and to the first Chinese private enterprise to purchase an overseas listed company, his legend not only shows us the past, but also reflects the future."

These were the words of Lu Guanqiu, chairman of the Wanxiang Group, when he was presented the award. He quit school at the age of 15, and worked as a blacksmith for some time. His story reflects the 20 years' history of reform and opening-up in China. From a small workshop which made farming tools to an outstanding township enterprise, his business grew steadily. Among numerous honors and titles, Lu Guanqiu succeeded in making his business an ever-green tree while many other private enterprises disappeared after a brief success. That was just a beginning. Lu Guanqiu made another legend as China joined the World Trade Organization (WTO). He became the first OEM manufacturer in mainland China to provide auto parts for General Motor. His capital investment extended to New York — the world's capital market center. On August 28, 2001, he initiated the purchase of UAL, which was listed in the NASDAQ stock exchange — becoming the first Chinese private enterprise to purchase an overseas listed company. At present, his business included two listed companies — UAL and "Wanxiang Qianchao". From a blacksmith to an entrepreneur in the context of globalization, a legendary story of a peasant was presented.

As an evergreen in private business, Lu Guanqiu had too many stories to tell, too many honors to promote, and too much experience to share. During the past 30 years, China's economy had witnessed numerous ups and downs. However, Lu Guanqiu has become steadier in his steps. From 2000 to 2004, his positions on the *Forbes* China rich list were respectively 6th, 7th, 4th, 4th and 5th. In 2005, he was ranked 5th on the Hurun's China rich list.

Hidden behind numerous honors and titles, some key issues still need to be addressed.

Firstly, the ownership issue. No one seems to be quite clear about the ownership of Wanxiang. Most people, including the employees, seem to believe that the business is experiencing an upturn, and this is not an urgent issue. Various evidence point to the fact that the property right boundary becomes blurred as it goes upward, especially when it reached the group level. Lu Guanqiu regards it a feature of Wanxiang. The property right belongs to the enterprise and to the employees as a whole. Everyone in Wanxiang is entitled to some privileges and preferences. Joint stocks are meant to be confusing. Just like people need privacy, the business should also enjoy "privacy". Lu Weiding, son of Lu Guanqiu as well as the CEO of Wanxiang, stated that "If everyone quarrels for a clear boundary of property right, no one will concentrate on work. And Wanxiang will decline as a result." Nevertheless, property right remains an issue to be solved.

The second issue is management handover. In choosing cars, Lu Guanqiu, the father, selected VOLVO S80 — the type with the highest safety index, while the son Lu Weiding chose BMW 745 for its speed. Their different choice of car reflected their personalities. In business operations, Lu Guanqiu favors safety and stability, while Lu Weiding values speed and courage. One is a conservative type, and the other is a typical "overseas returnee" who endorses modern management notion. Differences in management style contribute to mutual improvement, but pose challenges on succession.

Individual Contract System — Settling in Business

In 1945, Lu Guanqiu was born in a poor village in Ningwei, Zhejiang province. In 1960, due to poverty, Lu Guanqiu, without finishing his junior high school education, went to a blacksmith's store to be an apprentice. Before finishing his apprenticeship, a 3-year natural disaster set in. All of the enterprises and institutions had to trim staff. With a rural registered permanent residence, Lu Guanqiu had to go back home. But during these years of study, a special feeling towards the mechanical equipment production had already grow in his heart. Although he was fired, Lu Guanqiu realized that the only way to change the fate of poverty is to initiate industries. When he saw that the villagers had to mill flour in the town as far as 6 to 7 miles from their village, he decided to establish his own grain processing plant to resolve their inconvenience. With the support of his family, he raised about 3,000 yuan to purchase a mill and a rice polisher to establish an unregistered rice and flour processing plant. This plant was soon forced to close, under the reason of "cutting off the capitalists' tails". But before long, Lu Guanqiu seized the opportunity of "stopping production to make revolution", opening a blacksmith store to make shovels and hooks as well as repair bicycles for the farmers.

A turning point for Lu Guanqiu appeared in 1969, when Ningwei Commune Agricultural Repair Plant wanted to find a person to take it over because of its poor management. Lu Guanqiu decided to have a try. He sold all his property and raised about 4,000 yuan to invest into this repair plant. Since then, he stepped on the road of starting up. Depending on the workshop production mode and upholding the principle of choosing the profitable goods to produce, he began to make

ploughs, iron harrows and gimbals etc. His company struggled for survival and development in the cracks of the state-
owned economy. In the planned economy of that time, the
supplies of the materials and the sales of the products had targets. However, it is impossible for a communal enterprise to
make profits without these "plans".

In 1979, the reform and opening policies were implemented.
At the time when the township and village enterprises began to
take shape, Lu Guanqiu had already taken a lead due to his business experience accumulated in the previous years. At that time,
his company had hired about 40 employees. Besides the gimbals,
its products ranged from chains to agricultural equipments. In
the same year, Lu Guanqiu transformed his production from
multi-dimensional products to specialized products of gimbals.
In 1979 when the whole nation run short of energy supply, the
auto manufacturing industry shrank due to the insufficiency of
crude oil. Many key auto parts plants sequentially began to
change their lines of production. Thus, the demands for gimbals
were also decreasing rapidly. The gimbals plants of Lu Guanqiu
entered its difficult times. But Lu Guanqiu saw important information on the newspaper that in the 1981 National Economic
Plan, the freight target of the automobile would reach 540 million
tons. Therefore, there would be great demands for automobiles
and trucks. As an important auto component, the need for gimbals would also increase rapidly. As a result, Lu Guanqiu chose
gimbals as his main products, and abandoned the production of
the other products.

Joint Stock System — A Phase of Rapid Development

After 1979, Lu Guanqiu started the specialized production of
the gimbals. At that time, the Machinery Industry Ministry prepared to regulate the manufacturers of the gimbals, choosing 3
best of the 50 plants around the nation as the designated gimbals

suppliers. This was supposed to be the best opportunity for the gimbals plants to make a great progress, but since Lu Guanqiu's company was a township enterprise rather than a state-owned one, he was not qualified to compete for the deal. However, Lu Guanqiu strived to grasp this opportunity. He thought out a good idea: he secretly obtained the rectification document and based on its 400 items, he reformed his plant. The most difficult problem was the quality of the products. Therefore, Lu Guanqiu made great efforts to improve the quality of his products. In the early autumn of 1980, Lu Guanqiu assembled all the middle-level cadres and all his employees for a meeting in front of 30,000 sets of inferior gimbals. These inferior gimbals were collected by Lu Guanqiu from 28 provinces, cities and municipalities, based on the customers' opinions and his own experiences during the production. Lu Guanqiu made a breakthrough in quality by studying those inferior products. In 1980, his products had been ranked as the number one, with a mark as high as 99.4, in the national evaluation. Therefore, his company was selected as one of the three designated manufacturers of the gimbals, which won a place for his gimbals plant transformed from a township enterprise.

The contract system adopted in the 1980s did grant the private enterprises some degree of autonomy. However, the local government was still the "superior" in name. The so-called "management fee" was a big burden. In 1988, Lu Guanqiu divided the stock right. 7.5 million yuan was taken out of the 15 million yuan of net asset to be the government stock share. By so doing, the government shifted its status from a "superior" to a "shareholder". Without a superior, the enterprise obtained more independence in decision-making. Incurring no disputes, Lu Guanqiu solved the hardest problem of "red hat" enterprises successfully.

The years of 1979 to 1989 were the ten golden years of Wanxiang, during which the yearly income of the employees increased by six times, and yearly benefits increased by 40%, ranking the top in national auto parts industry.

Collectivized Management, Double-Track Property Right

In the 1990s, Lu Guanqiu and his Wanxiang came into the third stage of development, i.e., implementing "collectivizing the enterprise and internationalizing the operations". Wanxiang Group was formally established. The board was set up in 1994 to carry out corporation reforms in the subsidiaries, enabling the subsidiaries to become independent corporations directly facing the market competitions. Therefore, the organizational structure of "big outside and small inside" was formed, which helped to reduce the span of control and enhance the growth.

In 1994, Wanxiang Qianchao was listed in Shenzhen Stock Exchange, became the first township and public company that had ever been listed. At the same time, Wanxiang had organized its company in US.

Since 1996, Wanxiang group began to reorganize its assets. Wanxiang Qianchao — the listed subsidiary of Wanxiang Group — had acquired 60% of seven auto parts companies, including mechanism company, special bearing company, automobile bearing company and transmission shaft company, etc., most of which were growing companies with about hundreds of million yuan of sales income and tens of million yuan of profits. Since then Wanxiang began to step into a rapid development stage.

In August 1997, General Motors formally signed a supply contract with Wanxiang. Wanxiang thus became the first Chinese auto parts company that had entered the US main engine market.

On August 28, 2001, Wanxiang group successfully purchased UAI, a listed company on NASDAQ, creating a new history of Chinese township enterprise.

In 2001, Wanxiang group bought stock shares of Minsheng Insurance, which was the first Chinese insurance company organized mainly by civilian capitals. Wanxiang possessed about one-fifth of the total stocks. At the same time, through its solely holding subsidiary — Wanxiang American Corporation — Wanxiang group purchased the stock shares of Horton Insurance Inc which was the biggest un-listed insurance company in the US. On April 14, 2001, Wanxiang-Horton Insurance Group Inc was founded in Chicago, US, with 51% of its stock shares obtained by Wanxiang group with the form of providing intangible assets. In the joint venture company, Horton Insurance Group Inc was responsible for providing early investment with cash, and the "management supports" were given by Wanxiang American Corporation. After the Chinese insurance license was approved and the business went on the right track, Wanxiang American Corporation possessed 51% of the total assets by providing intangible assets.

In 2002, after 10 years of hard work and approval by 3 vice premiers, Wanxiang had eventually possessed its first financing company in Zhejiang province. Wanxiang Holding, Wanxiang Qianchao and Wanxiang Group had respectively invested 40%, 30% and 30% to organize Wanxiang Financing Company. With the exception of personal savings and other business forbidden by government, this financing company has all the functions of commercial banks, including banking, securities, entrusting, leasing, insurance agency, and financing consultation etc. The set-up of financing company had provided great support for Wanxiang for its involvement in the international financial operations.

In order to realize the strategy of globalization, Wanxiang had purchased 20% stock shares of the American listed company UAI, becoming its largest stockholder. By then, Wanxiang had owned 26 companies in eight foreign countries, including the US, Britain, Germany, and Canada. Most of them were solely held or controlled by Wanxiang. This was not the first time for

Wanxiang to purchase an overseas company. It spent US$420,000 buying the brand, technology patent, equipment, and customer net of Scheele, thus leading to an additional US$5 million in sales volume in the US market. Lu Guanqiu had accomplished a stride forward from "international marketing" and "international production" to "international resources allocation".

Lu Weiding: Taking Charge of 12 Billion Dollars at 23

As the only son of Lu Guanqiu, Lu Weiding, 23 years old then, replaced his father as the president of Wanxiang Group in 1994. After Wanxiang Qianchao was listed and Wanxiang Company in the US was established, it was Sr. Lu, rather than Jr. Lu, who took charge of everything in the group. During the years, Lu Guanqiu had been playing the role of a father, an educator, a cooperator and a mentor. According to Lu Guanqiu, he focused primarily on two things: one was the major direction. Any project that had not been listed in the plans should be thoroughly studied and carried out prudently. The other thing he focused on was the review of feasibility plans. However, he was not involved with the details, to avoid being confused and entangled.

Both Lu Guanqiu and the employees of the group confessed that the frequent actions in the capital operation level had a direct relation with the emergence of Lu Weiding as a real decision-maker. Crazy about riding motorcycles fast on the streets, Jr. Lu was hardly a good boy in his teens. He did not finish his high school course and was then sent to a college in Singapore by his father, majoring in business administration. Lu returned half a year later to work as a machine maintainer and fleet manager in the group.

Retaining is harder than winning. As the second generation of the family enterprise, Jr. Lu was brave enough to bear the responsibility of creating fortune. He was steady and dependable, and had his own way of judging situations. Aware that his position had been bestowed by his father, he tried even harder to prove his own value. Lu Weiding said, "The founder created the successes in the past, work hard for now, and will make new achievements in the future. Benefiting from the foundation they have made, we should achieve more."

He paid much attention to the control of financial risks. Lu appointed the financial managers of all the units under the group, established a unified financial system, and set up a 20-person supervision team to audit and review the accounts of every factory. In order to eliminate the pressure caused by cost increase, Lu put forward his own "Bring-It-Here-Ism". He employed two experts retired from Toyota to reconstruct the logistics and demand-supply flow, and thus eliminated the decrease of product profit margin by speeding up turnover. In practical operation, Sr. Lu has been bold, energetic and speedy. His comprehensive thinking, bold ideas and high spirit well complemented his father.

Lu Weiding, who is now the man at the wheel, often disagrees with the investment philosophy of "prudence and concession" upheld by his father. The 34-year-old Lu has been the president of Wanxiang Group for more than 10 years, and he had learned to keep low-profile as his father did. The difference is that Lu Guanqiu is frank and straightforward, and his son tends to be graceful and displomatic when facing the external world.

Challenges for Wanxiang

From the initial seven persons, 4,000 yuan and an iron workshop of 84 square meters in 1969, Wanxiang had developed into a big diversified enterprise with the annual taking of 25.2 billion yuan in 2005 and tens of thousand of employees. The development of Wanxiang could be summarized as "10 times' increase in total assets within 10 years". During the 1970s, Wanxiang had real-ized the goals of daily profit reaching 10,000 yuan and the high-est income of the employee reaching 10,000 yuan. During the 1980s, Wanxiang realized the goals of daily profit reaching 100,000 and the highest profit of the employee reaching 100,000 yuan. During the 1990s, Wanxiang realized the goals of daily profit reaching 1 million yuan, and the highest income of the employee reaching 1 million yuan. But to 2010, the goals of Wanxiang would become "daily profit reaching 10 million yuan, and the highest income of the employee reaching 10 mil-lion yuan". Trying to become the top 1,000 or the top 500 enterprises in the world, Wanxiang would undoubtedly face many challenges coming from both inside and outside.

The first challenge is the property rights

Currently, Wanxiang is perceived as a family enterprise. When *Forbes* listed the Chinese rich, they took Wanxiang as the personal property of Lu Guanqiu and his family. But in theory, Wanxiang Group is a collective enterprise in nature, whose property rights belong to the employees as a whole. And Lu Guanqiu took only his share of stock right. In this sense, it was controversial to attribute all the properties to Lu Guanqiu. Wanxiang had adopted the employee stock option scheme to stimulate the enthusiasm among the employees, but this system has not been perfectly implemented. Specifically speaking, the distribution of the stock shares was not clear. From the aspect of control rights, Wanxiang Group had been in tight control in the hands of the Lu family. But from the aspect of the property rights, the stock shares belonging to Lu Guanqiu is not enough to enable him to take the controlling position in the enterprise. Although he was the biggest stockholder, his shares only account for 0.19% of the total shares. The property rights of Wanxiang have the inherent historical features of the Chinese civilian-owned enterprises.

Due to the historical reasons, in the legal sense, Wanxiang's asset which was valued at nearly 10 billion yuan had actually no specific owners. Currently Wanxiang is still held tightly in the hands of Lu Guanqiu and his son Lu Weiding also has strong power over Wangxiang. What would happen after the distribution of the property rights? It could be said that if there was no Lu Guanqiu, then there would be no Wanxiang, but it is also not reasonable to say that all the assets of Wanxiang belong to Lu Guanqiu and his son. The problem of ownership and property right is a major issue of Wanxiang.

The second challenge is the succession problem of Wanxiang. Till 2004, Lu Guanqiu had been at the age of 60. Following Chinese traditions, Lu Guanqiu have pushed his son to the president position of Wanxiang Group, as his successor. Lu Weiding, born in 1971, is the only son of Lu Guanqiu. He entered Wanxiang at an early age, and had moved from one position to another. At the end of 1992, he assumed the position of vice president. And in 1994, he became the president of the group. Afterwards, he successively went to US, Singapore, and Tsinghua University to receive further education. In 1999, he came back to the position of president. Different from the old generations, who had founded their business through hard work, Lu Weiding was much better at capital management and investment. In November 2003, Lu Weiding was chosen by *Times* and American World News Network to be one of the most influential 20 entrepreneurs in the world. The other Chinese entrepreneur on the list was Li Zeju. Lu Weiding was not immune to mistakes, especially when pushing some new reform measures. When Lu Weiding first took over Wanxiang, he had conflicts with some old staff. At that time, Lu Weiding learned from many international big enterprises, and set up four big divisions to reorganize Wanxiang. The original subsidiaries were merged into these divisions to be managed by them. Lu Weiding appointed young or middle-aged business cadre men, i.e., the young turks, to be general managers of the divisions. The general managers of the subsidiaries and sub-subsidiaries were exclusively the old staff who accompanied Lu Guanqiu in the pioneer period. Due to their seniority, the old staff would not follow the report chain: They directly reported to Lu Guanqiu. Such behaviors upset the group's internal relations. As a result, Lu Weiding withdrew from Wanxiang from 1997 to 1999. It was not until the year 1999 when Wanxiang readjusted its organizational structure that Lu Weiding went back as the president of Wanxiang Group.

Besides his son Lu Weiding, Lu Guanqiu also had a son-in-law named Ni Pin, who was also very gifted and capable. As the vice president of Wanxiang, Ni Pin was in charge of the oversea development of Wanxiang. Ni Pin holds a MBA from Zhejiang University. In 1989 when he was appointed to work in the Zhejiang Social Science Association, he came to Wanxiang for training. In 1990, he went to the US to study for a doctoral degree. When Lu Guanqiu learned about it, he asked Ni Pin to work for his company to set up Wanxiang American Corporation. Due to the strict foreign exchange control. Ni Pin had to use his scholarship as original startup capital to set up Wanxiang American Corporation. Under the operation of Ni Pin, Wanxiang American Corporation rapidly progressed. When it registered in 1993, it had capital of less than $1 million. In 1995, its sales reached $3.5 million. Till 1997, its sales had broken through $20 million. It reached $35 million in 1998. By the end of 2001, it had been as much as $100 million. In the second year of establishment, the company got the order form from General Motors. Currently, Wanxiang American Corporation has already infiltrated into the American mainstream society, and had business relationship with many American famous enterprises. Besides US, Wanxiang has already established its marketing network in Canada, Britain, Germany, Italy, French and seven South American countries. At that time, the Foreign

Trading Minister Long Yongtu praised the outstanding accomplishments made by Wanxiang. Moreover, Huang Jiabi, the Chinese consul general in Chicago, also acclaimed Wanxiang American Corporation as a Chinese enterprise which had undergone the most rapid progress and possessed the most perfect management system in the mid-west US. The former US president Bill Clinton and vice-president Al Gore also had received and entertained Ni Pin. In 1996, as the representative of the preeminent Chinese-Americans, Ni Pin was invited to the White House. In 1999, he was chosen as the chairman of the Chinese enterprise sodality in the mid-west US. In the same year, he was granted the "Preeminence Award" by the Chinese-American Chambers. In 1998, during his visit to the US, former Premier Zhu Rongji received Ni Pin. When inspecting Wanxiang, Foreign Minister Li Zhaoxing complimented the accomplishments achieved by Wanxiang American Corporation, which had not only contributed to the American economy, but also contributed a lot to the economic cooperation as well as the friendship between the two countries. In 2001, Ni Pin became world-renowned because of the successful acquisition of UAI Company. Illinois, where Wanxiang American Corporation is located, named the day of purchase as the "Day of Wanxiang". All of the accomplishments made by Ni Pin had proven his outstanding capability in business management and international operations. Even Lu Guanqiu himself had announced publicly that Ni Pin was more outstanding. Therefore, Ni Pin had already become an important person in the future development of Wanxiang.

Consequently, succession had became a challenge for Lu Guanqiu. With the possibility of conflict, Lu Guanqiu had expressed that this problem might be solved by means of dividing family property. This however, would certainly weaken the competitiveness of Wanxiang. It would be a painful decision to make. Meanwhile, Lu Guanqiu has ever stated it clearly in public that if there emerged a better choice, he would have Lu Weiding replaced as the successor.

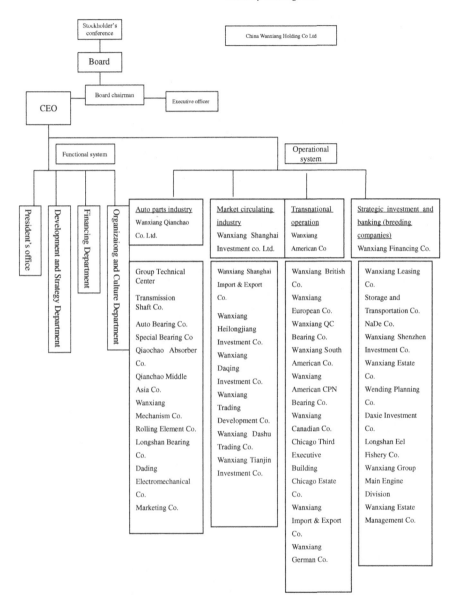

Figure 6.4: Structure of China Wanxiang Holding Co Ltd

7

Breakthrough of Chinese Family Enterprises

Due to various reasons, the culling ratio of Chinese family enterprises is rather high in China. Since the implementation of the open-door policy and reform policy, only 20%–30% of the total number of Chinese family enterprises survived. In the context of internationalization, the business has become much more competitive. It is essential for family enterprise to re-think about how to improve their competitiveness. The number of family enterprises keeps growing, and they contribute to almost half of the national economy. What is not in accordance with their position is that the family enterprises are still far from maturity, and therefore only few of them have the capability to win and sustain in the competitive markets. It is a necessity to re-examine the family enterprises in their current form.

With the ongoing opening and reform policy and the deepening of the economic system reform, the general economic condition in China has undergone great improvement, which has provided a favorable policy environment for the family enterprises. It could be said that Chinese family enterprises are facing the springtime for their development. The current development of the family enterprises has reflected the changes of the Chinese politics, economy and culture over time. It is a real challenge for the family enterprises to think about how to make steady and rapid progress in the new economic environment. Referring to the experiences and lessons from overseas Chinese family enterprises, this chapter will summarize the three dimension problems faced by the Chinese family enterprises and hopefully help the family enterprises to avoid the winding courses and enable them to realize their dream of making the family enterprises big and strong and sustainable over generations.

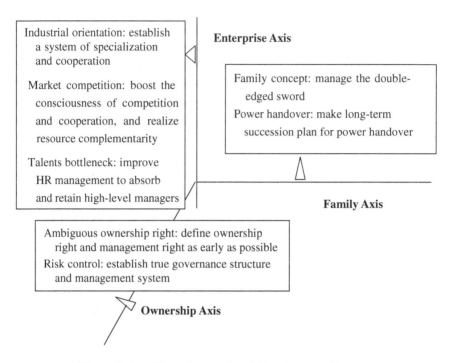

Figure 7.1:   Three-Dimensional Development Pattern

The Axis of Family

Family Concept — Manage the Double-Edged Sword

It was based on the strong family concept that many family enterprises made their success, such as the Ford family and Lee Kum Kee, whose wealth last for more than five generations. However, others were ruined in family conflicts, like Yeo Hiap Seng, or engulfed in the struggle for power, like Porsche and the Yellow River Group. Family concept is a double-edged sword, which may strengthen the competitive advantages of enterprises, or sometimes set them in crises. Nepotism will hinder the development of enterprises, which could be seen in the following areas: firstly, since the family enterprises attach too much importance to their personal interests, they are reluctant to provide more funds to research and development, and therefore there is little innovation and breakthrough in technology and management which restrict the enterprises to acclimatize themselves to the rapidly changing environment. Secondly, due to the family relations, the organizational structure and relationships within enterprises would become much more complicated, which would prohibit the information exchanges and coordination within the enterprises. Thirdly, family enterprises usually would exclude the professional talents from outside of the families to take up key positions. This is due to the low trust of outsiders and small talent pool. The professional manager market is far from maturity. Therefore, it is risky to assign management positions, especially the key positions, to the non-family members. In the long run, if Chinese enterprises only take family interests into account and appoint unqualified family members to the key positions, they may inhibit the long-term development of the companies. By so doing, the family enterprises would not get the optimized human resources while the motivation and commitment of the non-family employees might be negatively affected.

Nonetheless, the familism structure is not deemed to be inefficient. Under certain circumstances, it could be very efficient and competitive. In particular conditions, it could have more advantages, because the participation of family members enables the enterprise to organize resources with the lowest costs; it is much easier for the family members to establish common goals, pursue common interests and align cooperative actions; the nature of family enterprises could help to ensure the authority of the leadership and thus enhance the internal cohesion. Consequently, as a type of enterprise system, familism could fit well in the initial stage of the enterprises.

From the survey and analysis on the formation and development history of Chinese family enterprises, one can find that at certain stages (usually at the initial stage) the adoption of familism had helped rather than prohibited the development of some Chinese family enterprises. As a matter of fact, there is no almighty management structure in the world. At different developmental stages, under different social conditions, with different industrial characteristics, there is often one suitable management structure. As long as the family enterprises could fit well to the requirements of business conditions, the nature of the family enterprises would not necessarily hold back the development and expansion of the enterprises. Therefore, in the aspect of management reform, Chinese family enterprises could refer to the following suggestions:

1.   The necessity to adopt familism at the initial stage

The main features of the family management system are family and kinship. During the course of the family management, the property heritage relations are determined by the family relations. Key positions are usually assigned to the family members, the leading powers are centralized and the decision-making process is autocratic. Leadership in Chinese family enterprises are often based on blood relations. The underlying intention is at attempt to establish a natural confidence based on kinship to ensure the safety of the enterprise property.

Most of the initial funds of family enterprises come from family property or from a few relatives. This condition predetermines the limited resources, and the tight control held by the main investors and founders over the ownership, management personnel administration, in virtue of the stability and low cost of the operation. In this way, through fast decision-making and fast response to market opportunity, the family enterprises, with the characteristics of high flexibility and efficiency, could reduce the operational risks and achieve rapid growth. Furthermore, high unification and centralization also makes it easier for the decision-maker to command the first-hand information and therefore master the overall situation.

Under the conditions that the market economic order and legal system are far from consummated, with limited recourses, authoritative management could be seen as a more efficient and practical way of administration at the initial stages of enterprise development and capital accumulation.

2.   De-emphasize familism when entering the expansion stage

At the initial stage, with a small scale, a limited market and comparatively disadvantaged managerial techniques, the enterprise usually adopts a way of extensive operation, under which loyalty and obedience are more useful than the expertise and regulated operations. In this period, the scale effect of the family enterprises is not fully exerted, and the marginal efficiency is progressively increasing instead of decreasing.

With the expansion of the enterprises, the elements of the market competition are still undergoing changes. The natural closure to the outside world has prohibited the family enterprises from fully utilizing their external resources. For example, fund-raising, which is the key point for the expansion in both business scale and markets, is much easier for public companies than for family enterprises,.

Under special circumstances, family enterprises could become an efficient economic organization as the loyalty among the family members could reduce the communication costs and the family ethics could simplify the management control mechanism. However, when the limited resources and the low capability of the family members cause a higher transaction costs and a lower competitiveness than those non-family enterprises, then the family enterprise system would become inefficient. It is a common phenomenon that due to the close kinship, the family regulations often could not be used to restrain the rule-breaking behaviors and the factions, which may make the enterprise suffer a great loss. When the family enterprises enter the phase of expansion, it is inevitable that they will have to reform their management system.

3. Establish a proper and real organizational structure

The organizational structure of the family enterprises is essentially not established. It is only an ostensible phenomenon that the family enterprises also have the modern enterprise organizational structure. In practice, there is one simple way to judge whether one company is a family enterprise or not, i.e., to observe the final decision-making power. The most obvious indication of a family enterprise is that the decision-making power of operational management are tightly controlled by the "family patriarch", i.e., a centralized leadership. Many enterprises would assign high management positions to those professionals hired from outside, but it is often impossible for them to transfer the final decision-making power to those outsiders. In the Chinese family enterprises, the existing management structure could be changed at the will of the founders. The development of the enterprise requires a suitable organizational structure that could enable the established economic entity to operate well. Therefore, the family enterprises should adopt the pattern of professional management. During the course of the professional management, the enterprise should gradually overcome the negative effects of the familism pattern to the enterprise. The most prominent and pivotal problem lays in the separation of management rights from proprietorship, i.e., to employ non-family professional managers to be the CEO to administrate the enterprise businesses. Many family enterprises pluck up their courage to open their doors and accept the non-family members to carry out professional management. Some listed Chinese family enterprises have already implemented professional management. When entering the phase of expansion, the enterprises should establish a set of operational mechanism with high efficiency, and should utilize the power of organizational structure to overcome the shortcomings in the management systems. The stockholders meeting, the board and the supervision board of the modern enterprise system should form an effective mechanism in governing the decision-making and internal power balance.

4.   Move from family ethics to professional ethics

The enterprise culture of Chinese family enterprises often takes family as its core, and family ethics as its moral criterion. Many family enterprises have ostensibly exceeded the management pattern of family enterprises, but their nature is still entangled with the complicated family relations. Why is it not possible for family enterprises to expand to a large scale? Many people attribute it to familism, which attaches too much importance to nepotism and loyalty rather than talents. And the closure of the family enterprises has cut many channels to absorb talents. At the same time, the barriers in the family enterprises also weaken the cohesion of the non-family employees, which leads to "internal breeding", "denominationalism" and "circle culture" within the enterprises. The closed nature of the enterprises precludes the establishment of the systematic management pattern in the enterprise, but rather promotes the dependence on the emotions and relations, which would eventually weaken the "system consciousness" of the enterprise's managers.

In fact, all of these could be attributed to cultural impact. Both the family enterprises and their founders have been under the influence of cultures. They learn from the cultures and on contrary they are restrained by the cultures. Chinese family enterprises have both advantages and disadvantages. They must on one hard walk their own way of familism and on the other hand integrate Western management concepts into practice. In this sense, Chinese family enterprises need to be innovative to exploit the advantages of familism and modern management.

5. Develop shared management and governance

Experts on property rights believe that rights should be transferred to those who have the capability to perform and deliver. They should be motivated to use power to solicit cooperation. The implementation of the employee stock option scheme would help to realize the unification of the employees' interests, collective interests and family interests, and would help to set up an efficient management and governance structure.

The reorganization and re-structuring of enterprise stock holding has been regarded as the core of the "third time starting up". Liu Yongxing, ranking second in the *Forbes* top 50 successful businessmen in mainland China, faced the challenge of distribution of shares instead of delegation of power. The property rights of Hope Group are still centralized. With the exception that as a listed company New Hope Group has some circulating stocks, the rest are all sole property rights. But this might not be healthy for the further development of the enterprises. Lu Guanqiu, the board chairman of another large civilian-run enterprise — Wan Xiang Group — is relatively relaxed as Wan Xiang Group has already implemented the employee stock option scheme. As the decision-maker of the enterprise, Lu Guanqiu does not directly participate in the operational activities. He said that: "When the size of enterprise is still small, the roles of decision maker, manager and stockholder could be integrated. But after the enterprise is expanded and decentralized, the management must be changed. Sharing stocks to employees could help to motivate employees."

One feature of Chinese family enterprises is the introduction of employee stock option scheme. The family enterprises have formulated varieties of the stock holding, and have exercised the conception of "shared management" in the ownership arrangements. The employee stock option scheme is to reform the enterprise system in the precondition that the nature of the family enterprises would not be changed. By so doing, the family strength would be united with the professional strength.

Power Handover — Make Long-Term Plan for Succession

Although 80%–90% of the enterprises can be classified as family enterprises, only 70% of them can survive for one generation, 30% for two generations and 15% for more than three generations. What are the reasons for the short life span? Power handover is one of the primary reasons. Once an enterprise is turned from an individual ownership to a shared ownership, the power handover becomes a focus of attention. Passing on a profitable and well-performing company to the leader of a new generation is a target that the members strive for. An ideal process of the power handover is a process to realize shared visions. The handover is a process of integrating the dreams of both generations, and finding ways to put them into action.

Some family enterprises have plans for succession and some do not. Although there are different ways of power handover, it is often a very vulnerable and crucial moment for family enterprises. Any fault in the process may result in the loss of the control right by the family and consequently may become a turning point for the enterprise from zenith to valley. As John Wood, professor of KGSM, Northwestern University of US pointed out, 80% of the family enterprises can hardly be handed over to the second generation, whereas only 13% of all the family enterprises are still controlled by the third generation of the family. Those enterprises that failed to be passed to the second and the third generation have either gone bankrupt because of improper management, been forced to be sold to rivals or closed down permanently.

As Joachim Schwartz, professor of International Institute for Management Development in Switzerland said, the failure of power handover from the first generation to the next can be attributed to the founders to some extent. He said, "They are not willing to fade out from the power core, and they are not fully aware of the things they should do in grooming the successors." As Schwartz described, the second generation often end with disappointing and unexpected results.

The founders of Chinese family enterprises should clearly realize that their power has to be handed over sooner or later, which is an inevitable fact. However, some founders are not willing to give up the power with the worry that their children are not competent enough to shoulder the responsibility, and thus are reluctant to make long-term planning for power handover. Once the founders face sudden death or emergencies, the family enterprises will suffer from succession crisis and may lead to huge impact on business or even business failure.

The succession planning is not an easy case and involves some complicated process and considerations. The establishment of the potential successor's position requires a period of time. On the one hand, he needs recognition, trust and support from family members, senior followers, employees, suppliers, customers and banks, which is a long process. Potential successors need to receive training with the guidance of detailed plans. On the other hand, potential successors need time to penetrate and integrate into the enterprises.

Mao Lixiang, the managing director of Ningbo Fotile Kitchen Ware Co Ltd, is the founder of a typical family enterprise. He personally created the "World's Top Firing Gun". When talking about power handover of family enterprises, Mao took the example of Fotile and said that first of all, family-oriented management must be adopted in the initial stages. Secondly, the tone of family-oriented management must be decresed when the enterprises grow and expand. Thirdly, it is impossible to completely disgard family-oriented management in the current stage of China as the team of competent professional managers is far from being mature in China. In practice, Mao and his sons agree that family members should not enter the management team any longer. Moreover, he excluded his only daughter from the managerial circle of Fotile. As a mere shareholder, she does not participate in the operations of the company. Nevertheless, the complete control of decision-making rights at the top level of the company by the core members of the family should be guaranteed. He resolves the succession planning with the following considerations; first of all, set up the selection criteria. The criterion for selecting a family member as the candidate should focus on talent, whereas the criterion for selecting people outside the family should focus on virtue. The second factor is the timing and reason for succession. The power handover should be regarded as a strategic step and opportunity for the business development. In particular, the enterprises in growth stage should attach more importance to the strategic purpose of succession particularly when they are faced with complex and changing environment. The third factor is the procedures and process of power handover. For those in power, their changing roles are in this sequence: single owner → controller of highest power → consigner → advisor. For the successors, their changing roles are in such sequence: no role → assistant → manager → key decision-maker. In the process of power handover, how the founders should resign at an appropriate time and adjust their state of mind is crucial not only for the mental and physical health of the founders themselves, but also for the success of the power handover. The case of Fotile is a good example for Chinese family enterprises.

Put in a simple way, in order to solve the problem of succession, the founders of family enterprises should consider it a priority to develop the potential successor and manage the process of power handover with proper procedures and plans. In addition, they have to overcome the psychological block and hand over the power early. If their children are not suitable to be the candidates of successor, they should look for and train successors outside the family to facilitate the development of the family cause.

The Axis of Ownership

Define the Ownership Right and Management Right as Early as Possible

Generally speaking, China's family enterprises are still in their infancy. The founders rely on their experiences to run the enterprises. With luck and chance, the enterprises are provided with unprecedented opportunities for development. However, when the enterprises grow bigger and stronger, the bottleneck problem plaguing them is often the lack of proper management. The failure to adopt the right approach of management may restrict the further development of the enterprises or even result in evident losses and bankruptcy. Generally, Chinese enterprises at present can hardly rival the Western enterprises in their management. They have just started to pay more attention to management in the recent years, especially after China's entry into WTO. However, most of the enterprises are still in the initial stage for modern management. It will be an arduous and long process and a complicated task for family enterprises to transform their management model with innovative ideas and methods. Many have invited consulting companies for advice, but they can only obtain a set of solutions with short-term effect. It is difficult for the family enterprises to change their fundamentals. Accordingly, in order to achieve long-term target of development, the desire of the enterprises to seek management enhancement and long-term benefit become increasingly intense. In view of the development and interests of enterprises, the separation of ownership and management becomes inevitable and the class of professional managers and management companies emerge accordingly.

Since family enterprises have been operating under the patriarchal approach of management, they could hardly correct the shortcomings or flaws in a short period of time, thus obstructing the development of modern management system. The problems are manifested as follows: (i) the dominance of ownership makes it difficult to adopt a market-oriented management practice; (ii) the ineffective internal system and lack of flexibility and vitality are incommensurate with the requirements of market economy; (iii) the improper organizational structure of management team, which is often based on kinship, over-simplifies the decision-making process and decreases managerial efficiency; (iv) the professional quality and mindset of managers lag behind the development of enterprises, or their ideas and thoughts might be advance but they lack the experience and ability to execute. Their implementation is poor and coordination across departments is weak. Although many family enterprises are fully or partially aware of the problems, they are not willing to abandon the short-term effect with the implicit intention to keep ownership or due to their narrow-minded view of "never benefiting others with the profits of your own". Many enterprises at the initial stage only care about the short-term gain and fail to lead the enterprise to long-term development. Admittedly, long-term objectives and short-term gains may be contradictory. Should the owners hand out the right of management? Should they put the profits into the preparation for the future development? How should they balance the present interest and long-term development? These are important questions for family enterprises to ponder.

Risk Control — Establish True Governance Structure and Management System

Chinese family enterprises have grown in a special, historical time when the Chinese economy is changing from being planned to market-oriented. At the initial stage of this change, owing to the risks of establishing an enterprise, the pressure from competition, the difficulties in collecting fund and the friction of new and old systems, the constraints imposed on the family enterprises have been tremendous. They have to rely on kinship, affinity and geo-relationships to strive for survival. Under such conditions, the relationship of the members of the family enterprise is intimate and the managerial cost is low. Some family enterprises have gone through the hardship of the initial stages and a number of courageous and responsible entrepreneurs had emerged. However, with the changes of economic environment, family enterprises are facing new challenges. With the gradual maturity of the market economy, growing size of business expansion, increasing demand in management efficiency, sophistication of technology constant accretion of financial and market risks, increasing number of technical and management talents, explosion of information in knowledge economy, the authority and knowledge set of the family leaders are being shaken and challenged. In addition, due to the success of the enterprise and the accumulation of wealth, the conflict of interest becomes increasingly intense among family members, and ultimately challenging the patriarch-oriented management approach.

Compared with other enterprises, the greatest advantage enjoyed by the family enterprises lies in the managerial costs. However, the disadvantages of family enterprises are obvious as well. Nepotism is often seen in family enterprises. The result of inbreeding makes the choice of talents harder. Family enterprises always encounter such a dilemma: on the one hand they are short of talents, while on the other had, they lack the environment to nurture and retain talents. As a result, the family enterprises will move towards failure and falling apart. Among the typical examples are Wang Global overseas and Sanzhu in the country.

With the expansion of enterprise size and business scope, the requirement for size economy and division of management become increasingly urgent. Simple and closed managerial system and ownership system have displayed corrupt practices, thus becoming barriers for the further development of family enterprises. Family enterprises have distinct features in their internal governance structure: the oneness of capital, centralization of decision-making rights, and irregularity of daily management, closed and discriminatory characteristics of personnel system and irregularity of binding responsibility. These basic features are their advantages as well as the fundamental flaws. On the positive side, they have guaranteed the survival and development of private enterprises in the economic and historical environment when the market system was not perfect. Moreover, they will still, to a certain degree, promote the development of private enterprises in the years that follow. However, the fundamental disadvantages of the managerial pattern are becoming eminent with the enterprises having undergone several stages of development. Especially with the tide of knowledge and economic globalization floods, the flaws in the closed, controlled and centralized management will gradually become a major obstacle for the further development of family enterprises under the new trend of market integration, rule of law in economy, professional operation and scientific management.

How would the family enterprises break through the bottleneck problems and adapt to the new economic environment? In order to motivate the creativity and initiative of family members and employees, it is necessary to adopt modern management with advanced technology to ensure the performance and productivity. Aside from settling the problem of system, the patriarch-oriented management style should be changed to participatory management style so as to solve the conflicts in the development of family enterprises. The patriarch has to transfer part of his power to the talents from the employees. Only by sharing wisdom and managing collectively will the enterprises be more democratic and build up momentum.

In addition, family enterprises should get close to capital market and increase their competitive strength through broadened financial channels. When a family enterprise becomes a public one, it will be efficiently monitored by the securities market, which will create a favorable external conditions for the development of the enterprise. Moreover, the securities market has provided a convenient withdrawal mechanism for the original shareholders of family enterprises. Family enterprises can also overcome their own congenital deficiency by integrating social capital. From a global perspective, it is unnecessary to change all family enterprises into non-family enterprises. The existence of a large number of family enterprises is inevitable in any economic structure. However, in the modern economic growth, family enterprises must integrate with social capital for survival and development.

In conclusion, in order to obtain sustainable development in the environment of new economy, the family system must firstly be reformed to adapt to the enterprise development. Ownership should be clearly defined and shareholding rights be adequately open. The definition of ownership in family members will help to eliminate potential disputes in ownership. Moreover, it will also be very helpful for breaking the unified and closed shareholding structure and establishing the concept of socialization. It will not only help the enterprises to get the funds they need, but also guarantee the continuous and stable development of the enterprises.

The Axis of Enterprise

Industrial Orientation: Establish a System of Specialization and Cooperation

Small and medium in size, family enterprises can hardly rival the big enterprises and are often in disadvantageous positions. Moreover, it is quite difficult for them to get loans and funds. Moreover, they are very much affected by external environments such as governmental policies and industrial policies. Many small- or medium-sized family enterprises can hardly survive independently as a result of its internal and external constraints. They have to form alliances with major enterprises and become supplementary or subsidiary to them. However, the traditional concept of "small or inclusive" system has restricted family enterprises from developing itself through the specialization and cooperation with major enterprises. The specific manifestations are as follows:

a. At present, many large-scale enterprises in China pursue vertical integration or horizontal integration and neglect the cooperation with other enterprises, including those owned by families, thus making it difficult for family enterprises to cooperate with the major ones.
b. The "small and inclusive" system is still dominant in the family enterprises. They prefer independence and are not willing to play a supportive role and thus put themselves in a vulnerable position.
c. The barriers under traditional planned economy system are not fully dismantled. Local protectionism found its way, thus forming barriers for the division and cooperation between large-scale enterprises and small and medium-sized enterprises which may belong to different regions or administrative departments.

Due to the short history of the market-oriented economy in China, low maturity of market system, low social credit, low compliance rate and high transaction cost of trading are common in enterprises, thus obstructing the division and cooperation between large-scale enterprises and small-sized enterprises. Changes are needed to facilitate the cooperation between the large and small enterprises to develop complementary business relationships.

Market Competition: Enhance the Consciousness of Competition and Cooperation, and Emphasize Resource Complementarity

China's entry into WTO is a new opportunity for further development of the family enterprises in China. On the one hand, opportunities are presented on equal basis for competition; on the other, family enterprises are faced with fiercer challenge than ever. From then on, the domain of competition expands from the domestic market to foreign markets and the major rivals are no longer state-owned enterprises, but multinationals with abundant funds, advanced managerial system and broad markets. In order to adapt themselves to the rigorous situation of global competition, it is imperative for the family enterprises to consolidate their internal strength and enhance the overall quality of the enterprises in their second pioneering.

In recent years, competitiveness and growth of many multinationals have been greatly enhanced and reinforced through merger and acquisition, restructuring and expansion strategies. Evidence shows that 40,000 multinational groups account for 40% of the total production value, 60% of the trade volume, 70% of the direct investment and 80% of the R&D volume of the world's economy. In contrast, the consciousness of competition and cooperation of most family enterprises in China is still very weak. They often pursue the idea of being "small and inclusive". The competition within a certain industry is a life-and-death battle. For example, in Liushi Town of Yueqing City, the famous "Capital of Electrical Appliance in China", there are more than 1,000 enterprises manufacturing and distributing low voltage electrical appliances. They are similar in product category and structure, and identical in market orientation. The enterprises carry out unnecessary competition in prices and resources. They undermine the foundation of each other by taking away talents or technology. The situation can be found in many places in China. If the problem cannot be properly addresssed, many enterprises, including some promising ones, will die out quickly, not to mention participating in international competition.

Therefore, if family enterprises are to rival multinationals in the international markets, they have to enhance the awareness of competition and cooperation, fully exploit the advantages of local alliances and form industrial associations to share resources. Only by doing so, can funds be raised in a larger scale to focus on the development of potential projects. The irrational structure of "small and inclusive" can thus be changed to implement specialized production with effective division of labor; factors of production could be optimized to enable the reasonable flow of talents, funds, materials and information; the strategy of trademark and advantages of brands of the leading enterprises and the marketing channels of many enterprises could be fully utilized.

Bottleneck for Talents: Improve HR Management and Retain High-Level Managers

Human resource is of great importance to any organizations. In this respect, family enterprises, due to their unique characteristics, are more likely to run into limitations. Therefore, extra attention should be paid.

1. Arbitrariness, instead of standardization, in human resource management

In essence, family enterprises are different from state-owned corporations, for the former enjoys a higher degree of freedom and flexibility. Such characteristics make it easier for them to adapt to market demand. But when it comes to human resource allocation and utilization, it is certainly a challenge in family enterprises. Specifically, a lack of a scientific and formal the regulation and procedure in recruitment, training, promotion, and termination cause problems and limitations, resulting in low efficiency. Usually, family enterprise owners rely more on experience and emotion than on reason, and sometimes adopt different standards for family versus non-family members. Relatives and close friends are assigned to high positions regardless of their abilities. As for non-family employees, they are often face with heavy workload and responsibility, strict demands and control. Family enterprises often find it difficult to recruit good talents and are likely to fail in inspiring work enthusiasm among non-family employees. Therefore, after expansion in scale, family enterprises have to establish professional human resource and personnel management. Only by doing so can family enterprises meet the human resource demands of a diversified competitive environment.

2.   Emphasizing more on paper qualification than on capability

In most cases, family enterprises are developed from various individual entrepreneurs in towns or rural areas, and the owners are usually with a low level of education. According to statistics from 1998 "Development Report on China's Private Enterprises", 80% of the private owners received below-high school education. Due to personal experience, these people understand the importance of education, and are willing to recruit employees with higher education, which is a valuable aspect of their open-mindedness. But at the same time they tend to go too far in putting extreme emphasis on paper qualification. People with degrees are hired regardless of position and job-fit. A degree has become something to boast of. This is not only a waste of human resources, but also a burden on cost expenditure, which affects the enterprise's profit.

3.   Placing more importance on technical talents than managerial talents

In many family enterprises, employee profiles are more homogeneous, with an imbalanced emphasis on technical ability than on managerial ability. In most cases, the pioneers were technicians in the past, and often the experts in their industries.

Most of them spare little effort in searching for professional managers. Although the enterprise may have outstanding technology and their products are capable of excellent performance, poor management will inevitably result in high cost, low sales, and unsatisfactory customer service. As a matter of fact, a large-scale family enterprise is in great need of high-quality management talents, especially in the areas of planning, marketing, finance, and human resources management. Only by doing so can a family enterprise exert itself to the utmost of its potential and long-term development.

4. Focus on material rewards instead of non-material rewards in incentive system

Effective incentive system can greatly motivate employees and inspire work enthusiasm. Incentive system is a complicated matter involving company's philosophy and belief and professional design. Family enterprises should establish a scientific incentive mechanism based on their own unique conditions to foster morale and loyalty of its employees. In many family enterprises, the relation between the enterprise and its personnel is one of "employer" and "employee", or "order" and "obedience". Usually, the owners adopt an over-simplistic approach to understand the meaning of "incentive" and believe it to be a "praise or punishment" matter. Employees, in their eyes, are instrumental in achieving company's objectives. Instead of a long-term effective incentive mechanism, family enterprises often adopt materialistic incentive — raised salary for excellent performance, and reduced salary otherwise. Behavioral scientists believe that employees are not only "economic persons", but also "social persons". They are members belonging to a complex society. They have both material needs and social psychological needs. Therefore, a corporation should also apply innovation into its incentive system. A variety of measures, such as salary, bonus, dividend, profit-sharing, stock-holding, and stock options, can be adopted. Linking enterprise objective with employee benefit will bring about a strong sense of responsibility and belonging within employees. Work will be seen as challenging and employees will realize their self-value and sense of achievement. A good incentive system will also help enterprise to develop a unique culture that gain consensus.

5.   Emphasis on recruitment but not on training and retention

In family enterprises, talent-searching and cultivation is a long-term and meticulous job. Some family enterprises are eager for instant success and quick profits, therefore short-term acts are prevalent. In human resource management, such enterprises are reluctant to invest in talent cultivation and are unwilling to take the risk of investing in human capital. They prefer last-minute recruitment. Such hasty recruitment usually fails to ensure the right fit. From a long-term perspective, it is a must for family enterprises to establish their own talent cultivation and development and adopt a long-term and strategic approach in human resources management. Continuing education programs should be planned. Talent cultivation should be included as an important criterion in measuring performance of managers. It is the enterprises' responsibility to take care of the working atmosphere for the employees, offer chances for them to further their education and improve themselves, providing a stage for them to perform. Only by taking these measures can family enterprises attract and retain outstanding talents.

Section IV

CONCLUSION

8

Sustainable Development of Family Enterprises

Going Public: A Breakthrough in Capital and Governance

It is easy to understand that both family and non-family enterprises want to achieve further development. The precondition for further development lies in overcoming the limited capital and business expansion. In most cases, being listed in the securities exchanges is the best way to gain capital support. For most of the current Chinese family enterprises, financing is a common constraint. At the initial stage of the family enterprises, capital mostly come from relatives and friends based on kinship and geographical relations. With the development of the enterprises, when the capital accumulation of the enterprises themselves could not meet the demands of the development, raising money from outside becomes a vital way for the enterprises to obtain funds. According to some studies, the average life span of the family enterprises is usually about 20 years. Only 30% of them could last till the second generation, and only 15% of them could last till the third generation. This fact shows the difficulties for the family enterprises to actualize their sustainable development. Therefore, if the family enterprises could become public corporations, they could raise funds from the capital markets and enhance their reputations. This could make an excellent external condition for the development of the enterprises, as well as a good advertisement. Most of the international family enterprises have undergone this process.

Nevertheless, there are also risks involved during the listing process: the current regulations, laws and rules of the government policy and control authorities over the listed companies are far from perfect, which might possibly cause the stock shares of the family-holding corporations to be concentrated in the hands of one family or one family patriarch. This situation could impose more risks for the decision-making of the family enterprises. The external control and monitoring mechanism requires a much longer time, depending on the maturity and readiness of the external environment. Secondly, in the family-holding listed companies, the big stockholders would easily usurp the small stockholders, which is commonly found. For example, the families could maximize their own interests by controlling the asset-restructuring and stock transaction of the listed company. Under this circumstance, the interests of the listed company would be harmed and the interests of the small stockholders would be negatively affected.

Therefore, becoming a listed company does not guarantee long-term development of family enterprises. Financing cannot be regarded as the sole aim of being listed. The final goal should be stipulated as to regulate and perfect the governance structure and management systems in accordance with the criterions for the listed companies. The concrete measures include strengthening the stockholders' governance, and perfecting the functions of the boards, etc.

Theoretically, the shareholders' conference is the highest authority, and the board is the execution body responsible for the company's development. Since the Chinese family enterprises have a centralized stock rights structure and the big stockholders exert too much control over the board, the board and management levels lack sufficient rights. The stockholders conference structure must be planned properly, and the relationship between stockholders and board must be appropriately adjusted. As a non-standing body of the enterprises, if the stockholders conference fails to respond to the changes of the markets, it would be a negative factor for the effective management of the enterprises. The family enterprise management and even the goals of the enterprise development are often influenced by the will of the big stockholders (usually a certain family). The decisions made by those big stockholders are not always good for the enterprises. Therefore, in the small- and medium-sized enterprises, the big stockholders must rely on the board to operate and manage the enterprises, and thus the board would become the center of the management rights. By doing so, the operating efficiency of family enterprises could be raised and some strategic decisions that are favorable to the enterprises could also be made.

For a modern listed company, the board plays a critical role. In many Chinese family enterprises, the board has not exerted its full impact. So the functions of the board should be planned properly in order to exert its relative authority to strengthen the administration of the enterprises. Firstly, the board of the Chinese family enterprises should pay more attention to the formulation of the principles on risk elusion, moral criterion of career and transparency. The role of the board is to consult the above principles with the management level and then to come to an agreement with them. The board must regularly supervise the working conditions in those key fields, and exert its leading role in the emergencies. The board would justly and properly deal with the illegal behaviors of the management level. These transparent management regulations made by the board have played an important role in the administration of the enterprises, especially the family enterprises, where the regulations would counteract the disadvantages existing in the management level. Secondly, the board must possess necessary ways and methods to supervise the operational achievements of the enterprises. The board should ascertain some key measuring indexes connected to the strategic aims of the enterprise, and respectively set testing standards for each of the indexes. The establishment of the achievement testing standards is very essential. The board should not only consider the feasibility of these standards but also make them more challenging to continuously inspire the members of the management level. Moreover, the board should regularly assess the performance of the enterprises and provide feedback, in order to approve and modify the operational measures in time to meet the changes of the market. Thirdly, besides the supervision of the board, the establishment of incentive mechanism for the management level is a more important aspect. With the development of the family enterprises, the only way for further development is to introduce more and more managers and professionals from the outside. Consequently, the incentive mechanism for these employees would influence their working enthusiasm and their will to take risks in work. Being important to the business operation, a reasonable incentive system would also help the family enterprises to attract more managerial elites. During the 20-year development, the Chinese family enterprises have adopted work and efficiency connecting system, contracting system, award system and annual salary system to mobilize the working enthusiasm of the professional managers in the family enterprises. To some extent, these measures do help, but there are still some problems such as the impermanency of the management level's enthusiasm and the insufficiency of the rewards and punishments, etc. However, management level holding stock shares could be seen as a good way to establish a systematic incentive system. This approach could better resolve the problems of scale, expertise and "single big stockholders" existing in the development process of the family enterprises. It is an effective way for the family enterprises to obtain sustainable development. It will help to closely connect the interests of the management with the prosperity of the family enterprises. The rights-and-obligations balance of the management level would make for the set-up of the incentive mechanism and the increase of the risk endurance of the management level. At the level of practical operations, the board needs to adopt different measures in light of the realistic situations of the enterprises: for those family enterprises that have undertaken stock trading reforms, some of their stock shares should be allowed to be purchased by the professional managers; and for those sole family-holding enterprises, the total value of the stocks and the amount of the stock shares held by the management level should be fixed appropriately, in accordance with the total assets or net assets of the enterprises. Certainly in the operational practices, some difficulties and problems would emerge, such as the families holding too many stock shares, the limited purchase ability of the management level, and their lack of money to purchase relative stock shares, which makes the reasonable stock-holding system difficult to actualize. Therefore, the board should adopt some measures to solve these problems. For example, in the precondition that the interests of the original stockholders will not be hurt, they could provide some preference and advantages to the management level in share purchase; at the same time, various purchase channels must be set, such as bestowal of performance shares, i.e., taking part of the increment of the enterprise's assets as the performance share to bestow to management employees who are stay in their positions or are outstandingly dedicated to the development of the enterprises; or the management level is allowed to purchase the stock shares at a discount. For those management employees who have been contributing to the enterprises, they could buy the stock shares at a discount or they could choose divided payments. For those management employees who are unable to pay the money at one time, they could choose flexible payments based on their credits. In all, the realization of the management level holding stock share system would motivate the managers to contribute their wisdom and enthusiasm and eventually follow the ultimate goal of maximizing the interests of the stockholders.

The constitution of the board personnel is also very important. Besides the founders and the new external directors representing capitals and techniques, such as the foreign investors, the venture investment corporations and the strategic investors, etc., a reasonable board should also include the members from a third party: professional managers or key experts who represent the management level because of the importance of their positions; those old employees who represent the stock-holding employees through the "employee stock option plan"; the external independent directors, the solely independent third-party directors, such as economists, professors, high-level managers of the same industry or related industries, the high-level managers of the customers, the personnel from industrial association, the professionals of financing and securities, and the professionals of law and consultation. In the international key enterprises, the percentages of the independent directors in the boards are all very high. According to the reports of OECD, the percentages of the independent directors in the key international enterprises' boards respectively reach 62% in US, 34% in UK, and 29% in France. Generally

314　　*Jean Lee and Hong Li*

speaking, the independent directors could hold a more objective position to push the enterprises to move forward in accordance with the laws and regulations. With their participation in the board operations, some risk signals in the operation would be anticipated. Moreover, they would put forward warning advice on the illegal and improper behaviors of the enterprises, which would be good for improving the professional operations, increasing the rationality in the decision-making of the board, strengthening the governance function of the board, protecting the interests of the small and minority shareholders, increasing the transparency of the information disclosure, and eventually supervising and urging the enterprise to operate on the basis of laws and regulations. On August 16, 2001, CSRC issued *"Instructions on the Independent Director System Established in the Listed Companies"*. According to this Instruction, before June 30, 2002, all of the companies that had been listed in mainland China must include at least two independent directors in their boards; and before June 30, 2003, one-third of the board directors of the listed companies must be independent directors.

It is obvious that once the family enterprises are listed, they can not only raise money from the capital markets to overcome the choke point of the capitals and to expand the operational extent, but also seize this opportunity to regulate the management rules and structures and thus make the enterprises operate under a more normative system and eventually achieve the goal of long-term development.

Family Committee: Sharing Experiences

As mentioned above, the difference existing between family enterprises and enterprises of other types lay in their connections with a certain family or clan. This connection has brought many special problems to the family enterprises, such as the negative influences on the enterprises by the inner family conflicts, the familism management carried out by the family members, and the special heritage problems, etc. Therefore, family enterprises must accordingly have some special organizational structures to deal with these special problems, such as the Family Committee, which will be discussed in the following parts.

The emergence of this new structure — Family Committee — would create many opportunities and channels. The primary purpose of setting up this committee is to regularly gather the family members together to discuss some problems related to both the family and the enterprise. The committee is a platform on which the family members are free to express whatever they think about the enterprises. And most importantly, a set of reasonable and legal principles and regulations could be formulated to protect the family interests. In such a committee, all of the family members could find a proper channel to express their own ideas, which would be helpful to make a clear distinction between family and enterprise. Those family members who are not working in the enterprise would also have an opportunity to voice their opinions, which would reduce the possibility that the decision-making of the enterprise would be under the negative influences of the family ideas. Moreover, with the development of the enterprise, the obligations and rights assumed by every family member keep changing. Therefore, the family members must be kept informed. Then the Family Committee would informally provide an information channel for them. The Committee plays an even more important role when the family enterprise misses an authoritative patriarch. Moreover, although family members could also communicate with each other in some informal get-togethers, such as Spring Festival parties, holiday parties and birthday parties, it is far from enough. A Family Committee is essential for the discussion of some important issues, which would separate the enterprises discussions from the family celebrations and therefore differentiate the family issues from enterprise issues. What is the most important is that the Family Committee provides the best opportunities to solve the family conflicts. Since most of the family conflicts involve different interests, the Family Committee becomes a forum, where these conflicts and interests could be expressed. Besides, the more complicated the family structure is, the more necessary the set-up of the Family Committee would be. Furthermore, when the families develop to a certain stage, changes would also accordingly take place in the structure of the Family Committee.

The family members are probably not accustomed to deal with family businesses (in fact also enterprises businesses) in a formal way because they are used to informal and casual communication with each other. Under this circumstance, the Family Committee has to be well organized in setting a regulated meeting procedure so that family members would gradually understand the goals and functions of the Family Committee.

In light of different situations in different family enterprises, the questions needed to be discussed in the Family Committees vary from one to another, but some questions need to be repeatedly discussed in the Family Committees during the development of the families, such as what is the most important thing to the families; how to exhibit these importance through proper behaviors; and how to maintain the family values and traditions and pass them on to the next generations. These questions seem to be abstract rather than specific, irrelevant to business, but they are fundamental principles to family business that should be emphasized and discussed seriously among family members. By so doing, the family members could draw a consensus on these fundamental questions about both families and enterprises, and therefore the specific contradictions and conflicts could be properly managed and resolved. For example, whether the family members have drawn an agreement seems to be especially important, when the following problems are encountered: the heritage of the family enterprises; diversification of business operations; support to the family members' careers; and other difficulties like hiring or firing family members.

Certainly, Family Committee takes on different tasks at different stages. When the next generation emerges in the family, the Family Committee will spend most of its time on the education of the younger generation and on the career choice for the grown-up offspring, such as whether to encourage them to work in the family enterprises; whether to propose some requirements before the members of the younger generation enter the enterprises; how to set these requirements; how to formulate a salary system to attract those family members who are capable of assuming the positions in the management level or leadership level; and how to distribute the stock rights to the next generations.

When the family members from different generations and different branches enter the family enterprises, the problem on operation management would become one of the most important agendas for the Family Committee. At this stage, the Family Committee needs to discuss the following questions such as how to connect the family core values with the enterprises' strategy and operations; whether some behavioral norms should be established to regulate those family members working in the family enterprises; how should the family members working in the enterprises communicate with those not working in it; how to balance the discrepancies existing among the interests obtained from the enterprises by different family members; how to help those economically disadvantaged family members; and what are the specific rights, obligations and functions of different family stockholders.

When it becomes necessary to pass the family enterprises to the next generations, the problem of heritage will be the key issue for discussion, including: whether the enterprises still need to be controlled by the next generation of the family; how to divide the proprietorship and the stock-holding rights, in order to maintain a better operation for the enterprises; how to deal with stock trade and other transaction among family members or families; how to help the older generation in their retirement plan, etc. Furthermore, the following questions could also be discussed in the Family Committee, such as how to pass on the family traditions and values to the next generations; how to enhance the public image and reputation of the family enterprises; and how much social responsibility family enterprises must bear.

Besides providing a platform for the family members to brainstorm and exchange views, the Family Committee has another important function, that is to formulate family plans, which is as important as the enterprise's plan. The family plan is essential for the development of the family. It enables the family to be forward-looking and develop a long-term vision for the family. As the enterprises are closely connected with the families, the family plan developed by the committee would directly and indirectly affect the development of the family enterprises. A proper family plan should include family history, family future design, family mission and concrete action plans. Recording the family history would help to protect the spiritual heritage of the founders and the older generations. In the development process of the family enterprises, every founder has undergone various hardships and difficulties. In some sense, these precious spiritual heritage are much more valuable than the material property they have gained. If these heritage could be maintained, they would be the best education for the next generations, and would be very powerful to inculcate a sense of family honor and a sense of responsibility. Besides the written documents, some pictures, craftworks, photographs and gifts could also be protected as the family history. Moreover, the future design for the family could also inspire the family members to strive for a better future. The family history would be something that allows the family members to lean on when they face pressures and problems of the current reality. It would inspire the members to imagine what the family and enterprises would be like in the next 5 or 10 years. At the same time, they could imagine the future for themselves. Once they identify the gap, they will ascertain the things they need to do. The power of family mission, which is generated from the pursuit of dream, could never be underestimated. The illustration of the family mission includes: why does the family try to maintain this enterprise; what kind of social, enterprise, and family responsibilities the family members should assume; what kind of moral criteria they should follow; and under what kind of framework could the individuals realize the self-development. This kind of family mission illustration could remind the family members of what they should do for the enterprise. The action plan is the last step of the family plan, which could help the family to turn objectives into realities. The concrete steps include providing training for the family members, ranging from knowledge on enterprise management, cultivation of the leadership, the resolution of the conflicts and various seminars on the family enterprises; creating a set of behavior criteria for the family; establish a procedure for resolving the family conflicts; and organizing family activities such as holidays and traveling. It is necessary to manage a family in the way of managing enterprise. The management of family and enterprise shares the same ultimate goal: to establish a dynamic and growing enterprise system; at the same time, to sustain a dynamic and growing family system.

A well-operated Family Committee indeed could play an essential role. What are the steps needed to set up an effective Family Committee? According to the experiences of many foreign family enterprises, the experts have suggested the following constructive suggestions to the family enterprises: firstly, a meeting schedule needs to be formulated and strictly followed. The prearrangement of the regular meeting dates could ensure active participation of the family members. Generally speaking, the meeting could be held quarterly or annually. Secondly, the agenda and procedure of the meeting should be reasonably arranged. It is important to create a consultative atmosphere, in which the family members could speak freely. Only by so doing so would the family members be willing to express their own opinions. The close relations among the Family Committee members are equally important. This would be very crucial in an expanding family. The Family Committee could combine the important matters with some relaxing topics, such as asking each other about the current living situations, new-born babies and health conditions. In this way, the intimate relations and bonding could be established. The venue could be in resort areas with beautiful scenery, which will create more relaxing atmosphere. Thirdly, there must be a good leader in the Family Committee. Generally speaking, the leader of the Family Committee should be a senior member of the family, but not the leader of the family enterprises. In this way, the enterprise could be separated from the family, which would be helpful for creating an open atmosphere. Fourthly, the strength of the different sub-groups or levels in the Family Committee should be capitalized. For example, the family members of the same gender, or the same generation might have much more common topics with each other, so some problems could be discussed first within a smaller circle and then be brought to the whole committee. By so doing, it would be easier to reach an agreement. Finally, the Family Committee can engage experts and professionals to organize such meetings. The expertise of the professionals would also serve an education purpose by sharing their professional knowledge, which will enable family members to openly share their opinions about management, family and family enterprises.

Shaping "Enterprise Family Culture": Separation of Ownership and Management

Integrating the merits of the family enterprise system and professional management system is probably the only way out for the family enterprises. In order to set up a modern canonical enterprise system, the family enterprises need to start from two aspects: first, they need to establish professional and systematic management and operation, which are the basis for the family enterprises to survive and develop in a constantly changing market; second, they need to set up a reasonable heritage system, which is fundamental for family enterprises to maintain sustainable development.

The modernization and standardization of family enterprises management system is first demonstrated in the aspect of employment. One feature of the familism management lies in nepotism, which encourages the trend that most of the key leader positions are occupied by the family members or those closely related to the family. This characteristic of family enterprises has prohibited the development of the enterprises to a large extent. Nepotism leads to the phenomenon that the emotions weigh more than the rationality. Management principles are often overridden by family relationships. Therefore, the standardization personnel system has been regarded as one of the key condition for the smooth development of the family enterprises. Take DuPont Company, which has a history of more than 100 years, as an example. We can learn from the case how important the personnel system reforms can be to the family enterprises. DuPont is a typical family enterprise, which had been under the control and management of the family for as long as 170 years. Till 1917, the enterprise was still held in the hands of the proprietors. In the 1930s, the number of high-level managers exceeded the number of the DuPont family members on the board. In the 1970s, the enterprise was taken over by the professional managers. According to the study on the DuPont management reforms, it was discovered that unless the family members are as outstanding, capable or hardworking as the non-family members, they would be persuaded to leave the management positions of the enterprise. DuPont has offered a "privilege" to the male family members by allowing them to do the inceptive jobs leading to the management level of the enterprise. In the following five years, there will be four to five family elders to evaluate their performances. If they are estimated to be unsuitable for the high-level managers, then they would be persuaded to leave the management positions of the enterprise. Due to the persistence of this by Pierre, the grandson of the DuPont founder and the CEO of DuPont in 1906, a serious family conflict was provoked. As a result of the persistence on this principle, the DuPont family as the proprietors still enjoy a larger share of the enterprise's earnings, although the family no longer participate in the important decision-making on operational and management matters. In fact, only the experienced members could be chosen into the executive committee, and most of them have graduated from MIT or other technical institutes. Hundreds of DuPont family members have become qualified managers, but very few of them are working in DuPont Company. Among them, only 5 to 6 family members attend the 25-member board as non-voting delegates, and only one has entered the high management level. Such examples can also be found in Standard Oil Trust, Harkness family, Platt family and Rockefeller family. It is obvious that with the expansion of the enterprises, the principle of "competence", instead of nepotism must be adopted. Some specific measures have to be adopted to carry out this principle: with the development of the enterprises, when the family members, who are originally assigned the managerial positions, could not fit their positions due to incompetence or lack of relevant knowledge and capabilities, the family must make a prompt decision to ask them to leave the management position. The withdrawal of the family members could choose the following options: the first one is to conform to the regulations, i.e., the authoritative patriarchs formulate the regulations forcing the family members to leave the enterprise; the second one is to adopt an indirect way that when the enterprise starts to reorganize new companies, they must be established strictly based on the management requirements, and siblings and relatives should not be allowed to work in the new companies. Subsequently, the focus of the enterprise would be transferred to the new companies, and the family members would gradually withdraw from the enterprises. The first approach is straightforward and agile. Its shortcoming lies in the possibility of inviting an undesirable family conflict. The second approach is relatively moderate, but the process would be longer and it would not provoke conflicts. The adoption of the two approaches has to be based on the actual situation of the family enterprises. Besides withdrawal, family members could also be converted to become professional managers. This could be particulary helpful for the younger generations, who could be cultivated to be excellent managers. This will be the prerequisite to enter management position. Otherwise, they should also leave the enterprise. In fact, many family enterprises hope that they could have more competent managers from their families. But if the members are not performing, they should be replaced by outside talents. The key to success lies in the talents. Only those who have a pool of talents could make a great success. As for talent selection, one must learn how to recognize the talents and pay special attention to their morality and capability. In terms of employment, family enterprises should firsting develop contractual relations with the talents based on to prevent potential conflicts in the future. Secondly, hired talents should be respected and treasured. They should be assigned proper positions and responsibility. Thirdly, the cultivation and training of talents should be stressed, no matter where they come from — inside or outside of family. Family enterprises should build up its philosophy of talents. They should adopt a two-way traffic — "sending the current employees out for training and recruiting outside talents to join the new blood". They should also constantly provide opportunities for talents to revitalize their knowledge and skills. The family enterprises should build good and balanced talents profile, forming echelons for long-term development. Only with a group of talents could the family enterprises be in an advantageous position in the market competition.

Secondly, formalization of professional management system should be developed with objectivity and rationality in decision-making. The set-up of scientific decision-making mechanism would help to reduce risk and failure in decision-making process. Factors affecting decision-making mechanism are mainly structural elements, including leadership, organization to employee profile, and procedural elements ranging from decision-making procedure, decision-making methods to communication and information transfer. Therefore, the establishment of scientific decision-making mechanism could start from two aspects. Structurally, besides the board, there should be another platform, i.e., Family Representative Committee to facilitate decision making. The Family Committee has been discussed in the former section. Most of the family members may have withdrawn from the enterprise, as the proprietors still have a voice on the development of the enterprise. In order to avoid the conflicts between the board and the family stockholders, the Family Committee would represent the family members to review the decisions made by the board, to put forward advice to reach a final consensus. This committee is regarded as the lubricant to ensure the proper operation of the governance structure of the family enterprise. It is also seen as the communication channel between family members and the board, and among the managers. Simultaneously, the enterprises should spare no expense to exploit the "outside brains". Most of the board directors are the professional managers, some of them are even professional independent directors, but due to the complexity of the external environment, the enterprises should introduce "outside brains" at any cost in order to ensure the scientific operations and to avoid mistakes. A standing consultation body, constituted by professionals, should be set up within the enterprises. Consequently, the decision-making system of the family enterprises should comprise of three components: board, Family Committee, and "outside brains". The tripartite system will be mutually supported and restricted, and to ensure quality of decisions and control risks.

From the procedural element, the family enterprises should make rational decisions through scientific methods. The diversity of the composition of decision-makers would help to balance the interests of enterprises and stockholders and balance of professional knowledge and experiences, so as to ensure objectivity in decision-making. Furthermore, the decision-making should employ the principles of voting and majority rule, which could minimize the impact of absolute authority on decision-making, and thus ensure rationality in any business activity from beginning. At the same time, during the process of decision-making, the interests of different parties should be repeatedly measured and calculated, in order to draw coherence to a maximum extent, to balance the short-term and long-term interests, to eliminate the potential internal conflicts, and to reduce the costs of future implementation. In this perspective, decision-making is regarded not only as objective science, but also a transactional relationship, in which everyone's interest could be addressed. This is indeed the core value in decision-making.

Thirdly, a professional management system should include an effective incentive system. A good incentive system could help the family enterprise to inspire enthusiasm and commitment of the employees and to drive them to excel and achieve the enterprise's goals. There are a variety of incentive measures. The stimulus of income could directly affect the employees' contribution. It has relatively strong pertinence, but lacks short-term effects. The employee stock option scheme has a long-term effect and can help to increase wealth of the employees. In addition, it also enables them to share the success and sorrows of the enterprise. By doing this, the employees would have a better sense of ownership and be willing to make changes to help build the enterprise. The stock option system may also help to reduce employee turnover. Besides the material reward, the non-material reward is also crucial. Work autonomy for non-family employees is particularly important because it shows a sense of trust and confidence. Challenging jobs should be provided to employees to allow them to learn and grow, and achieve a sense of satisfaction. Excellent employees should be provided with opportunities of advanced studies, position training and travels to ensure them to get enough exposure for personal development. Through this method, the employees would feel a sense of recognition and appreciation. When their personal wisdom and talents are in full play, the enterprises would benefit from it, and achieve a win-win situation.

With an effective incentive system, the family enterprises also need to establish a effective control system. Incentive co-exists with discipline. While providing motivation to employees, the control mechanism should also be established. The specific control methods include: establishing strict regulations and explicit reprimand to ensure penalty for wrongdoings; imposing control through personal credit system — before the completion of the credit system in China, the high-level managers could be asked to pay partial income of the stocks or personal tangible assets (such as house) as the credit guarantee using public opinion as a control on the ethical behaviors of professional managers. Unprofessional wrongdoings such as corruption, gambling and infringing upon the enterprises' interests, would be feedback to the market to devaluate the credits of the person. Those who have caused great losses to the enterprises would be investigated and accused for their civil and criminal responsibilities; the monitoring function of the governance committee should be strengthened. The performance evaluation should be seriously conducted. Only through both internal and external control and monitoring on the performance of employees and professional managers, would enterprise interests be protected.

Equally important as the establishment of the professional management, the succession planning is a long-term and systemic project. The challenge of succession is of great importance for both the ordinary enterprises and the family enterprises. On surface, the problem of succession is a transfer of power and authority or proprietorship, but in reality it changes the organizational structure, power core, resource allocation and repartition of the interest distribution systems, which could lead to a pretty profound reform. We all know that reform means concussion and instability, which would severely threaten the development of the enterprises. In view of the history of the world enterprises, we find that the problem of succession is a major challenge and one of the core issues concerning the long-term survival of the enterprise. In this sense, it is important to ask what kind of succession system should the Chinese family enterprises set up?

In the 1990s, the Chinese family enterprises have gradually entered the peak period of succession. The first generation of successful entrepreneurs is silently retiring from public life after their great accomplishments. A large number of young managers have gradually stepped up to the center stage under the guidance and support of the older generation. The problem of succession becomes an inevitable issue that many founders have to address. For the first generation, the family enterprises are not only a ground to make fortunes, but also a form of the existence of their lives. Therefore, the selection of a right successor determines the sustainability of their lives. Consequently, the succession problem of the family enterprises becomes prominent enough to urge the founders to take a careful consideration. The take-over of the enterprises' rights is not an oversimplified behavior. It is a complicated system, as well as a procedure, involving a series of processes ranging from planning, implementation, and effects control. Subsequently, when this systematic project is carried out, there are some problems to be noticed: a proper succession plan is necessary to avoid the instability of the enterprises induced by the change of the leadership. Mere planning without good implementation is not sufficient for the accomplishment of the succession. In the family enterprises, the structures are usually the extension of the proprietor's personality. Sometimes the implementation of the plans would be prohibited by the founders. As long as they have realized the importance, they would impel the completion of this plan. Furthermore, the culture of the family enterprises is also a most important factors influencing the succession. A failed succession often results from a peculiar cultural structure, such as patriarchic management, conflicting families, and rubberstamp-like board. In contrast, with an open and participating leadership style, cooperating family culture and consultative boards, the succession plan would be much easier to achieve. Furthermore, some reasonable intervention from the consultating committee would be of great help to the success of succession.

Different forms of succession have been used by different family enterprises in different countries. The selection of the succession forms mainly depends on the cultural environment, different stages of development, the nature of the proprietorship, the mindset of the core leaders and the trust system, etc. The developmental stage has influenced the form of succession to a large extent. It is very difficult to objectively analyze the development of the family enterprises, if the developmental stage is not taken into consideration. In the early, middle and even late middle stages of the family enterprises' life-cycle, the power is mainly passed from one generation to the next. But after entering the stage of maturity, the family enterprises are possibly controlled by the non-family members. Therefore, the management rights would probably be passed to the outside professional managers. The features of the proprietorship could influence the succession form through balancing the internal and external powers. The development of proprietorship of the family enterprises basically follows the track of moving from homogenity to diversity. Many factors such as the separation of property, the degree of separation affect the balance of the internal and external power and eventually affect the form of succession. For enterprise in a low trust culture, the succession of power would tend to be carried out within the family enterprise. Trust plays a crucial role in the selection of the succession forms. Generally speaking, those enterprises in high trust society would tend to accept the external-oriented approach in succession. In contrast, enterprise in the low trust society, would tend to choose the internal-oriented approach.

For the current Chinese family enterprises, the "inside strong and outside weak" feature is pressed by factors such as the development stage of the enterprises, the insufficiency of the social credits, the immaturity of professional managers' market and the over-powerful families. Therefore, the internal-oriented form of succession is thus more preferred and becomes the primary choice of the current Chinese family enterprises. In fact, "sons inheriting the businesses of their fathers" is still the dominant practice of many Chinese family enterprises. If the internal-oriented approach is a preferred approach, systematic planning of the succession process, omni-directional reviewing training the successors, and the establishment of the successors' new authorities would be key considerations.

From the execution viewpoint, the succession procedure consists of four parts: training, evaluation, confirmation and eventual establishment of the authority. They are closely related and interdependent. Leadership is never accomplished and shaped overnight, but through long-term development. If the family enterprises have decided to pass their businesses to the next generation, they must try their best to train the potential successors, with a design of knowledge competency training, the edification of the family culture and the opportunities to be exposed to all-rounded practical training. The successors of the family enterprises to some extent will have to work harder than those outside managers, because as family members, their capabilities will be suspected and challenged. Therefore, they must work much harder to accumulate enough experiences and capabilities both within and outside of the family enterprises to build their credibility and authority. The evaluation on the "potential successors" includes evaluation on their actual achievement and performance, evaluation by the family patriarchs, peer evaluation, self-evaluation and subordinate evaluation. After the overall evaluation, other assessments such as personality test, qualification, competency test and team leadership will also be taken into consideration before a final candidate is identified. However, the simple transfer of power does not guarantee the establishment of the successor's actual authority. It is also important, in the succession process, to eliminate interference from other also-rans. More importantly, the philosophy and values of the successors must be put into reality. In this regard, it is advisable for the successors not to rush into changing the old management and operation at the initial stage of their tenure of position. It will take time for them to get accustomed to the new situation and gradually develop their management authority. According to some organizational behavior studies, during the processes of power takeover, the successor has the tendency to exhibit rebellious behaviors by rejecting past practices, the past management team, changing the strategy and style. They would also implement new thoughts imprinted with their own features. Although this kind of acts has some senses of renovation and reforms, it could probably bring negative influences to the development of the enterprises. In order to reduce the risks in decision-making at the initial stage of takeover, a decision-making mechanism, featuring better communications with the management level of the enterprises, should be set up within the family to review the practicality and feasibility of the new initiatives.

Generally speaking, the succession planning of the Chinese family enterprise must be brought into the framework of the strategic planning. And its concrete measures at different stages should be guided by systematic ways of thoughts, including formulating heritage plans, developing enterprises, instructing the successors, gradually handing over the management rights and providing support during the transitional period of the takeover. If there were delays or obstacles during the succession process, conflicts would happen and may obstruct the long-term development of the family businesses

There are several aspects to be considered during the process of implementation as they are often dealt with arbitrarily and as a result have affected the stability and effects of the succession. Firstly, the selection of the successors must be made by the incumbent leaders on the basis of a comprehensive understanding of the future, the obligations assumed by the senior managers and the family patriarchs, and the potential changes. Secondly, the current leaders of the enterprises must fully evaluate the communication and the decision-making style of the successors, so as to properly arrange the future position for successors to assume. Besides the leadership ability, the cultivation of the family concept and the experience of the family roles are also important factors for consideration. In addition, the working experiences outside the families and the experiences on certain positions within the families are indispensable for them. The current leaders should not only gradually release the control rights, but also positively support the succession procedure and help the successors to build their new authority and style.

Of course, in reality, there might be many other factors that would impair the stability in power succession. For example, firstly, there must be candidates who can meet the requirements and have the capability to manage the enterprises. Compared with enterprises of other kinds, the scope of selection could be smaller. Secondly, the family members must reach an agreement on the cultivation plan of the successors, including the supports to the procedure and the process. Thirdly, the succession procedure must be planned as early as possible and must be implemented when the enterprises are still under the stable control of the current leaders, in case the businesses of the enterprises are in decline or the current leaders pass away before the plan could be carried out. Timing is also critical. The current leaders must ponder over and get prepared for the problem of successor's selection and cultivation in advance, as advance as ten years before the retirement of the current leaders.

Due to the complexity of the business environment and the perculiarity of different enterprises or families, different forms of the ownership structure, organizational design and management style would emerge in the new family enterprises in China. Nonetheless, they share one thing in common, i.e., only with the modern and professional management system in place, would the succession and continuity of the family enterprises be realized. In addition, the family enterprises should especially foster their strengths and circumvent their weakness, and try to turn the family features into the advantages that could bring positive effects for the enterprises. The familism atmosphere should be created, "family" conception to the whole enterprises expanded and the non-family members should be integrated into the conception of "taking enterprises as our own homes" to build up a family culture in the enterprises. At the very beginning of the establishment, the enterprises are filled with the "family" culture of Confucianism, which pushed the enterprises forward rapidly. With the expansion of the scale, the establishment of all the systems, and the introduction of the outside competent mangers, family enterprises have to include those new members into the big "families", rather than being limited in the original blood relations or kinships. In fact, many of the practices of the Japanese enterprises are worthy of reference to the Chinese family enterprises. The Japanese enterprises stress that the employees are the members of the enterprises, and the enterprises are the families of the employees. They encourage employees to devote to the enterprises for their lifetime. Take the world-renowned manufacturer Toyota as an example. We could obtain some enlightenment from its business culture building. Each and every employee of Toyota is trained on the corporate culture, which includes both the job-related aspect, and the personal life aspect. Through these trainings, the employees are mobilized, and their common values are established by the informal activities, including the group activities inside company, personal contact, program of establishing happy dormitories, and Toyota club activities. Take the inside group activities as an example. In light of different standards, various groups are organized, such as classmates group, hometown fellow group, educational group and gym group etc. The employees could participate in different groups based on their own interests, which would be very helpful in the cultivation of the team awareness and promotion of team bonding among the employees. Moreover, the venues and expenses are provided by the company. Toyota has established a comprehensive gym center and a women club to make every employee feel the warmth and belonging to the big family. Every new employee would be entrusted to a "senior", who will instruct and guide the newly-employed for six months. The seniors would help them to coordinate the personal relations within the company. It is through this arrangement that Toyota has established their own enterprise culture in a proper sequence.

The Chinese family enterprises should also establish the enterprise culture with their own unique features. The following factors should be noticed:

a. Collectively set up the long-term goals for the enterprises. Goals are the basis for enterprise business and management activities. They guide the actions and behaviors of employees, and provide foundation of corporate culture. The set-up of the enterprises' goals is the precondition of the build-up of the enterprises' culture, and it should involve the opinions and suggestions of the employees. In the process, it will inculcate a sense of confidence and psychological contract with the enterprises.

b. Take advantage of the original "family" culture and expand the conception of a "family" to the employees. By so doing, the cohesion of the enterprises would be enhanced. For example, in Japanese enterprises, employees would receive a greeting card on their birthdays, which would increase their sense of belonging.

c. The leaders should walk the talk and be the role models in the enterprises. As the "family patriarchs", leaders themselves should be the incarnation of the enterprises' common values. They should earnestly practice what they advocate and be the role models for the employees. They should attempt to communicate with the employees, treat them equally and fairly, and guide the employees to recognize and abide by the enterprises' values. They should also try to create a coherent, tacit and cooperative team.

d. Develop an enterprise spirit with zeitgeist and unique characteristics. Corporate spirit is an awareness advocated by the leaders, recognized by the employees and understood by the public. It is the exhibition of the enterprises' common values or the soul of the enterprises' culture.

In general, cultures are created by humans, and conversely, humans are also shaped by cultures. Shaping an unique business culture is one of the most important conditions for the development of the family enterprises. Only through the constructions and innovations of enterprise system and culture could the family enterprises actualize their fundamental reforms and break through various restrictions. Through the construction of the modern enterprise culture, the reform and development of family enterprises be expedited. Consequently, the dream of family enterprise development and prosperity in the Chinese economy would eventually come true.

Innovation: Source of Longevity

Through observation of enterprises, we could find out that if an enterprises adopts a new technique, develops a new product, explores a new market, controls a new resource of raw materials, restructures or reorganizes, the enterprise will be raised to a new level of challenge. These measures are called innovations, which are crucial for all enterprises, including family enterprises.

1. System innovation

In terms of management system, the pattern of "only one man's words count" in family enterprises should be changed into joint-stock companies with separated ownership and management. Within the companies, human relations may be an influential factor, but it is not the case in the markets. When an enterprise is in its elementary stage, maximization of profits is the main target and traditional paternalism works well. However, when it reaches a certain scale, the enterprise needs to promote its overall value while pursuing the maximization of profits. An advanced management system is essential. Known to all, to institutionalize and formalize management is a difficult task in family enterprises, since most key managers are family members. The nature of family enterprises makes it even harder to implement rules and regulations. In the worst scenario, family members are the destructive force of rules and regulation. What ties family members and family enterprises together is not only the contract relations, but also familial affection and kindness. Dismissal of family members from the enterprise will not only terminate the contract, but also destroy the family relations. In the face of family relations, rules and regulations become a mere scrap of paper. Irregularity and inconsistency in the management system results in poor quality and high costs, and thus leading to the low competitive advantage and difficulties in achieving continuous growth and long-term development.

In terms of personnel system, family enterprises must recruit a group of professional experts into the management team to facilitate the standardization and formalization of management. If family enterprises are unable to recruit and retain good talents, the long-term development of family enterprises will inevitably be affected. If talents within the enterprises are not put in important positions, the non-family members will lose commitment and may ultimately leave. At present, some domestic family enterprises have taken the step of accepting outside talents and consequently become leaders in their industries. For example, Shenzhen Taita Pharmaceutical is a family enterprise owned by the family of Zhu Baoguo. The enterprise introduced many state-of-the-art marketing directors, sales directors and financial directors in the industry. Mrs. Gu Yueyue, vice general manager and marketing director of the group, is a senior manager employed with good compensation package. She worked in Unilever for 17 years and in GSKT for 3½ years. Another example is Guo Ziwen, president of Guangdong Jinye Group and Olympic Investment Corporation. In ten years, he changed the local board of directors into an international one. Nobody in the board of directors has personal relations to the president. The general manager of the group is from Hubei and obtained his dual academic degree in Peking University. The president of Shanghai Olympics, an affiliated company of the group, got his PhD in Australia. The company also hired many students with academic experience overseas. The diversification of personnel structure ultimately brings good returns to the enterprises.

As far as talent attraction is concerned, corporate culture often plays a significant role. Generally speaking, family enterprises value traditional culture such as family traditions, kinship relations and materialistic orientation. At the present stage, many family enterprises gave undue emphasis on pragmatic materialistic outcomes in their decision-making, reward structure and management system. It lacks the emphasis on a healthy culture featuring innovation, learning and integration that are necessary for modern knowledge economy. Therefore, it is quite difficult for family enterprises to attract talents with high quality to join.

2. Business innovation

It can be said that the establishment and growth of many Chinese family enterprises is dependent on their successful market strategy. However, performance of these enterprises depends on innovations in a great measure. Only by unceasingly bringing forth the new products and services can an enterprise secure its own position in the fierce market competition.

In terms of products, innovation is the breakthrough for the development of enterprises. Most of the Chinese family enterprises started their businesses by processing low-quality daily necessities or by distributing others' products. However, when Chinese family enterprises want to achieve long-term development, they have to establish their own brands, and move from the small local market to cross-ownership, cross-industry, cross-regions and cross-national international strategy. Product innovation and variety are essential for the growth and development of family enterprises. Zhejiang CHINT is a good example. Formerly a family workshop producing low-voltage electric appliances, CHINT is now a large-scale group focusing on the production of unitized apparatus, instruments and communication apparatus. It is the first enterprise in China to obtain the international ISO9000 quality certificate in this industry. For more than ten years since the 1990s, CHINT has independently developed more than 80 kinds of new products with world-class quality. Its complete set of equipments are not only provided for medium-sized clients, but also the appointed and priority products for China's large-scale construction projects (Three Gorges Project, Wuhan Steel Factory, Shengli Petroleum and so on).

In terms of investment finance, capital has always been a bottleneck problem plaguing the development of the enterprises. Generally speaking, family enterprises seldom set foot on the capital market at their elementary stages. It is inevitable for them to enter the capital market and involve in capital operation. Surviving fierce market competition, some excellent family enterprises can easily enter capital market and carry out further capital operation with their good performances and clearly-defined property rights. For example, the Oriental Group spent 140 million yuan to purchase the shares of Jinzhou Port in 1995. As the largest shareholder, it controls 30.4% of the total shares of Jinzhou Port. After that, the group accelerated its pace of expansion by entering other industries, including banks and insurance. By doing so, the group succeeded in acturalizing multi-directional operations, reduced risks and enhanced competitive strength. Another example is Hope Group, a leading family enterprise. In July 1995, Liu Yonghao assumed the office of vice board chairman of China Minsheng Banking Corporation Ltd. In 1998, New Hope Group, controlled by the family of Liu Yonghao with 80% shares, was listed in Shenzhen. In November 2000, China Minsheng Banking Corporation Ltd was listed. The Liu's brothers individually held 203 million shares in the names of Sichuan New Hope Agribusiness Co Ltd and Sichuan South Hope Co Ltd, thus holding 12% of the total capital. Another example is Wanxiang Group. Before 1998, due to the exchange control by the central government, the funds of Wanxiang could not be remitted to other countries, so the capital operational scope of Wanxiang America became limited and their business operations were restriced. From 1999, Wanxiang Group carried out vertical mergers overseas to invest in the existing manufacture field and the supplementary fields with automobile spare parts, the main focus of Wanxiang Group. It purchased a lot of American companies, including LT, TD, QAI and HMS. On the other hand, it carried out risk investment to enter the fields, including high tech, finance, insurance, pharmaceutical, software and Internet. On August 23, 2001, Wanxiang Group successfully acquired UAI (Universal Automotive Industries, Inc).

The entry of family enterprises into capital markets carries both benefits and harms. The benefits are that the investors of Chinese family enterprises are clear, unlike the state-owned enterprises; their primary business is often clear, and profit is centralized. Generally speaking, the total capital stock and circulating capital stock of family enterprises are small, if they are not used in capital operation, and thus they tend to attract the attention of major investors. However, the exclusive holding of shares by a family brings harm as well. The first and major risk is in morality. When family enterprises are listed, the holding family shareholders have a good chance to illegally impair the interests of ordinary shareholders. For example, they may maximize their benefit by controlling capital restructuring and shareholding rights trading of listed companies, which is detrimental to the interests of the listed companies and small- and medium-sized shareholders. Moreover, the associated trading in listed family companies can be processed secretly, making it hard and complicated to prevent and monitor. In addition, the operations of listed family enterprises tend to be influenced by internal conflicts within the family. The exclusive holding of shares will increase risks in decision-making process. These are the problems in the listing of family enterprises.

How are problems being addressed in the West? Many well-known multinationals are family enterprises, for example, Microsoft, Ford, DuPont, GM and Motorola. Foreign family enterprises are keen on becoming listed public enterprises. Generally speaking, the lifespan of foreign family enterprises is 23 years. 39% of them can last for two generations and only 15% can last for three. If they want to achieve sustainable development, the enterprises need to unceasingly add capital. In this regard, family enterprises make every effort to turn themselves into listed companies, so they can win full support in finance to create favorable external conditions for the rapid growth of the enterprises. Moreover, since there is a convenient exit system in the stock market, being listed can also help to solve potential huge unrest in the operations and power transfer of family enterprises. If a family enterprise is listed, the shareholders can monetize their shares at any time. What the family members inherit are shares of the enterprises and the property inheritance is conducted in the form of shares. Therefore, in international markets, almost all large-scale family enterprises have experienced the process of being listed. But, even in international stock markets, special attention is given to the listed companies completely controlled by families, since complete control of shares may exert some unfavorable influences on economic policies and even judiciary system. First of all, family enterprises may be favored and the odds are higher if any family member takes senior governmental positions.

Secondly, family monopoly may even influence the development of judiciary system in the long run. When a few families dominate the business market as a whole and the government is zealously involved in it, it is very likely that the judiciary system cannot play the role of encouraging legal and fair competition and protecting small- and medium-sized shareholders. Nevertheless, even in America where capital market is highly developed and the inspection system is mature, the power of family enterprises is far beyond the imagination of ordinary people. Even when some family enterprises are already socialized, family's control over the enterprises remains tight. DuPont, Amway and Motorola are cases in point. This is an indication that the socialization, market-oriented operation and strength do not necessarily contradict with the nature of family enterprises. With reasonable governance structure and managerial systems, the Chinese family enterprises will hopefully become world-class enterprises in the near future.

In order to solve the abuses brought by the exclusive holding of shares by families after they are listed, we can consolidate the internal monitor mechanism and establish a modern enterprise system in accordance with laws and regulations. In addition, it is also very important for the family enterprises to take measures themselves. Specifically, the listed enterprises under families control should transform the management system. This can define the property right clearly, establish a system and also gradually disperse the stock rights. Outstanding employees should be allowed to have shares, which is necessary for the establishment of a professional manager team. Thus, the tone of family enterprises will be diluted and any changes in the enterprises will be conducted based on institutional regulations. Only by doing so can family enterprises achieve safe and sound development. Being listed is only one of the approaches to improve corporate management and governance structure, but it is far from enough. Recently, some family enterprises and private enterprises are listed by assets reconstruction. They do not make the effort to realize optimization and integration of industry and fund chain by improving their governance structure and regulating management. On the contrary, they make the listed companies a tool to make money. Such action harms the small and medium-sized shareholders and disarray the economic order of capital market, thus bringing bad influences and outcomes.

Therefore, family enterprises must rectify their attitudes and regard the small shareholders as their bosses. The magnates should never be lost in their success, with their billions in assets and inclusion in lists of millionaires. Without the support and investment of small and medium-sized shareholders, family enterprises will not become successful public listed companies. Without the support and investment from numerous small- and medium-sized shareholders, family enterprises cannot become public companies, let alone qualify as listed companies. Being listed means huge economic interests, but also corresponding responsibility as well as obligations.

After being listed, the wisest way for family enterprises to become bigger and stronger is to change the concepts, dilute the family-oriented system, get rid of patriarch management, establish scientific and reasonable modern enterprise system and management system, and employ more talents to launch innovations. Of course, family enterprises should try to reshape themselves with self-consciousness. Powerful corporate governance environment is also needed. Till now, there have been some successful stories. For example, some family members can be asked to quit with certain share rights benefit through the policy of "buying out" and introduce talents in HR market. The Chinese listed family enterprises should pay attention to the following problems: firstly, the founder of the enterprise should occupy a proper ratio of shares. Secondly, only a clearly defined share rights structure can motivate the employees. Thirdly, the enterprises should use stocks and share rights reasonably to attract and retain talents. At the same time, the mechanism of selection and appointment should also be established to prevent incompetent relatives or friends of the founders from being promoted to important positions. The enterprises should attach more significance to, rely on and care about the talents.

In terms of organizational pattern, innovations conducted by family enterprises to adapt to external environment can achieve unexpected results, which can hardly be explained by traditional economic theories. The family enterprises cluster in Wenzhou is a good example. Being an individual, the small and medium-sized enterprise does not enjoy the competitive force as major modern enterprises do. But from a collective point of view, their cooperation network is a one-up manufacture pattern in the world. For example, CHINT Group, the leading enterprise in Liushi Town, manufactures only 10% of the key parts by itself and invites tenders for the rest 90% with 800 cooperating factories. By doing so, its cost stands at one-third of that in state-owned enterprises. In the lighter industry of Wenzhou, 500 finished products factories are at the top of the pyramid, beneath which there are 2,000 factories of spare parts. The finished products factories produce only 50% of the spare parts of a lighter, and the rest is provided by the 2,000 lower stream factories. The relationship among the factories of spare parts is competitive, whereas that between parts-factories and finished-products-factories is cooperative. The factories manufacturing parts do not adhere to the finished products factories. One factory can provide parts for many finished products factories. So, technical progress in one parts factory can benefit 500 finished products factories. In addition, the competitive relationship among spare parts factories may avoid the rigescent administrative costs in coordinating the workshops of major enterprises. An example is the sock-making industry in Wenzhou. There are more than 8,000 family enterprises in Cixi Town and each has only 8 knitting machines averagely. The manufacturing process of socks there is divided into 10 parts in the town: 1,000 factories focusing on raw materials, 300 factories on sewing, 100 factories on design, 300 factories on packaging, 200 factories on machine fittings, 600 distribution dealers, and 100 transportation merchants. The division of labor is very definite and clear. When combined, they are a titanic in the industry capable of finishing orders of any size. The annual production of the town stands at 4.8 billion pairs and the production value reaches as much as 9 billion yuan. The family enterprise Jinxiang Badges Factory is also very typical, which has only 100 pressure machines and 50 ovens. Small as it is, the enterprise presents huge flexibility and is capable of finishing any kind of orders. The factory will allot manufacturing tasks to hundreds of other enterprises to jointly finish a major order. And when the number of orders shrinks, it dismisses its 100 workers who may find jobs in other small-sized factories. Any factory in the town is confident enough to accept big orders, since they may share the orders with the peer factories. Under such pattern, the small- and medium-sized family enterprises focusing on manufacturing may achieve rapid development even when the micro-economy is in its valley. It is mentionable that any merchant in any area of Wenzhou can enjoy the sales network throughout the region, for there are thousands of independent salesmen in the area of Wenzhou. At its elementary stage, with the help of independent salesmen, CHINT set up 800 sales companies for free. With the salesmen as coordinators, the manufacturing system and sales system can cooperate well with each other, thus avoiding the situation of poor communication between two systems as in the Western enterprises. The number of products manufactured by small-sized enterprises in Wenzhou is quite small, but the enterprise cluster produces more kinds of products than a single big enterprise of the same size. This enables Wenzhou to overpass the rest of the country in product categories. At present, lamps produced in Wenzhou occupy 30% of the national market, bread tickets 89%, certificates 91%, low-voltage apparatus 35%, leather products 20%, magnetic pumps 70% and valves 30%. Although the size of individual enterprises is small, the region as a whole dominates 20% of the market, which benefits from the innovations and flexibility in organizational structure of the family enterprise cluster in Wenzhou.

The last factor is the innovative spirit of the entrepreneurs, which lies at the core of its pioneering process for family enterprises. China's family enterprises are significantly different from each other as they are involved in different fields and have different sizes and organizational structure. However, all the successes more or less rely on the spirit of entrepreneurs, i.e., the innovative spirit, which includes: courage in bearing risks, skill of problem-solving, energetic personality, confidence, reason in dealing with personal issues. It is fair to say that the founders of the family enterprises are innovation-driven and the key is to keep the spirit and promote the long-term development of family enterprises. To fulfill this goal, it is a priority to improve the innate character of the entrepreneurs, who must accomplish the transformation from the traditional bosses to the entrepreneurs adaptable to global economic competition. If the first pioneering depends on courage and painstaking efforts, the second one relies mainly on knowledge and personality. Family entrepreneurs will be aware of the importance of personality in the fierce domestic and international competition. "Computers cannot replace human brain, and the wisdom of others cannot replace the boss himself". Although some of the entrepreneurs, limited by historical conditions, cannot receive sound education, they must raise their internal quality by learning unceasingly. A successful family industrialist does not necessarily need high educational success, but he must be keen to learn. He should at the same time promote the learning atmosphere within the entire enterprise and try to turn the family enterprise into a learning-oriented one, thus promoting the competitive strength of the enterprise.

Through the analysis of some family enterprises with sound development prospect, we can summarize their similarities. We hope these points can be used as reference for sustainable and stable development of other family enterprises.

a. *Standard operation and management, and modern enterprise system.* From the angle of establishing standardized managerial system, the environment, strategy and organization should be highly syncronized and relevant to the growth of enterprises. For example, since the beginning of the 1990s, Wanxiang Group began to gradually establish standardized managerial system, which is in line with its strategy in specialized production and expanding into international market. The New Hope Group adopted modern management methods and technology to satisfy the requirements for enterprises in the growth stages and adapt to the changes in the industrial environment. UFIDA has already established a perfect governance structure, in which the shareholders meeting, board of directors, supervisory committee, management meeting and independent directors could participate in business decisions within their own purview. They employ experienced professional managers, recruit and train high-level management talents. Taita improves its managerial level by exploring managerial concepts unceasingly. Zhu Baoguo, board chairman of Taita Pharmaceutical, often encourages his employees to express innovative ideas. He managed to find suitable ways to balance the interests for the senior followers and employ high quality talents, which helped to form a healthy interactive relationship between family members and professional managers. This provided a solid foundation for sustainable development of the enterprise.

b. *Making long-term plans.* In terms of a long-term plan, governance structure and strategic planning should be highly relevant and adapted to both the internal and external environment. For example, Wanxiang Group effectively combines long-term planning with short-term planning. Lu Guanqiu's son Lu Weiding takes charge in specialized production management and the son-in-law Ni Pin is responsible for the development of international market and capital operations. The governance pattern and strategy of Wanxiang Group satisfy the demands of industrial environment and internal environment after China's entry into WTO. New Hope Group takes a leading role in entering banking, securities and insurance industries. By doing so, it achieves its goal of capital operations and self-expansion, and is quite prudent with the strategy of diversification as well. The strategy is made after thorough analysis of internal and external environments. UFIDA purchases a series of software enterprises after being listed to obtain the technology and resources it needs, which is of great significance to a high-tech software company. It is obvious that UFIDA's acquisition strategy also adapts to the industry environment.

c. *Cultivate core competitive competency.* Adopting the specialized production system, Wanxiang Group unceasingly promotes its core competitive edge. On this basis, it formulates strategies to explore international mainstream market, and to diversify business operation and to seek new growth. UFIDA has always been focusing its primary business in software system, and thus targeting acquisition only in software industry. Bird Company boosts its core competitive strength by improving its image and enhancing brand values.

d. *Manage family relationships wisely within the family enterprise.* The human resources management system in Wanxiang Group is quite flexible. Lu Guanqiu said he had two principles in hiring and promotion: the first one is to never appoint people by favorism, and the second is to never be afraid of promoting able people from the family. According to Lu, whether to put someone in an important position or not depends on his ability to do the job, instead of his family connections. The flexibility helps to recruit talents from the outside and allow the strength of family members to excel as well. New Hope Group insists on the principle of never putting family members in important positions. By doing so, it is able to recruit and retain a number of excellent professional managers, which is an important progress for the group in its matured stage. UFIDA properly deals with the senior members of the company and introduces experienced professional managers, thus making a sound preparation for the entry into its maturity stage.

e. *Adopt the strategy of diversification.* Guanghui Stock constantly expands its business fields. Its primary business had changed from the catering industry to oil trade, and then the industry of construction materials and finally, the energy industry. So Guanghui Stock adopts the strategy of diversification to find ways to adapt itself to the changes of external environments. The business scope of Youngor Group includes garment industry, international trade, real estate and finance, among which garment industry is the primary business and the rest are supplementary business. Youngor has made its development strategy in light of long-term planning, which enables the balanced development of the group as a whole and helps the company to adapt to fierce competitive environment and find out new points of growth.

f. *Restructuring at the Group level and promoting integration at the industrial level through capital investment management.* Taita Pharmaceutical set its advantages in capital operations into full play and enhances the integration at the industrial level through the strategy of consolidating industry, capital and technology. Taita cultivates its core competitive strength by way of merger, controlling and establishing core business and technical departments, which adapts to the industry changes and satisfies the requirements of internal environment. Youngor sponsors the establishment of CITIC Securities to adjust the industrial structure and enhance the capability and comprehensive strength of the whole Group, and to find out the effective combination of garment business and capital market. By doing so, it adapts to the changes of industrial environments and discovers new rooms for development. Oriental Group lays its emphasis on both capital market and core business operation.

g. *Establish market-oriented management and distribution model.* Youngor Group pays much attention to the establishment of a comprehensive distribution network. Since Youngor formerly focused on garment production, it has a sales network in place, which is an advantage when it shifts to the field of channels. In light of the demands of regional economy, the marketing strategy of Guanghui Stock makes use of the regional resource advantages to expand the market..

From the above, it can be concluded that only when family enterprises possess some competitive advantages, will they lay a sound foundation for further sustainable development.

Epilogue

The vigorous development of China's economy will certainly foster a number of world-class enterprises. With advantages in resources and scale, the state-owned enterprises will come into the world stage. Privately-owned enterprises also strive to be the best, trying to expand their business throughout the world. Can Chinese family enterprises ride the wave and be passed from one generation to another? Can the curse of "wealth does not sustain beyond three generations" be broken? The answer has not yet been revealed.

History is a mirror. The experiences of others can save us from twists and turns. Hopefully, this book can be a useful reference for the Chinese family enterprises.

References

1. Poutziouris, P., Smyrnios, K., and Klein, S. (2006). *Handbook of research on family business.*
2. Shaheena Janjuha-Jivraj (2006). *Succession in Asian family firms.* New York: Palgrave Macmillan.
3. Liu, Haiming (2005). *The transnational history of a Chinese family: immigrant letters family business and reverse migration.* New Brunswick NJ: Rutgers University Press.
4. Edmund Terence Gomez and Hsin-Huang Michael Hsiao (2004). *Chinese enterprise, transnationalism and identity.* New York: Routledge.
5. Wu Xiao An (2003). *Chinese business in the making of a Malay state, 1882–1941.* New York: Routledge Curzon.
6. *East Asian business systems in evolutionary perspective: entrepreneurship and coordination (2003).* Nova Science.
7. Nam, Sang-Woo (2001). *Business groups looted by controlling families, and the Asian crisis.* Asian Development Bank Institute
8. *Family corporations in transition* (2001). Asian Institute of Management.
9. Ming-Jer Chen (2001). *Inside Chinese business: a guide for managers worldwide.* Boston, Mass.: Harvard Business School Press.
10. Leo Douw, Cen Huang and David Ip (2001). *Rethinking Chinese transnational enterprises: cultural affinity and business strategies.* Richmond, Surrey: Curzon.
11. Chan, Eunice Shan (2001). *The institutional constraints of turnaround in East Asia.*
12. Claessens, Stijn (2000). *East Asia corporations: heroes or villains.* World Bank.
13. Henry Wai-chung Yeung and Kris Olds (2000). *Globalization of Chinese business firms.* Hampshire: Macmillan.
14. Elvis, P. J. (1999). *The strategy and structure of the large, diversified, ethnic Chinese organisations of Southeast Asia* [electronic resource].

15. Claessens, Stijn (1999). *Who controls East Asian corporations?*. World Bank.
16. Cathernine, C. H. (1998). *Small family business in Hong Kong: accumulation and accommodation*. Hong Kong: Chinese University Press.
17. *Prominent Asian family businesses* (1997). Political & Economic Risk Consultancy.
18. Rajeswary, A. B. (1995). *Chinese business enterprise in Asia*. New York: Routledge.
19. Li Yu-ning (1992). *Chinese women through Chinese eyes*. Armonk, New York: M.E. Sharpe.
20. Gary Hamilton (1991). *Business networks and economic development in East and Southeast Asia*. Hong Kong: Centre of Asian Studies, University of Hong Kong.
21. International Conference on Business History (10th: 1983: Fuji Education Center). *Family business in the era of industrial growth: its ownership and management: proceedings of the Fuji Conference*. University of Tokyo Press.
22. Redding, S. G. (1990). *The spirit of Chinese capitalism,*. W. de Gruyter.
23. 席守诚 (1991). *家庭经济理论与实践*北京: 新华出版社。
24. 国务院研究室个体、私营经济调查组编 (1990). *中国的个体和私营经济* (1990). 北京: 改革出版社。
25. Redding, S. G. (1993). *海外华人企业家的管理思想: 文化背景与风格*. 上海: 上海 三联书店。
26. 冯邦彦 (1997). *香港华资财团, 1841–1997*. 香港: 三联书店。
27. 林圃, 林耕 (1998). *华人财团大观*. 成都: 四川人民出版社。
28. 克林·盖尔西克 (1998). *家族企业的繁衍*. 北京: 经济日报出版社。
29. *OECD 公司治理原则* (1999). 世界经济合作与发展组织 (OECD).
30. 郎咸平 (2001). *家族企业敛财秘笈*. 新财富. No. 1.
31. *世界竞争力报告* (2000). 洛桑国际管理学院。
32. 森岛通夫 (2000). *透视日本*（中译本）. 北京: 中国财政经济出版社。
33. 盛柯著 (2002). *打造新型家族企业*. 北京: 中国致公出版社。
34. 兰德尔. S. 卡洛克 (2002). *家族企业战略计划*（中译本）. 北京: 中信出版社。
35. 迟双明 (2002). *刘永好创造财富的 66 策略*. 北京: 当代世界出版社。
36. 甘德安 (2002). *中国家族企业研究*. 北京: 中国社会科学出版社。
37. 张翼 (2002). *国有企业的家族化*. 北京: 社会科学文献出版社。
38. 姚贤涛、王连娟著 (2002). *中国家族企业现状问题与对策*. 北京: 企业管理出版社。
39. 张厚义主编 (2001) *中国私营企业发展报告*. 北京: 社会科学文献出版社。
40. 付文阁 (2004). *中国家族企业面临的紧要问题*. 北京: 经济日报出版社。

41. 储小平 (2004). *家族企业的成长与社会资本的融合*. 北京: 经济科学出版社。

42. (美)埃德温·A·胡佛, (美)科利特·L·胡佛 (2004). *关系商: 家族企业经营的迷思*（中译本）. 上海: 译文出版社。

43. 周立新 (2005). *转轨时期中国家族企业组织演进研究*. 北京: 经济管理出版社。

44. 李新春主编 (2005) *家族企业: 组织、行为与中国经济* (2005). 上海: 上海人民出版社。

45. 应焕红 (2005). *家族企业制度创新*. 北京: 社会科学文献出版社。

46. 中国国家工商行政管理局办公室. *工商管理行政管理统计汇编* (1991–1999).

47. 家族企业网络 (The Family Business Network), 瑞士。

48. 罗纳德. 耶茨著 (2003年). *龟甲万公司的营销创举*. 北京: 机械工业出版社。

49. 解放, 法国家族企业制度分析与借鉴。硕士论文. 2004.

50. 罗晓扬, 国外家族企业权力传接模式研究及对中国的启示。硕士论文。2004.

51. 朱红萱, 台湾家族企业发展概况, 海峡产业与科技, 2006 年第1期。

52. 赵颖、戴树芬. 意大利模式对促进我国家族企业技术创新的启示。现代管理科学, 2005年第6期。

53. 刘剑, 意大利企业经营之道—家族管理模式, 北京经济, 2002年 第12期。

54. 刘洪钟, 曲文轶, 公司治理、代理问题与东亚家族企业: 以韩国财阀为例。世界经济, 2002年第2期。

55. 龚振, 钟爱群。中韩家族企业治理模式的比较。企业经济, 2005年第8期。

56. 陈向阳, 剩余价值索取与控制在家族企业亲缘关系分析中的运用。2004年 第1期。

57. 应立芬, 家族企业继任机制与创新研究。硕士论文, 2003年11月。

58. 刘建强, 家族企业的德国前世和中国今生。中国家族企业, 2004年1月。

59. 李国富, 家族控股上市公司治理结构问题研究。硕士论文, 2002年6月。

60. 史蒂夫 巴龙, 牛文文, 中德家族企业的对话。中国家族企业, 2003年8月。

Index